MATH NATION – How It Works

Welcome to Math Nation! Our goal is to help you master 8th Grade Math and beyond. Here's how to get started:

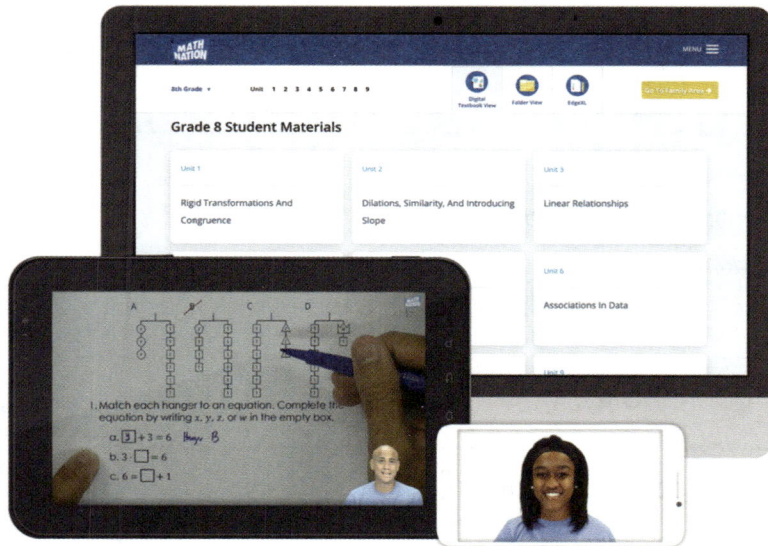

1. Visit us at MathNation.com to log in on the web. To download our free app, just search 'Math Nation' in the Google Play Store (all Android devices) or the App Store (iPhones and iPads) on your mobile phone or tablet.

2. Use this workbook as you watch the videos, which have been organized into 9 units across two volumes. You can use Math Nation in the classroom, at home, and on the go.

Unit 1: Rigid Transformations and Congruence

Section 1: Rigid Transformation

Section 2: Properties of Rigid Transformations

Adapted from Open Up Resources 6-8 Math (authored by Illustrative Mathematics).
See inside front cover for details.

Unit 1: Rigid Transformations and Congruence

MATH NATION

Section 3: Congruence

Section 4: Angles in a Triangle

Section 5: Let's Put it to Work

Adapted from Open Up Resources 6-8 Math (authored by Illustrative Mathematics).
See inside front cover for details.

Unit 1: Rigid Transformations and Congruence

3

Let's describe ways figures can move in the plane.

1.1.1 Warm-Up: Which One Doesn't Belong: Diagrams

Which one doesn't belong?

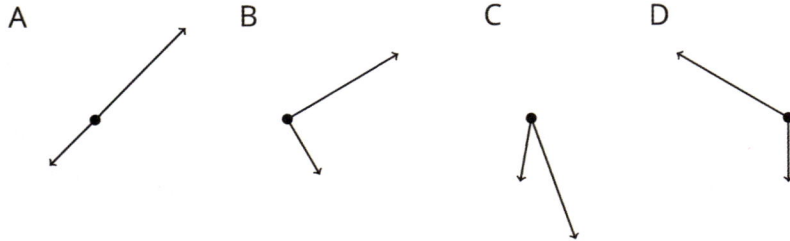

A   B   C   D

1.1.2a Exploration Activity: Triangle Square Dance

Your teacher will give you three pictures. Each shows a different set of dance moves.

1. Arrange the three pictures so you and your partner can both see them right way up. Choose who will start the game.

   o The starting player mentally chooses A, B, or C and describes the dance to the other player.

   o The other player identifies which dance is being talked about: A, B, or C.

2. After one round, trade roles. When you have described all three dances, come to an agreement on the words you use to describe the moves in each dance.
3. With your partner, write a description of the moves in each dance.

1.1.2b Exploration Extension: Are you ready for more?

We could think of each dance as a new dance by running it in reverse, starting in the 6th frame and working backwards to the first.

1. Pick a dance and describe in words one of these reversed dances.

Unit 1: Rigid Transformations and Congruence

2. How do the directions for running your dance in the forward direction and the reverse direction compare?

Lesson 1 Summary

Here are two ways for changing the position of a figure in a plane without changing its shape or size:

- Sliding or shifting the figure without turning it. Shifting Figure A to the right and up puts it in the position of Figure B.

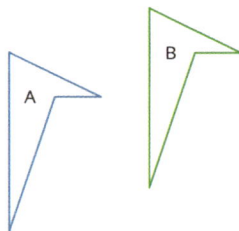

- Turning or rotating the figure around a point. Figure A is rotated around the bottom vertex to create Figure C.

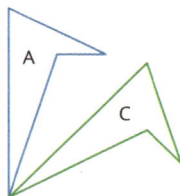

1.1.4 Practice Problems

1. The six frames show a shape's different positions.

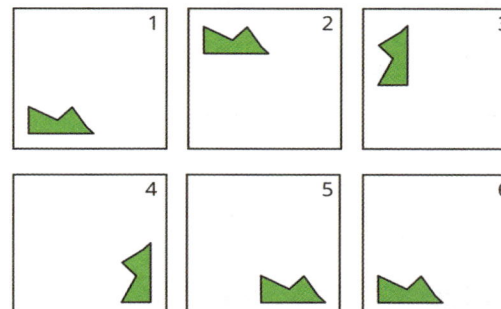

Describe how the shape moves to get from its position in each frame to the next.

2. These five frames show a shape's different positions.

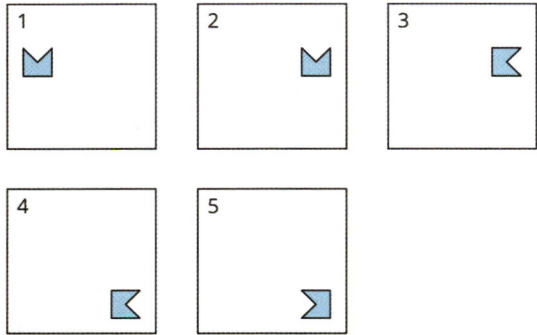

Describe how the shape moves to get from its position in each frame to the next.

3. Diego started with this shape.

Diego moves the shape down, turns it 90 degrees clockwise, then moves the shape to the right. Draw the location of the shape after each move.

Unit 1: Rigid Transformations and Congruence

Let's be more precise about describing moves of figures in the plane.

1.2.1 Warm-Up: A Pair of Quadrilaterals

Quadrilateral A can be rotated into the position of Quadrilateral B.

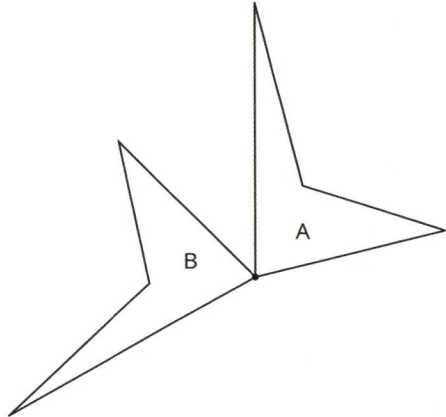

Estimate the angle of rotation.

1.2.2 Exploration Activity: How Did You Make That Move?

Here is another set of dance moves.

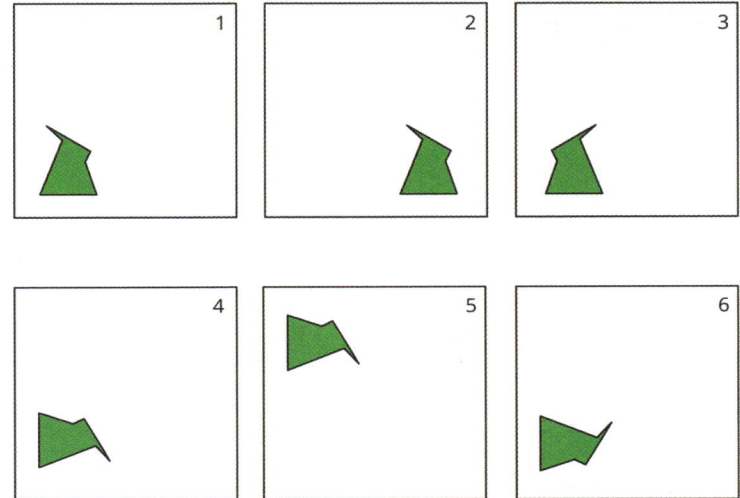

1. Describe each move or say if it is a new move.

   a. Frame 1 to Frame 2.

   b. Frame 2 to Frame 3.

   c. Frame 3 to Frame 4.

   d. Frame 4 to Frame 5.

   e. Frame 5 to Frame 6.

2. How would you describe the new move?

1.2.3 Exploration Activity: Move Card Sort

Your teacher will give you a set of cards. Sort the cards into categories according to the type of move they show. Be prepared to describe each category and why it is different from the others.

Lesson 2 Summary

Here are the moves we have learned about so far:

- A **translation** slides a figure without turning it. Every point in the figure goes the same distance in the same direction. For example, Figure A was translated down and to the left, as shown by the arrows. Figure B is a translation of Figure A.

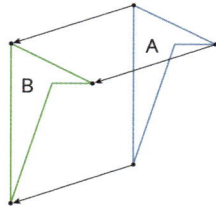

- A **rotation** turns a figure about a point, called the center of the rotation. Every point on the figure goes in a circle around the center and makes the same angle. The rotation can be **clockwise**, going in the same direction as the hands of a clock, or **counterclockwise**, going in the other direction. For example, Figure A was rotated 45° clockwise around its bottom vertex. Figure C is a rotation of Figure A.

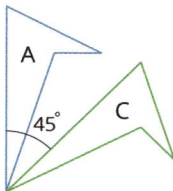

- A **reflection** places points on the opposite side of a reflection line. The mirror image is a backwards copy of the original figure. The reflection line shows where the mirror should stand. For example, Figure A was reflected across the dotted line. Figure D is a reflection of Figure A.

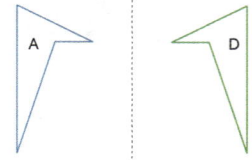

We use the word **image** to describe the new figure created by moving the original figure. If one point on the original figure moves to another point on the new figure, we call them **corresponding points**.

1.2.5 Practice Problems

1. Each of the six cards shows a shape.

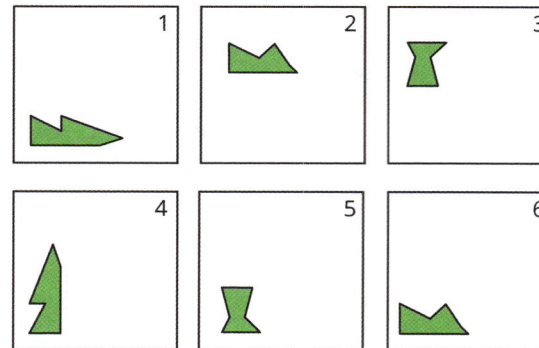

   a. Which pair of cards shows a shape and its image after a rotation?

   b. Which pair of cards shows a shape and its image after a reflection?

Unit 1: Rigid Transformations and Congruence

2. The five frames show a shape's different positions.

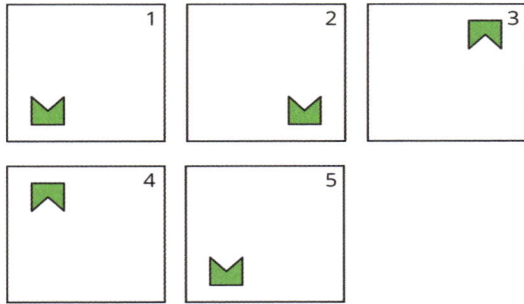

Describe how the shape moves to get from its position in each frame to the next.

3. The rectangle seen in Frame 1 is rotated to a new position, seen in Frame 2.

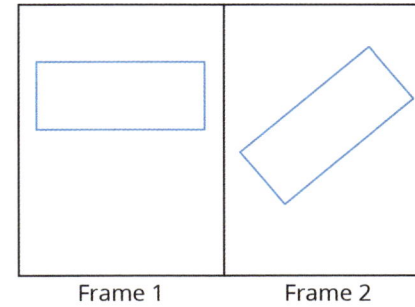

Frame 1   Frame 2

Select **all** the ways the rectangle could have been rotated to get from Frame 1 to Frame 2.

☐ 40 degrees clockwise

☐ 40 degrees counterclockwise

☐ 90 degrees clockwise

☐ 90 degrees counterclockwise

☐ 140 degrees clockwise

☐ 140 degrees counterclockwise

Unit 1, Lesson 3: Grid Moves

Let's transform some figures on grids.

1.3.1 Warm-Up: Notice and Wonder: The Isometric Grid

What do you notice? What do you wonder?

1.3.2a Exploration Activity: Transformation Information

Your teacher will give you tracing paper to carry out the moves specified. Use A', B', C', and D' to indicate vertices in the new figure that correspond to the points A, B, C, and D in the original figure.

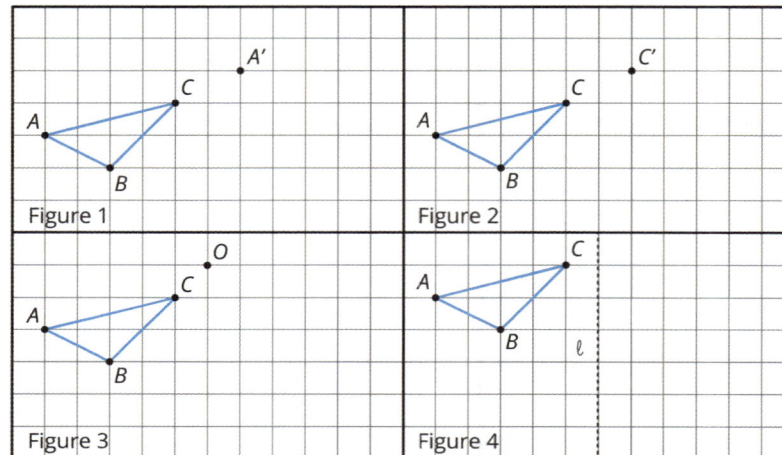

1. In Figure 1, translate triangle ABC so that A goes to A'.

2. In Figure 2, translate triangle ABC so that C goes to C'.

3. In Figure 3, rotate triangle ABC 90° counterclockwise using center O.

4. In Figure 4, reflect triangle ABC using line ℓ.

Unit 1: Rigid Transformations and Congruence

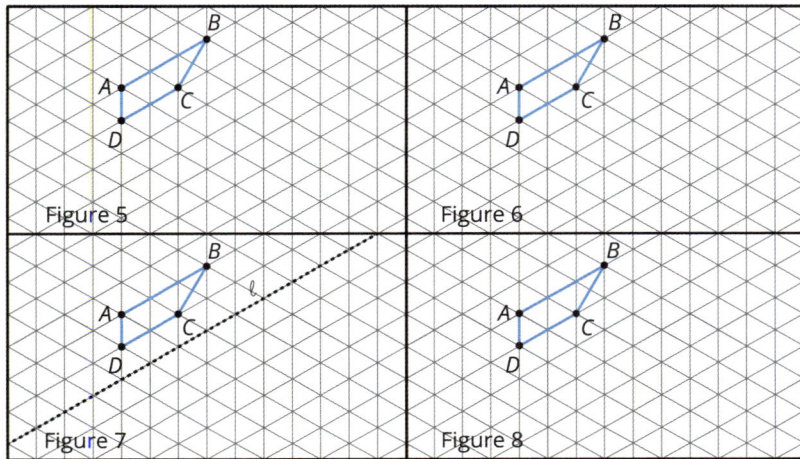

Figure 5

Figure 6

Figure 7

Figure 8

5. In Figure 5, rotate quadrilateral $ABCD$ 60° counterclockwise using center B.

6. In Figure 6, rotate quadrilateral $ABCD$ 60° clockwise using center C.

7. In Figure 7, reflect quadrilateral $ABCD$ using line ℓ.

8. In Figure 8, translate quadrilateral $ABCD$ so that A goes to C.

🔴 1.3.2b Exploration Extension: Are you ready for more?

The effects of each move can be "undone" by using another move. For example, to undo the effect of translating 3 units to the right, we could translate 3 units to the left. What move undoes each of the following moves?

1. Translate 3 units up

2. Translate 1 unit up and 1 unit to the left

3. Rotate 30 degrees clockwise around a point P

4. Reflect across a line ℓ

📕 Lesson 3 Summary

When a figure is on a grid, we can use the grid to describe a transformation. For example, here is a figure and an image of the figure after a move.

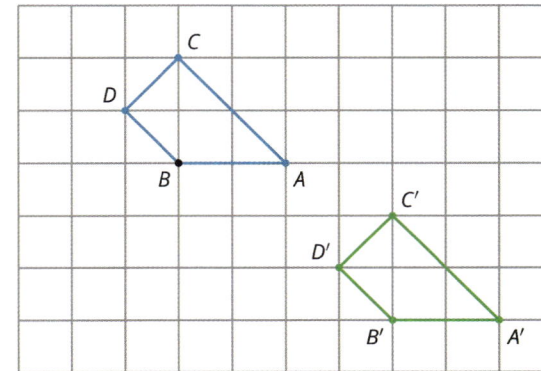

Quadrilateral $ABCD$ is translated 4 units to the right and 3 units down to the position of quadrilateral $A'B'C'D'$.

A second type of grid is called an *isometric grid*. The isometric grid is made up of equilateral triangles. The angles in the triangles all measure 60 degrees, making the isometric grid convenient for showing rotations of 60 degrees.

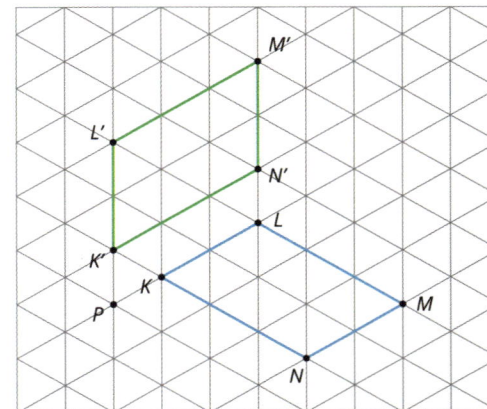

Here is quadrilateral $KLMN$ and its image $K'L'M'N'$ after a 60-degree counterclockwise rotation around a point P.

1. Apply each transformation described to Figure A. If you get stuck, try using tracing paper.

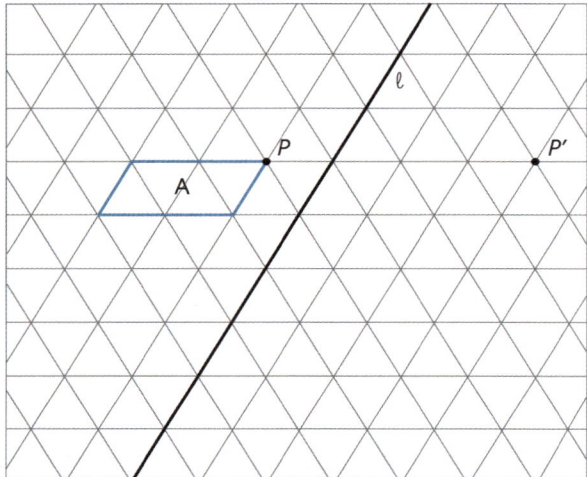

   a. A translation which takes P to P'
   b. A counterclockwise rotation of A, using center P, of 60 degrees
   c. A reflection of A across line ℓ

2. Here is triangle ABC drawn on a grid.

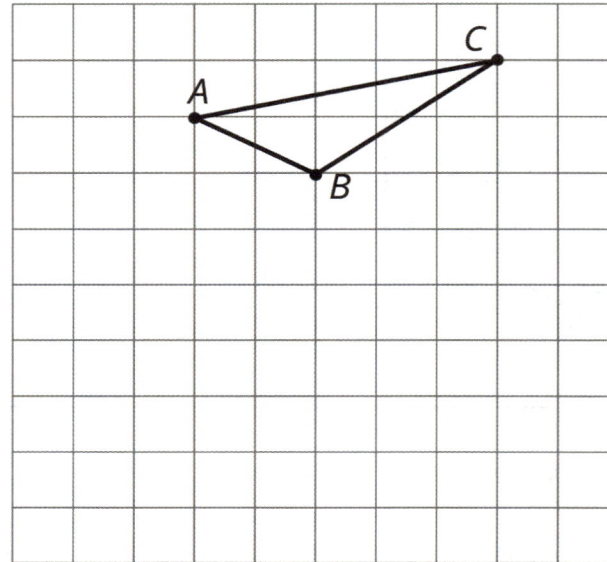

   On the grid, draw a rotation of triangle ABC, a translation of triangle ABC, and a reflection of triangle ABC. Describe clearly how each was done.

3.
   a. Draw the translated image of $ABCDE$ so that vertex C moves to C'. Tracing paper may be useful.

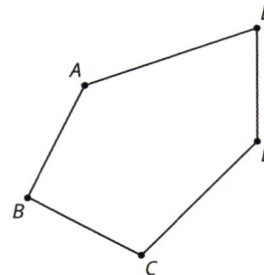

b. Draw the reflected image of Pentagon *ABCDE* with line of reflection ℓ. Tracing paper may be useful.

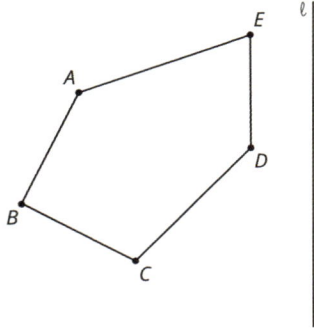

c. Draw the rotation of Pentagon *ABCDE* around *C* clockwise by an angle of 150 degrees. Tracing paper and a protractor may be useful.

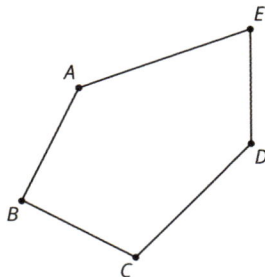

Let's draw and describe translations, rotations, and reflections.

1.4.1 Warm-Up: Reflection Quick Image

Here is an incomplete image. Your teacher will display the completed image twice, for a few seconds each time. Your job is to complete the image on your copy.

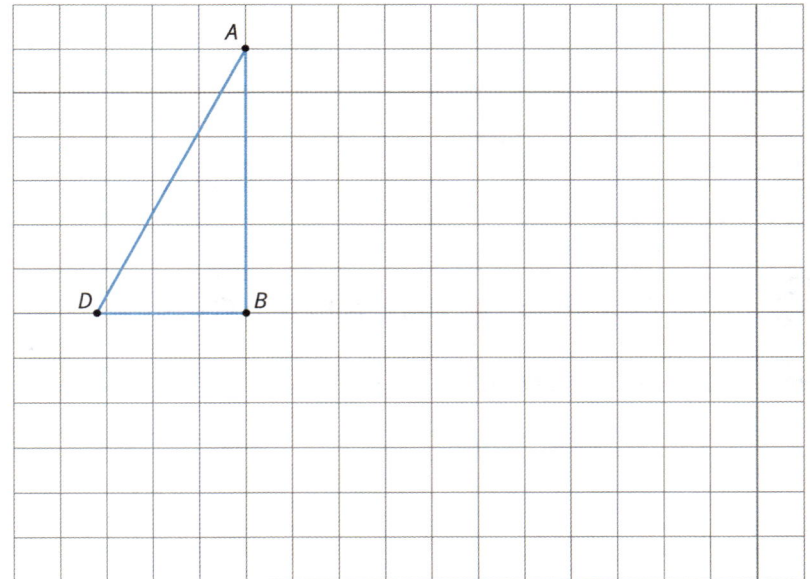

1.4.2 Exploration Activity: Make That Move

Your partner will describe the image of this triangle after a certain **transformation**. Sketch it here.

1.4.3a Exploration Activity: A to B to C

Here are some figures on an isometric grid.

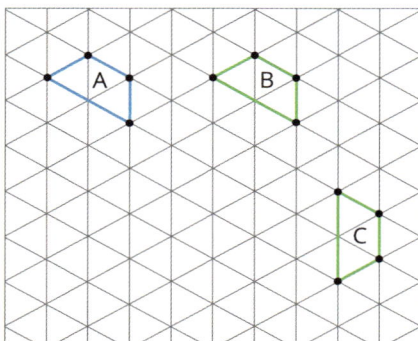

1. Name a transformation that takes Figure *A* to Figure *B*. Name a transformation that takes Figure *B* to Figure *C*.

2. What is one **sequence of transformations** that takes Figure *A* to Figure *C*? Explain how you know.

1.4.3b Exploration Extension: Are you ready for more?

Experiment with some other ways to take Figure *A* to Figure *C*. For example, can you do it with. . .

- No rotations?

- No reflections?

- No translations?

Lesson 4 Summary

A move, or combination of moves, is called a **transformation**. When we do one or more moves in a row, we often call that a **sequence of transformations**. To distinguish the original figure from its image, points in the image are sometimes labeled with the same letters as the original figure, but with the symbol ' attached, as in *A'* (pronounced "A prime").

- A translation can be described by two points. If a translation moves point A to point A', it moves the entire figure the same distance and direction as the distance and direction from A to A'. The distance and direction of a translation can be shown by an arrow.

  For example, here is a translation of quadrilateral $ABCD$ that moves A to A'.

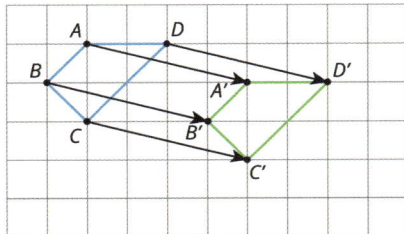

- A rotation can be described by an angle and a center. The direction of the angle can be clockwise or counterclockwise.

  For example, hexagon $ABCDEF$ is rotated 90° counterclockwise using center P.

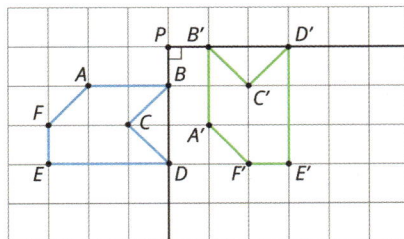

- A reflection can be described by a line of reflection (the "mirror"). Each point is reflected directly across the line so that it is just as far from the mirror line, but is on the opposite side.

  For example, pentagon $ABCDE$ is reflected across line m.

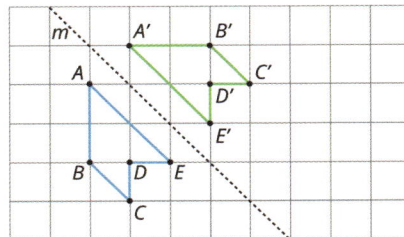

1. For each pair of polygons, describe a sequence of translations, rotations, and reflections that takes Polygon P to Polygon Q.

a.

b.

Continued on next page

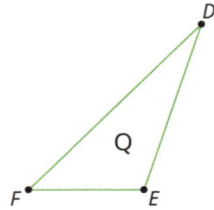

C.

2. Here is quadrilateral $ABCD$ and line ℓ.

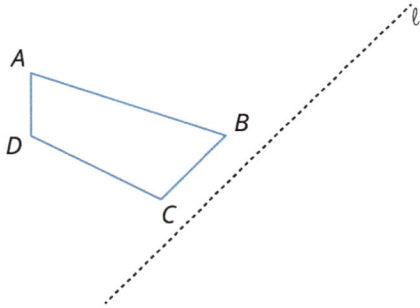

Draw the image of quadrilateral $ABCD$ after reflecting it across line ℓ.

3. Here is quadrilateral $ABCD$.

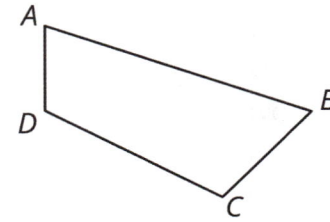

Draw the image of quadrilateral $ABCD$ after each rotation using B as center.

a. 90 degrees clockwise

b. 120 degrees clockwise

c. 30 degrees counterclockwise

Unit 1: Rigid Transformations and Congruence

Let's transform some figures and see what happens to the coordinates of points.

1.5.1 Warm-Up: Translating Coordinates

Select all of the translations that take Triangle T to Triangle U. There may be more than one correct answer.

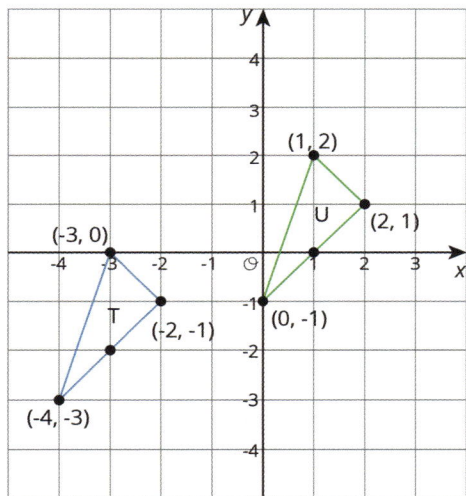

☐ Translate $(-3,0)$ to $(1,2)$.

☐ Translate $(2,1)$ to $(-2,-1)$.

☐ Translate $(-4,-3)$ to $(0,-1)$.

☐ Translate $(1,2)$ to $(2,1)$.

1.5.2 Exploration Activity: Reflecting Points on the Coordinate Plane

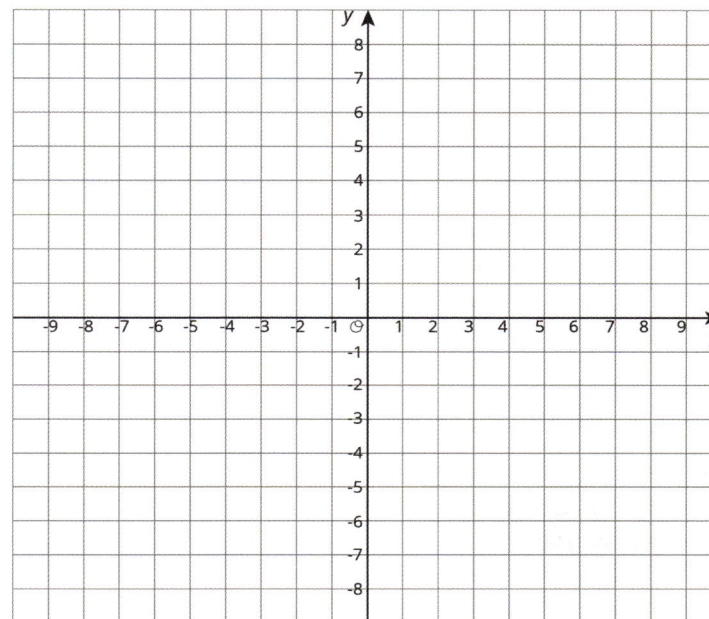

1. Here is a list of points

   $A = (0.5,4)$ $B = (-4,5)$ $C = (7,-2)$ $D = (6,0)$ $E = (0,-3)$

   On the coordinate plane:

   a. Plot each point and label each with its coordinates.
   b. Using the x-axis as the line of reflection, plot the image of each point.
   c. Label the image of each point with its coordinates.
   d. Include a label using a letter. For example, the image of point A should be labeled A'.

2. If the point (13,10) were reflected using the x-axis as the line of reflection, what would be the coordinates of the image? What about (13,−20)? (13,570)? Explain how you know.

3. The point R has coordinates (3,2).

   a. Without graphing, predict the coordinates of the image of point R if point R was reflected using the y-axis as the line of reflection.

   b. Check your answer by finding the image of R on the graph.

   c. Label the image of point R as R'.

   d. What are the coordinates of R'?

4. Suppose you reflect a point using the y-axis as line of reflection. How would you describe its image?

1.5.3a Exploration Activity: Transformations of a Segment

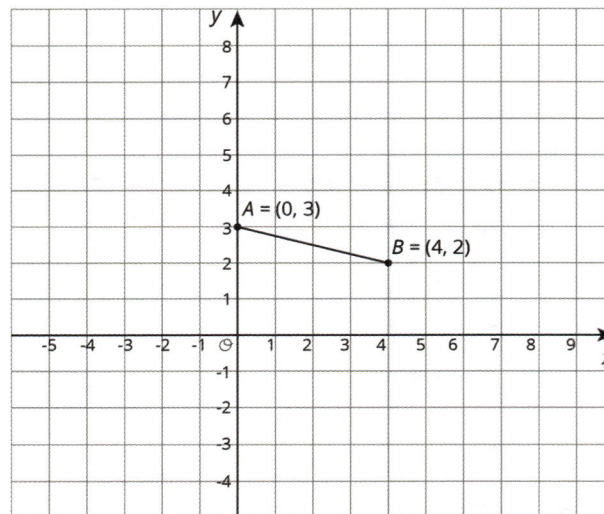

Apply each of the following transformations to segment AB.

1. Rotate segment AB 90 degrees counterclockwise around center B. Label the image of A as C. What are the coordinates of C?

2. Rotate segment AB 90 degrees counterclockwise around center A. Label the image of B as D. What are the coordinates of D?

Unit 1: Rigid Transformations and Congruence

3. Rotate segment AB 90 degrees clockwise around (0,0). Label the image of A as E and the image of B as F. What are the coordinates of E and F?

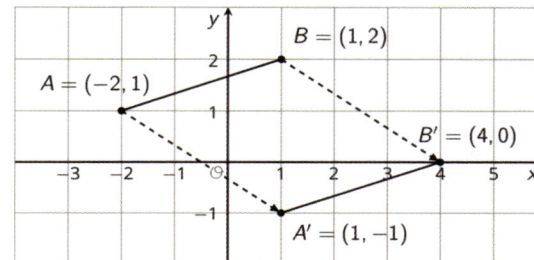

4. Compare the two 90-degree counterclockwise rotations of segment AB. What is the same about the images of these rotations? What is different?

Reflecting a point across an axis changes the sign of one coordinate. For example, reflecting the point A whose coordinates are $(2, -1)$ across the x-axis changes the sign of the y-coordinate, making its image the point A' whose coordinates are $(2,1)$. Reflecting the point A across the y-axis changes the sign of the x-coordinate, making the image the point A'' whose coordinates are $(-2, -1)$.

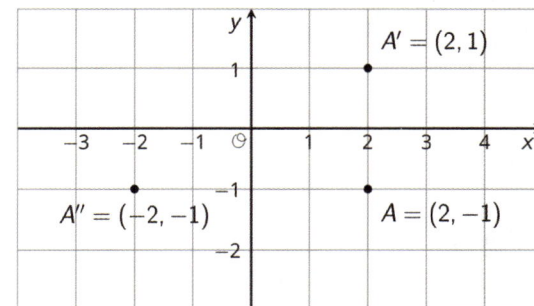

⚙ **1.5.3b Exploration Extension: Are you ready for more?**

Suppose EF and GH are line segments of the same length. Describe a sequence of transformations that moves EF to GH.

Reflections across other lines are more complex to describe.

We don't have the tools yet to describe rotations in terms of coordinates in general. Here is an example of a 90° rotation with center (0,0) in a counterclockwise direction.

📖 **Lesson 5 Summary**

We can use coordinates to describe points and find patterns in the coordinates of transformed points.

We can describe a translation by expressing it as a sequence of horizontal and vertical translations. For example, segment AB is translated right 3 and down 2.

Point A has coordinates $(0,0)$. Segment AB was rotated 90° counterclockwise around A. Point B with coordinates $(2,3)$ rotates to point B' whose coordinates are $(-3,2)$.

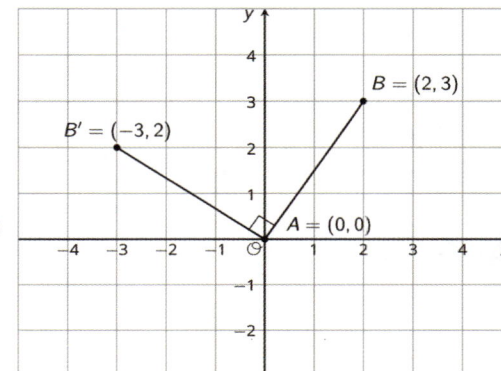

1.

a. Here are some points.

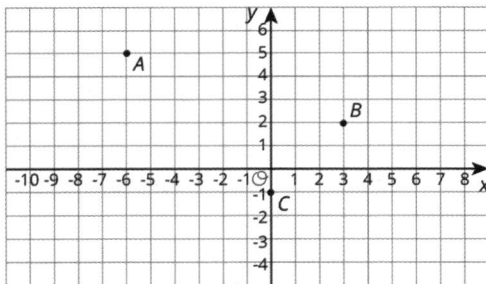

What are the coordinates of A, B, and C after a translation to the right by 4 units and up 1 unit? Plot these points on the grid, and label them A', B', and C'.

b. Here are some points.

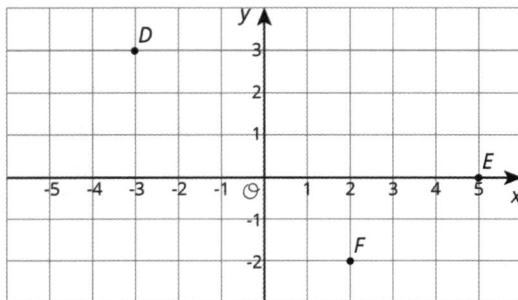

What are the coordinates of D, E, and F after a reflection over the y axis? Plot these points on the grid, and label them D', E', and F'.

c. Here are some points.

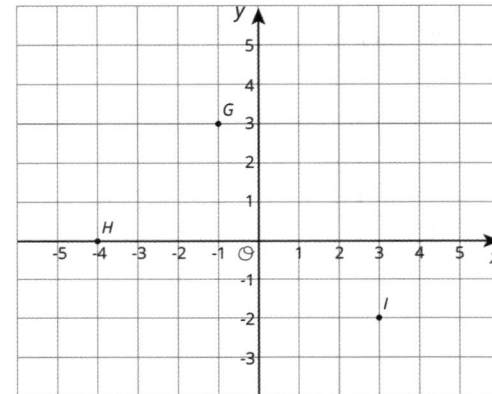

What are the coordinates of G, H, and I after a rotation about $(0,0)$ by 90 degrees clockwise? Plot these points on the grid, and label them G', H', and I'.

2. Describe a sequence of transformations that takes trapezoid A to trapezoid B.

3. Reflect polygon *P* using line ℓ.

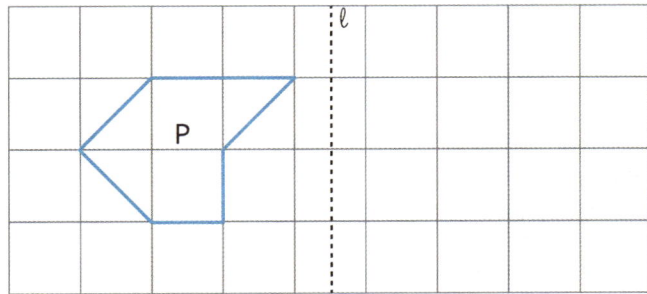

Let's transform some polygons in the coordinate plane.

1.6.1 Warm-Up: Finding a Center of Rotation

Andre performs a 90-degree counterclockwise rotation of Polygon P and gets Polygon P', but he does not say what the center of the rotation is. Can you find the center?

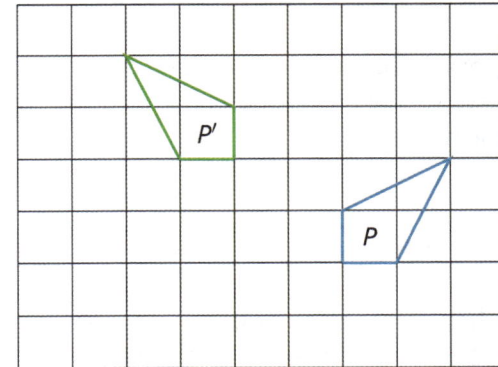

1.6.2a Exploration Activity: Info Gap: Transformation Information

Your teacher will give you either a problem card or a data card. Do not show or read your card to your partner.

If your teacher gives you the *problem card*:

1. Silently read your card and think about what information you need to answer the question.
2. Ask your partner for the specific information that you need.
3. Explain to your partner how you are using the information to solve the problem.
4. Solve the problem and explain your reasoning to your partner.

If your teacher gives you the *data card*:

1. Silently read the information on your card.
2. Ask your partner "What specific information do you need?" and wait for your partner to *ask* for information. *Only* give information that is on your card. (Do not figure out anything for your partner!)
3. Before telling your partner the information, ask "Why do you need that information?"
4. After your partner solves the problem, ask them to explain their reasoning and listen to their explanation.

Pause here so your teacher can review your work. Ask your teacher for a new set of cards and repeat the activity, trading roles with your partner.

1.6.2b Exploration Extension: Are you ready for more?

Sometimes two transformations, one performed after the other, have a nice description as a single transformation. For example, instead of translating 2 units up followed by translating 3 units up, we could simply translate 5 units up. Instead of rotating 20 degrees counterclockwise around the origin followed by rotating 80 degrees clockwise around the origin, we could simply rotate 60 degrees clockwise around the origin.

Can you find a simple description of reflecting across the x-axis followed by reflecting across the y-axis?

Lesson 6 Summary

The center of a rotation for a figure doesn't have to be one of the points on the figure. To find a center of rotation, look for a point that is the same distance from two corresponding points. You will probably have to do this for a couple of different pairs of corresponding points to nail it down.

When we perform a sequence of transformations, the order of the transformations can be important. Here is triangle ABC translated up two units and then reflected over the x-axis.

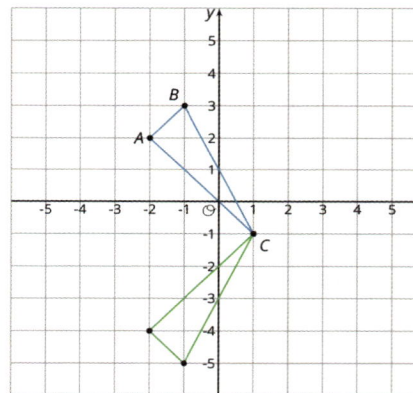

Here is triangle ABC reflected over the x-axis and then translated up two units.

Triangle ABC ends up in different places when the transformations are applied in the opposite order!

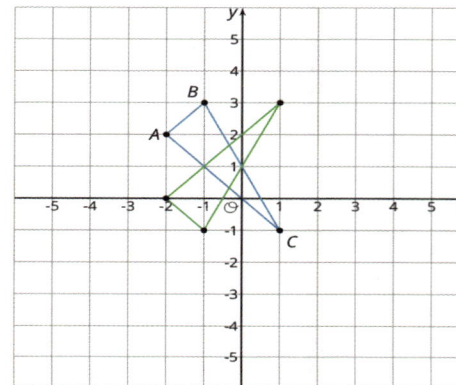

Unit 1: Rigid Transformations and Congruence

1.6.4 Practice Problems

1. Here is Trapezoid A in the coordinate plane:

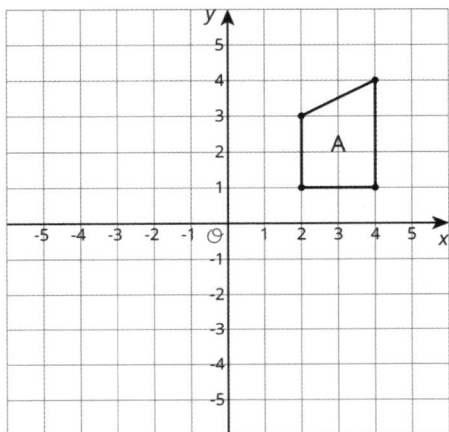

a. Draw Polygon B, the image of A, using the y-axis as the line of reflection.

b. Draw Polygon C, the image of B, using the x-axis as the line of reflection.

c. Draw Polygon D, the image of C, using the x-axis as the line of reflection.

2. The point $(-4,1)$ is rotated 180 degrees counterclockwise using center $(-3,0)$. What are the coordinates of the image?

A. $(-5,-2)$

B. $(-4,-1)$

C. $(-2,-1)$

D. $(4,-1)$

3. Describe a sequence of transformations for which Triangle B is the image of Triangle A.

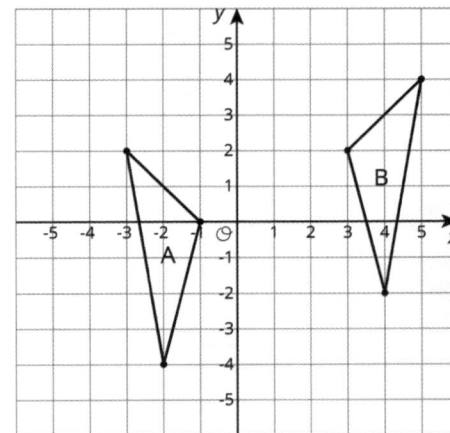

4. Here is quadrilateral $ABCD$.

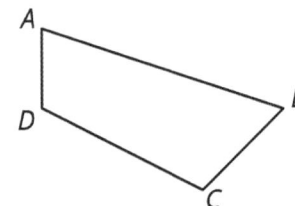

Draw the image of quadrilateral $ABCD$ after each transformation.

a. The translation that takes B to D.

Continued on next page

b. The reflection over segment BC.

c. The rotation about point A by angle DAB, counterclockwise.

Let's compare measurements before and after translations, rotations, and reflections.

1.7.1 Warm-Up: Measuring Segments

For each question, the unit is represented by the large tick marks with whole numbers.

1. Find the length of this segment to the nearest $\frac{1}{8}$ of a unit.

2. Find the length of this segment to the nearest 0.1 of a unit.

3. Estimate the length of this segment to the nearest $\frac{1}{8}$ of a unit.

4. Estimate the length of the segment in the prior question to the nearest 0.1 of a unit.

1.7.2 Exploration Activity: Sides and Angles

1. Translate Polygon *A* so point *P* goes to point *Q*. In the image, write the length of each side, in grid units, next to the side.

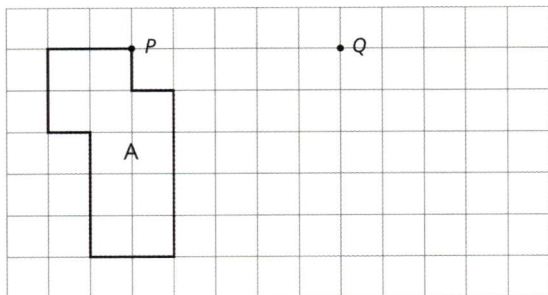

2. Rotate Triangle *B* 90 degrees clockwise using *R* as the center of rotation. In the image, write the measure of each angle in its interior.

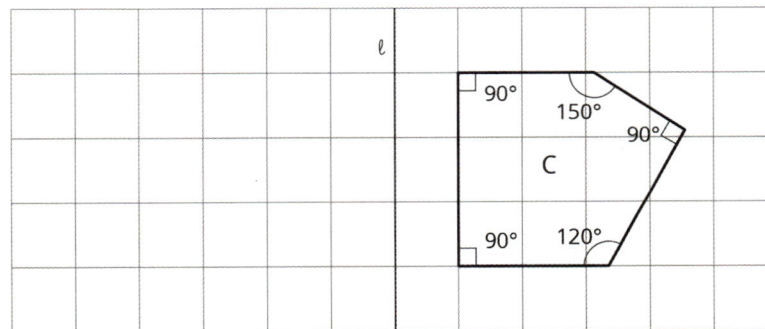

3. Reflect Pentagon *C* across line *ℓ*.
   a. In the image, write the length of each side, in grid units, next to the side. You may need to make your own ruler with tracing paper or a blank index card.

   b. In the image, write the measure of each angle in the interior.

1.7.3a Exploration Activity: Which One?

Here is a grid showing triangle *ABC* and two other triangles.

You can use a **rigid transformation** to take triangle *ABC* to *one* of the other triangles.

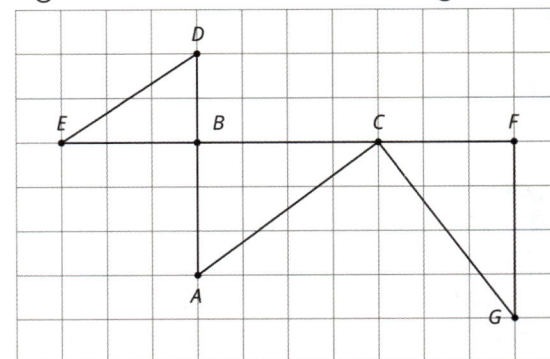

1. Which one? Explain how you know.

2. Describe a rigid transformation that takes ABC to the triangle you selected.

1.7.3b Exploration Extension: Are you ready for more?

A square is made up of an L-shaped region and three transformations of the region. If the perimeter of the square is 40 units, what is the perimeter of each L-shaped region?

Lesson 7 Summary

The transformations we've learned about so far, translations, rotations, reflections, and sequences of these motions, are all examples of **rigid transformations**. A rigid transformation is a move that doesn't change measurements on any figure.

Earlier, we learned that a figure and its image have corresponding points. With a rigid transformation, figures like polygons also have **corresponding sides** and **corresponding angles**. These corresponding parts have the same measurements.

For example, triangle EFD was made by reflecting triangle ABC across a horizontal line, then translating. Corresponding sides have the same lengths, and corresponding angles have the same measures.

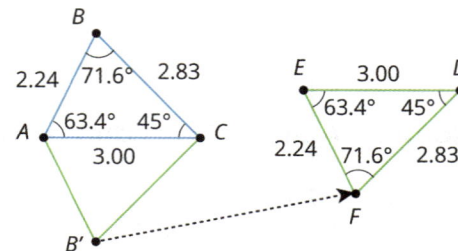

measurements in triangle ABC	corresponding measurements in image EFD
$AB = 2.24$	$EF = 2.24$
$BC = 2.83$	$FD = 2.83$
$CA = 3.00$	$DE = 3.00$
$m\angle ABC = 71.6°$	$m\angle EFD = 71.6°$
$m\angle BCA = 45.0°$	$m\angle FDE = 45.0°$
$m\angle CAB = 63.4°$	$m\angle DEF = 63.4°$

1.7.5 Practice Problems

1. Is there a rigid transformation taking Rhombus P to Rhombus Q? Explain how you know.

2. Describe a rigid transformation that takes Triangle A to Triangle B.

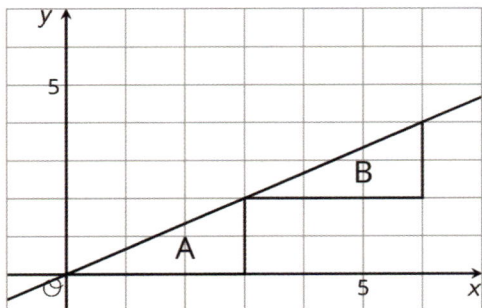

3. Is there a rigid transformation taking Rectangle A to Rectangle B? Explain how you know.

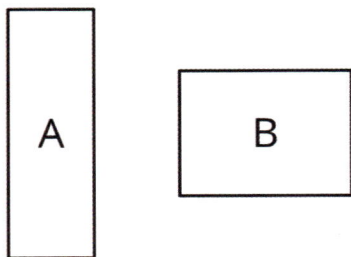

4. For each shape, draw its image after performing the transformation. If you get stuck, consider using tracing paper.

a. Translate the shape so that A goes to A'.

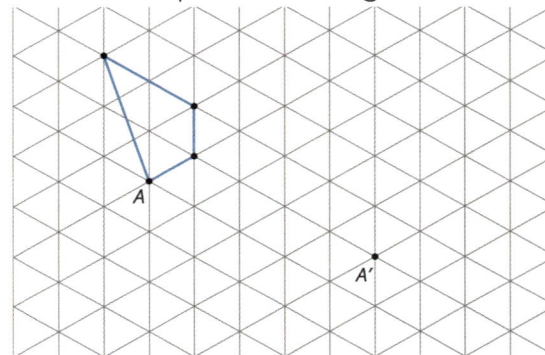

b. Rotate the shape 180 degrees counterclockwise around B.

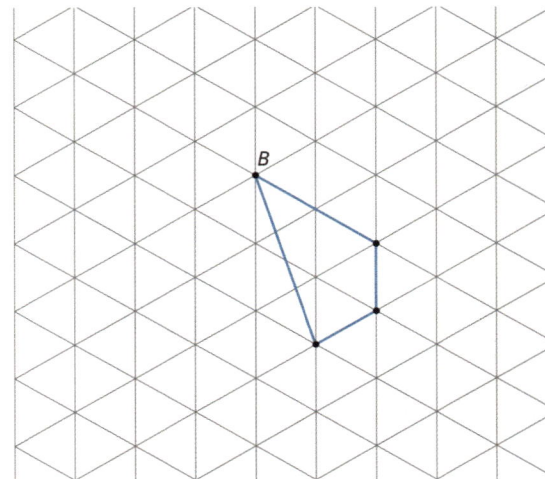

Continued on next page

c. Reflect the shape over the line shown.

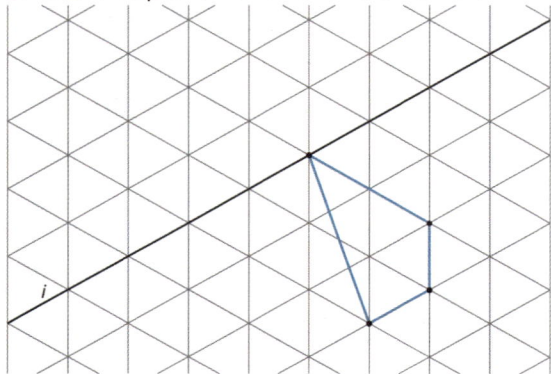

Let's rotate figures in a plane.

1.8.1 Warm-Up: Building a Quadrilateral

Here is a right isosceles triangle:

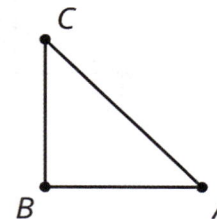

1. Rotate triangle ABC 90 degrees clockwise around B.
2. Rotate triangle ABC 180 degrees clockwise round B.
3. Rotate triangle ABC 270 degrees clockwise around B.

4. What would it look like when you rotate the four triangles 90 degrees clockwise around B? 180 degrees? 270 degrees clockwise?

3. Rotate segment CD 180 degrees around its midpoint, G. What is the image of C?

4. What happens when you rotate a segment 180 degrees around a point?

1.8.2a Exploration Activity: Rotating a Segment

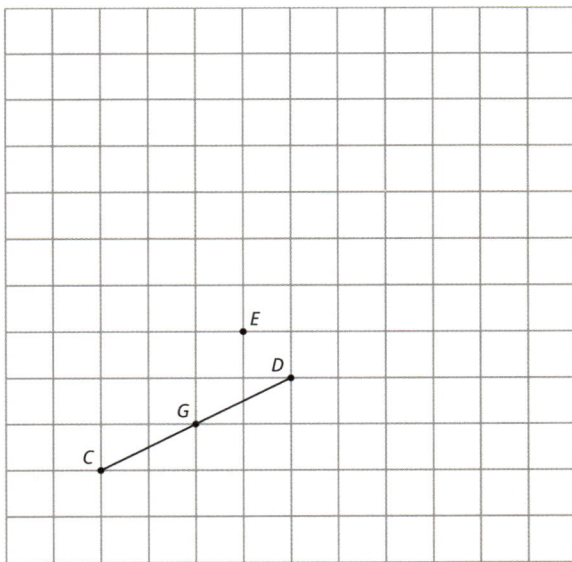

1. Rotate segment CD 180 degrees around point D. Draw its image and label the image of C as A.

2. Rotate segment CD 180 degrees around point E. Draw its image and label the image of C as B and the image of D as F.

1.8.2b Exploration Extension: Are you ready for more?

Here are two line segments. Is it possible to rotate one line segment to the other? If so, find the center of such a rotation. If not, explain why not.

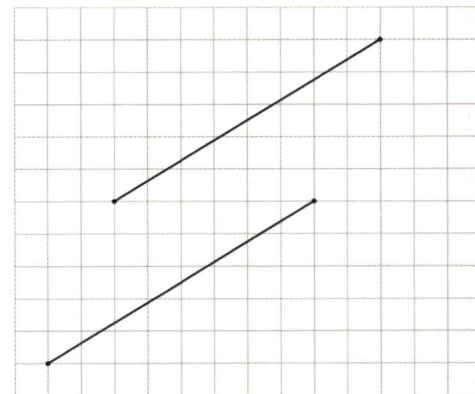

1.8.3 Exploration Activity: A Pattern of Four Triangles

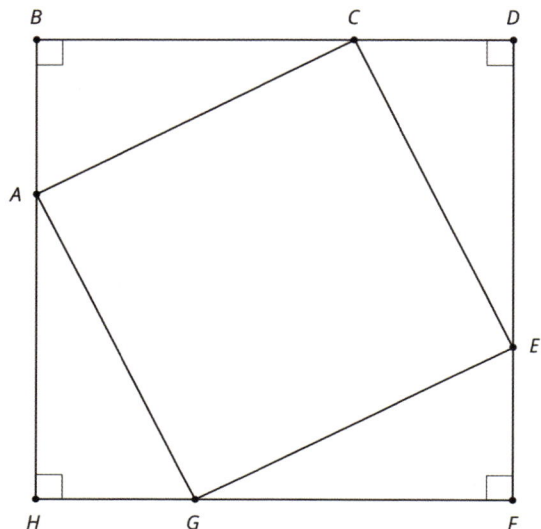

You can use rigid transformations of a figure to make patterns. Here is a diagram built with three different transformations of triangle ABC.

1. Describe a rigid transformation that takes triangle ABC to triangle CDE.

2. Describe a rigid transformation that takes triangle ABC to triangle EFG.

3. Describe a rigid transformation that takes triangle ABC to triangle GHA.

4. Do segments AC, CE, EG, and GA all have the same length? Explain your reasoning.

Lesson 8 Summary

When we apply a 180-degree rotation to a line segment, there are several possible outcomes:

- The segment maps to itself (if the center of rotation is the midpoint of the segment).
- The image of the segment overlaps with the segment and lies on the same line (if the center of rotation is a point on the segment).
- The image of the segment does not overlap with the segment (if the center of rotation is *not* on the segment).

We can also build patterns by rotating a shape. For example, triangle ABC shown here has $m(\angle A) = 60$. If we rotate triangle ABC 60 degrees, 120 degrees, 180 degrees, 240 degrees, and 300 degrees clockwise, we can build a hexagon.

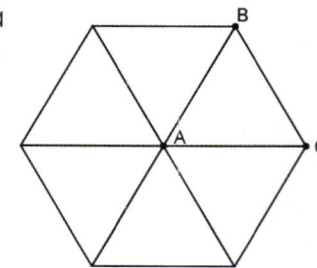

Unit 1: Rigid Transformations and Congruence

1. For the figure shown here,

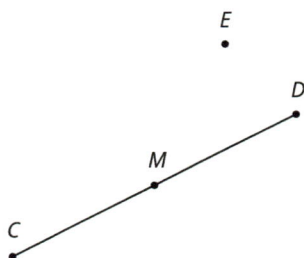

  a. Rotate segment CD 180° around point D.
  b. Rotate segment CD 180° around point E.
  c. Rotate segment CD 180° around point M.

2. Here is an isosceles right triangle:

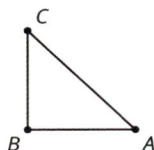

Draw these three rotations of triangle ABC together.

  a. Rotate triangle ABC 90 degrees clockwise around A.
  b. Rotate triangle ABC 180 degrees around A.
  c. Rotate triangle ABC 270 degrees clockwise around A.

3. Each graph shows two polygons $ABCD$ and $A'B'C'D'$. In each case, describe a sequence of transformations that takes $ABCD$ to $A'B'C'D'$.

  a.

  b.

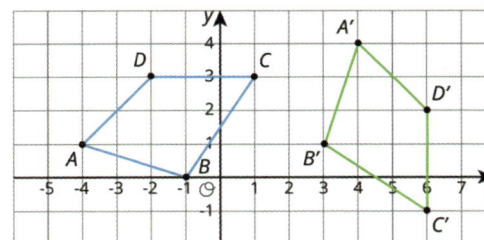

4. Lin says that she can map Polygon A to Polygon B using *only* reflections. Do you agree with Lin? Explain your reasoning.

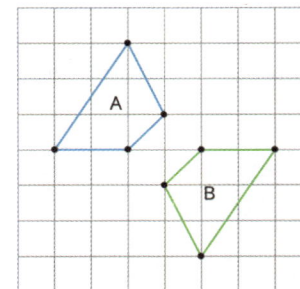

Let's transform some lines.

1.9.1 Warm-Up: Line Moves

For each diagram, describe a translation, rotation, or reflection that takes line ℓ to line ℓ'. Then plot and label A' and B', the images of A and B.

1.

2.

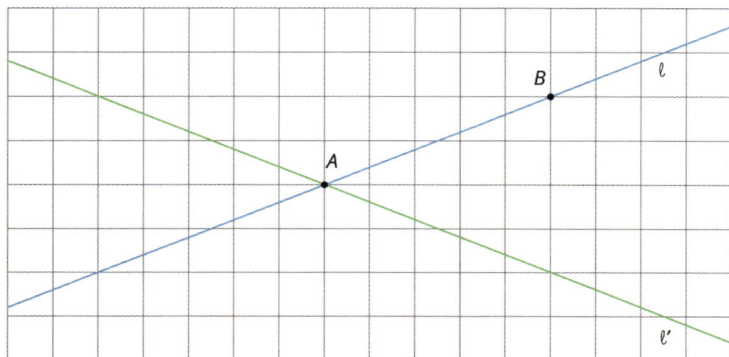

1.9.2a Exploration Activity: Parallel Lines

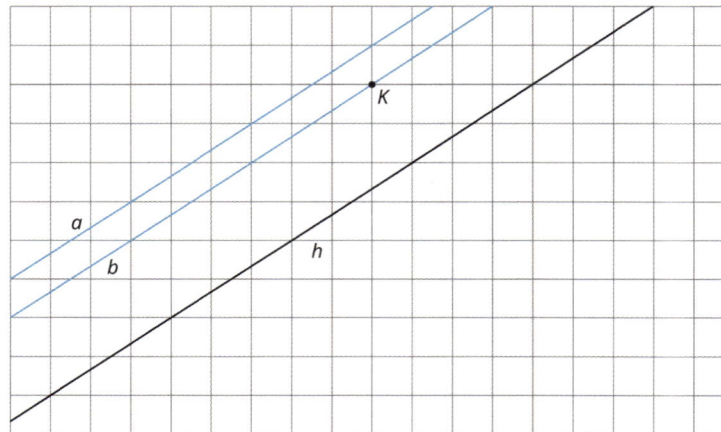

Use a piece of tracing paper to trace lines a and b and point K. Then use that tracing paper to draw the images of the lines under the three different transformations listed.

As you perform each transformation, think about the question:

What is the image of two parallel lines under a rigid transformation?

1. Translate lines a and b 3 units up and 2 units to the right.

    a. What do you notice about the changes that occur to lines a and b after the translation?

    b. What is the same in the original and the image?

2. Rotate lines a and b counterclockwise 180 degrees using K as the center of rotation.

   a. What do you notice about the changes that occur to lines a and b after the rotation?

   b. What is the same in the original and the image?

3. Reflect lines a and b across line h.

   a. What do you notice about the changes that occur to lines a and b after the reflection?

   b. What is the same in the original and the image?

1.9.2b Exploration Extension: Are you ready for more?

When you rotate two parallel lines, sometimes the two original lines intersect their images and form a quadrilateral. What is the most specific thing you can say about this quadrilateral? Can it be a square? A rhombus? A rectangle that isn't a square? Explain your reasoning.

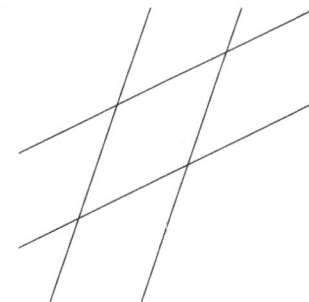

1.9.3 Exploration Activity: Let's Do Some 180's

1. The diagram shows a line with points labeled A, C, D, and B.

   a. On the diagram, draw the image of the line and points A, C, and B after the line has been rotated 180 degrees around point D.

   b. Label the images of the points A', B', and C'.

   c. What is the order of all seven points? Explain or show your reasoning.

2. The diagram shows a line with points A and C on the line and a segment AD where D is not on the line.

   a. Rotate the figure 180 degrees about point C. Label the image of A as A' and the image of D as D'.

   b. What do you know about the relationship between angle CAD and angle $CA'D'$? Explain or show your reasoning.

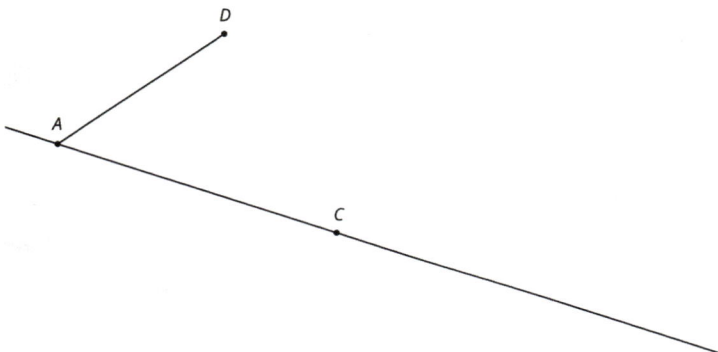

3. The diagram shows two lines ℓ and m that intersect at a point O with point A on ℓ and point D on m.

   a. Rotate the figure 180 degrees around O. Label the image of A as A' and the image of D as D'.

   b. What do you know about the relationship between the angles in the figure? Explain or show your reasoning.

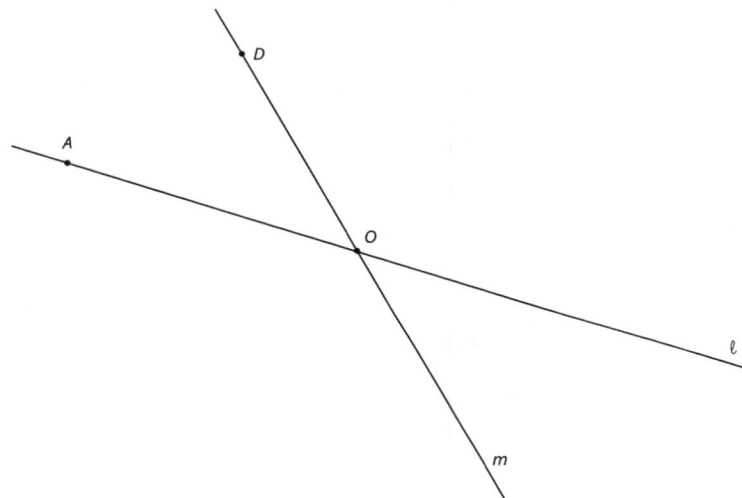

📔 Lesson 9 Summary

Rigid transformations have the following properties:

- A rigid transformation of a line is a line.

- A rigid transformation on two parallel lines results in two parallel lines that are the same distance apart as the original two lines.

- Sometimes, a rigid transformation takes a line to itself. For example:

Unit 1: Rigid Transformations and Congruence

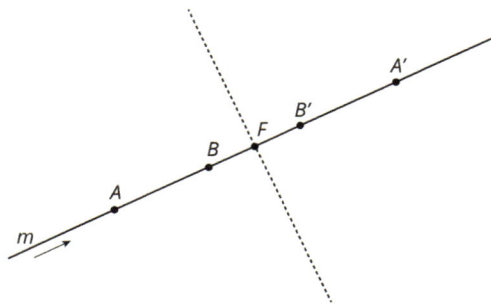

o A translation parallel to the line. The arrow shows a translation of line m that will take m to itself.

o A rotation by 180° around any point on the line. A 180° rotation of line m around point F will take m to itself.

o A reflection across any line perpendicular to the line. A reflection of line m across the dashed line will take m to itself.

These facts let us make an important conclusion. If two lines intersect at a point, which we'll call O, then a 180° rotation of the lines with center O shows that **vertical angles** are congruent. Here is an example:

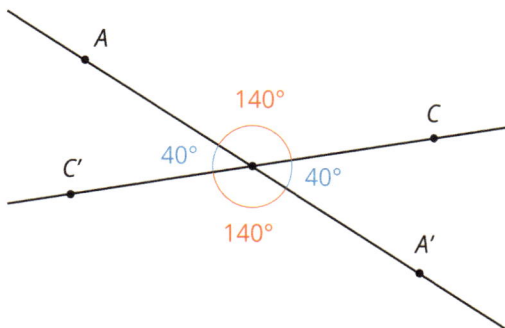

Rotating both lines by 180° around O sends angle AOC to angle $A'OC'$, proving that they have the same measure. The rotation also sends angle AOC' to angle $A'OC$.

1.
   a. Draw parallel lines AB and CD.
   b. Pick any point E. Rotate AB 90 degrees clockwise around E.
   c. Rotate CD 90 degrees clockwise around E.
   d. What do you notice?

2. Use the diagram to find the measures of each angle. Explain your reasoning.

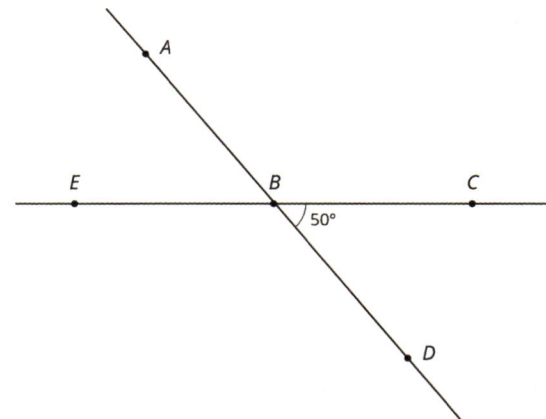

   a. $m\angle ABC$

   b. $m\angle EBD$

Continued on next page

c. $m\angle ABE$

3. Points P and Q are plotted on a line.

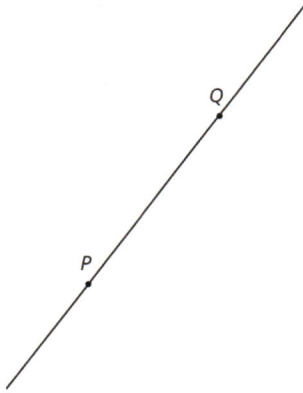

a. Find a point R so that a 180-degree rotation with center R sends P to Q and Q to P.

b. Is there more than one point R that works for part a?

4. In the picture triangle $A'B'C'$ is an image of triangle ABC after a rotation. The center of rotation is D.

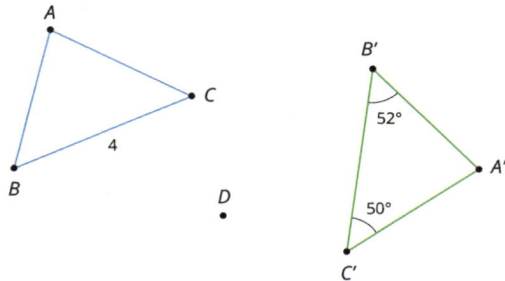

a. What is the length of side $B'C'$? Explain how you know.

b. What is the measure of angle B? Explain how you know.

c. What is the measure of angle C? Explain how you know.

5. The point $(-4,1)$ is rotated 180 degrees counterclockwise using center $(0,0)$. What are the coordinates of the image?

    A. $(-1,-4)$
    B. $(-1,4)$
    C. $(4,1)$
    D. $(4,-1)$

Unit 1, Lesson 10: Composing Figures

Let's use reasoning about rigid transformations to find measurements without measuring.

1.10.1 Warm-Up: Angles of an Isosceles Triangle

Here is a triangle.

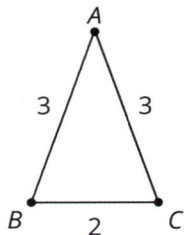

1. Reflect triangle ABC over line AB. Label the image of C as C'.
2. Rotate triangle ABC' around A so that C' matches up with B.
3. What can you say about the measures of angles B and C?

1.10.2a Exploration Activity: Triangle Plus One

Here is triangle ABC.

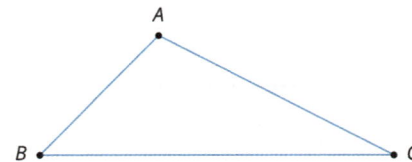

1. Draw midpoint M of side AC.
2. Rotate triangle ABC 180 degrees using center M to form triangle CDA. Draw and label this triangle.
3. What kind of quadrilateral is $ABCD$? Explain how you know.

1.10.2b Exploration Extension: Are you ready for more?

In the activity, we made a parallelogram by taking a triangle and its image under a 180-degree rotation around the midpoint of a side. This picture helps you justify a well-known formula for the area of a triangle. What is the formula and how does the figure help justify it?

1.10.3 Exploration Activity: Triangle Plus Two

The picture shows 3 triangles. Triangle 2 and Triangle 3 are images of Triangle 1 under rigid transformations.

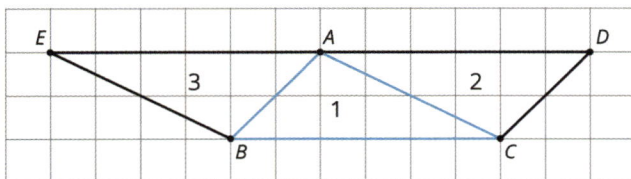

1. Describe a rigid transformation that takes Triangle 1 to Triangle 2. What points in Triangle 2 correspond to points A, B, and C in the original triangle?

2. Describe a rigid transformation that takes Triangle 1 to Triangle 3. What points in Triangle 3 correspond to points A, B, and C in the original triangle?

3. Find two pairs of line segments in the diagram that are the same length, and explain how you know they are the same length.

4. Find two pairs of angles in the diagram that have the same measure, and explain how you know they have the same measure.

1.10.4 Exploration Activity: Triangle ONE Plus

Here is isosceles triangle ONE. Its sides ON and OE have equal lengths. Angle O is 30 degrees. The length of ON is 5 units.

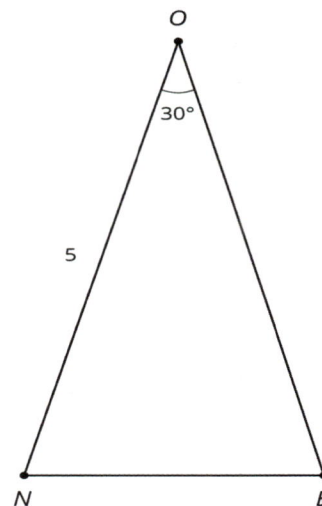

1. Reflect triangle ONE across segment ON. Label the new vertex M.

2. What is the measure of angle MON?

3. What is the measure of angle MOE?

4. Reflect triangle MON across segment OM. Label the point that corresponds to N as T.

5. How long is $\overline{OT}$? How do you know?

6. What is the measure of angle TOE?

7. If you continue to reflect each new triangle this way to make a pattern, what will the pattern look like?

Lesson 10 Summary

Earlier, we learned that if we apply a sequence of rigid transformations to a figure, then corresponding sides have equal length and corresponding angles have equal measure. These facts let us figure out things without having to measure them!

For example, here is triangle ABC.

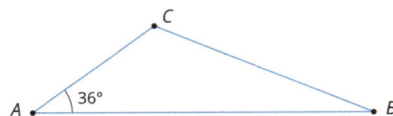

We can reflect triangle ABC across side AC to form a new triangle:

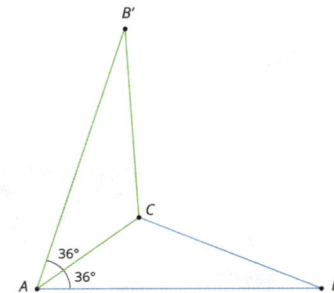

Because points A and C are on the line of reflection, they do not move. So the image of triangle ABC is $AB'C$. We also know that:

- Angle $B'AC$ measures 36° because it is the image of angle BAC.
- Segment AB' has the same length as segment AB.

When we construct figures using copies of a figure made with rigid transformations, we know that the measures of the images of segments and angles will be equal to the measures of the original segments and angles.

1.10.6 Practice Problems

1. Here is the design for the flag of Trinidad and Tobago.

Describe a sequence of translations, rotations, and reflections that take the lower left triangle to the upper right triangle.

2. Here is a picture of an older version of the flag of Great Britain. There is a rigid transformation that takes Triangle 1 to Triangle 2, another that takes Triangle 1 to Triangle 3, and another that takes Triangle 1 to Triangle 4.

a. Measure the lengths of the sides in Triangles 1 and 2. What do you notice?

b. What are the side lengths of Triangle 3? Explain how you know.

c. Do all eight triangles in the flag have the same area? Explain how you know.

3.

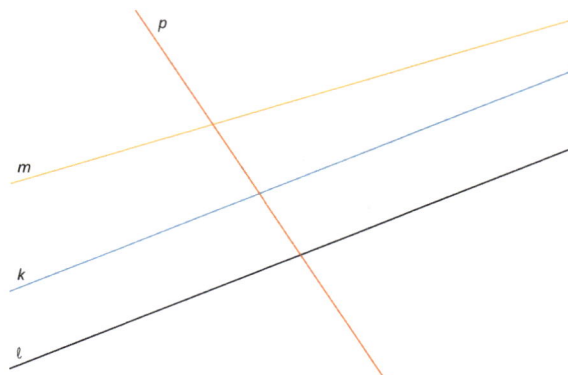

a. Which of the lines in the picture is parallel to line ℓ? Explain how you know.

b. Explain how to translate, rotate, or reflect line ℓ to obtain line k.

c. Explain how to translate, rotate, or reflect line ℓ to obtain line p.

4. Point A has coordinates (3,4). After a translation 4 units left, a reflection across the x-axis, and a translation 2 units down, what are the coordinates of the image?

Unit 1: Rigid Transformations and Congruence

MATH NATION

5. Here is triangle *XYZ*:

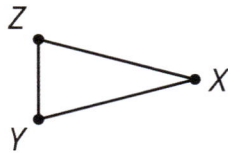

Draw these three rotations of triangle *XYZ* together.

  a. Rotate triangle *XYZ* 90 degrees clockwise around *Z*.

  b. Rotate triangle *XYZ* 180 degrees around *Z*.

  c. Rotate triangle *XYZ* 270 degrees clockwise around *Z*.

Unit 1, Lesson 11: What Is the Same?

Let's decide whether shapes are the same.

1.11.1 Warm-Up: Find the Right Hands

A person's hands are mirror images of each other. In the diagram, a left hand is labeled. Shade all of the right hands.

1.11.2 Exploration Activity: Are They the Same?

For each pair of shapes, decide whether or not they are the same.

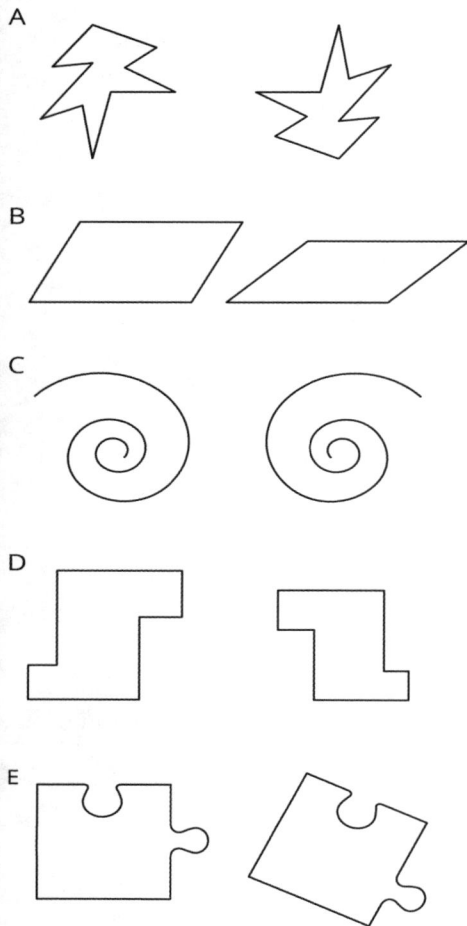

A

B

C

D

E

1.11.3a Exploration Activity: Area, Perimeter, and Congruence

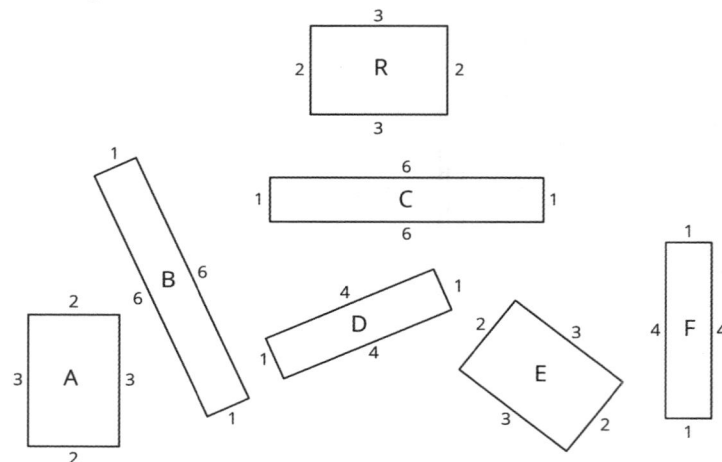

1. Which of these rectangles have the same area as Rectangle R but different perimeter?

2. Which rectangles have the same perimeter but different area?

3. Which have the same area *and* the same perimeter?

4. Use materials from the geometry tool kit to decide which rectangles are **congruent**. Shade congruent rectangles with the same color.

Unit 1: Rigid Transformations and Congruence

MATH NATION

In square $ABCD$, points E, F, G, and H are midpoints of their respective sides. What fraction of square $ABCD$ is shaded? Explain your reasoning.

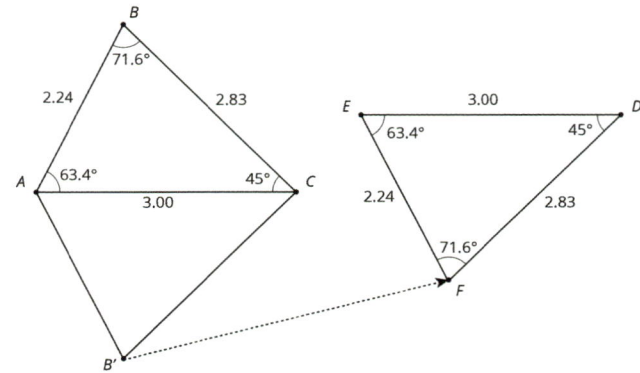

Here are some other facts about congruent figures:

- We don't need to check all the measurements to prove two figures are congruent; we just have to find a sequence of rigid transformations that match up the figures.

- A figure that looks like a mirror image of another figure can be congruent to it. This means there must be a reflection in the sequence of transformations that matches up the figures.

- Since two congruent polygons have the same area and the same perimeter, one way to show that two polygons are *not* congruent is to show that they have a different perimeter or area.

📝 **1.11.5 Practice Problems**

1. If two rectangles have the same perimeter, do they have to be congruent? Explain how you know.

📖 **Lesson 11 Summary**

Congruent is a new term for an idea we have already been using. We say that two figures are congruent if one can be lined up exactly with the other by a sequence of rigid transformations. For example, triangle EFD is congruent to triangle ABC because they can be matched up by reflecting triangle ABC across AC followed by the translation shown by the arrow. Notice that all corresponding angles and side lengths are equal.

2. Draw two rectangles that have the same area, but are *not* congruent.

b.

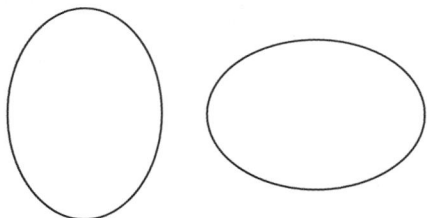

3. For each pair of shapes, decide whether or not it appears that the two shapes are congruent. Explain your reasoning.

a.

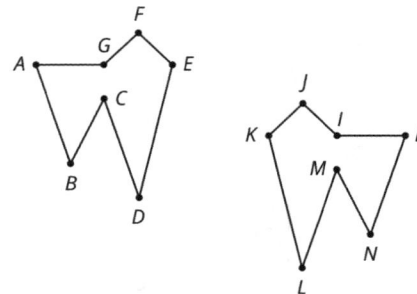

4.

a. Reflect Quadrilateral A over the x-axis. Label the image Quadrilateral B. Reflect Quadrilateral B over the y-axis. Label the image C.

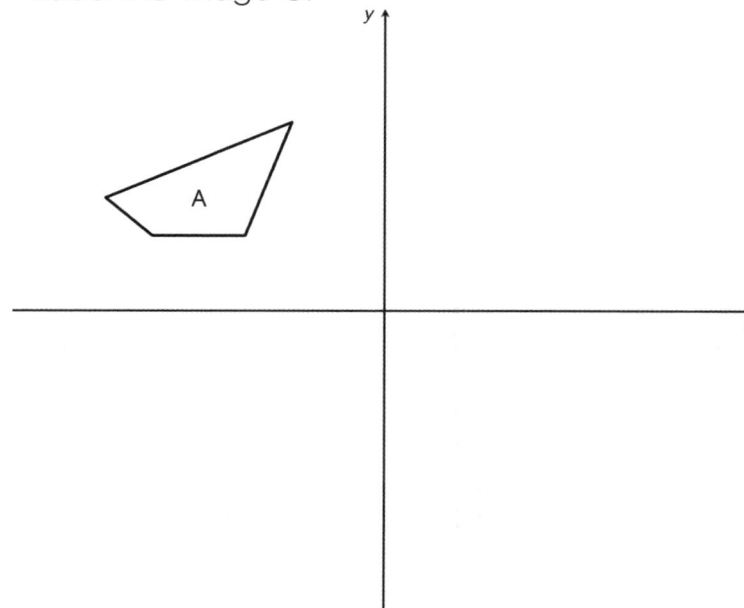

Unit 1: Rigid Transformations and Congruence

b. Are Quadrilaterals A and C congruent? Explain how you know.

5. The point $(-2, -3)$ is rotated 90 degrees counterclockwise using center $(0,0)$. What are the coordinates of the image?

   A. $(-3, -2)$
   B. $(-3, 2)$
   C. $(3, -2)$
   D. $(3, 2)$

6. Describe a rigid transformation that takes Polygon A to Polygon B.

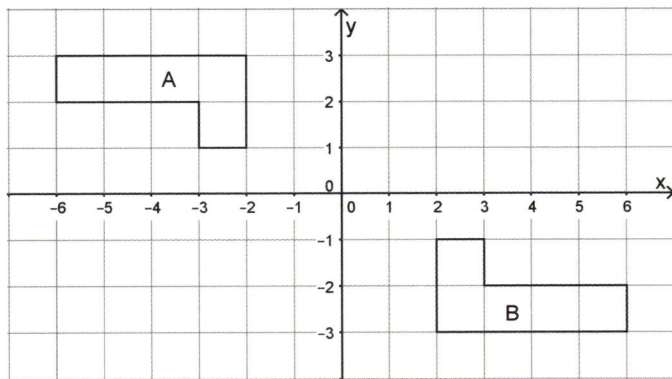

Unit 1, Lesson 12: Congruent Polygons

Let's decide if two figures are congruent.

1.12.1 Warm-Up: Translated Images

All of these triangles are congruent. Sometimes we can take one figure to another with a translation. Shade the triangles that are images of triangle ABC under a translation.

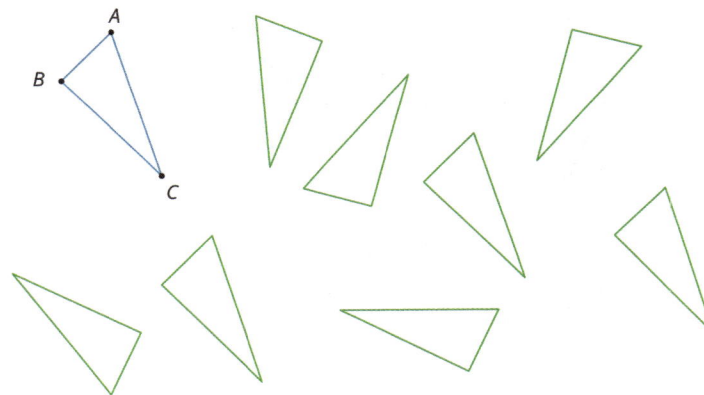

1.12.2 Exploration Activity: Congruent Pairs (Part 1)

For each of the following pairs of shapes, decide whether or not they are congruent. Explain your reasoning.

1.

2.

3.

4.

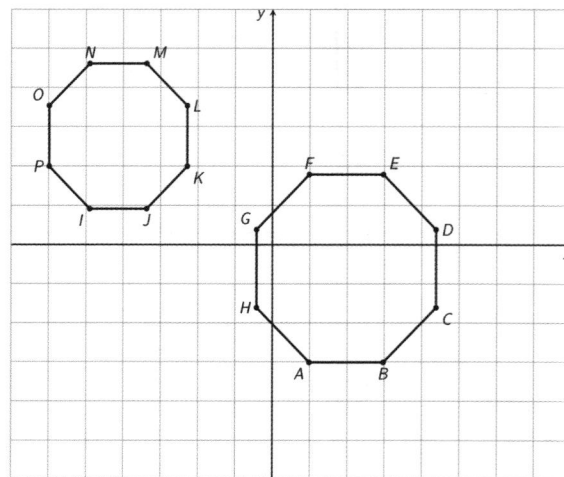

1.12.3a Exploration Activity: Congruent Pairs (Part 2)

For each pair of shapes, decide whether or not Shape A is congruent to Shape B. Explain how you know.

1.

2.

3.

4.

MATH NATION

5.

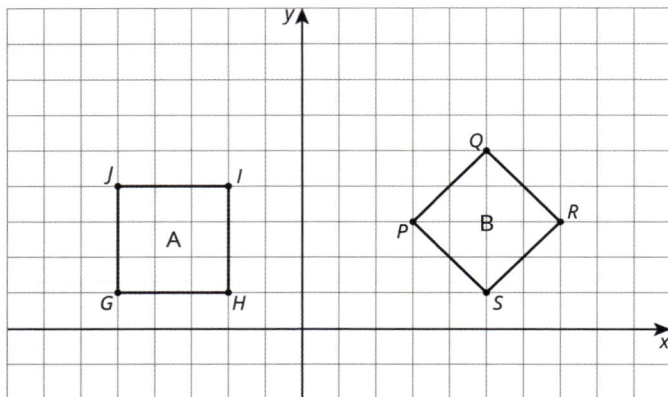

1.12.3b Exploration Extension: Are you ready for more?

A polygon has 8 sides: five of length 1, two of length 2, and one of length 3. All sides lie on grid lines. (It may be helpful to use graph paper when working on this problem.)

1. Find a polygon with these properties.

2. Is there a second polygon, not congruent to your first, with these properties?

1.12.4 Exploration Activity: Building Quadrilaterals

Your teacher will give you a set of four objects.

1. Make a quadrilateral with your four objects and record what you have made.

2. Compare your quadrilateral with your partner's. Are they congruent? Explain how you know.

3. Repeat steps 1 and 2, forming different quadrilaterals. If your first quadrilaterals were not congruent, can you build a pair that is? If your first quadrilaterals were congruent, can you build a pair that is not? Explain.

How do we know if two figures are congruent?

- If we copy one figure on tracing paper and move the paper so the copy covers the other figure exactly, then that suggests they are congruent.

- We can prove that two figures are congruent by describing a sequence of translations, rotations, and reflections that move one figure onto the other so they match up exactly.

How do we know that two figures are *not* congruent?

- If there is no correspondence between the figures where the parts have equal measure, that proves that the two figures are *not* congruent. In particular,

  o If two polygons have different sets of side lengths, they can't be congruent. For example, the figure on the left has side lengths 3, 2, 1, 1, 2, 1. The figure on the right has side lengths 3, 3, 1, 2, 2, 1. There is no way to make a correspondence between them where all corresponding sides have the same length.

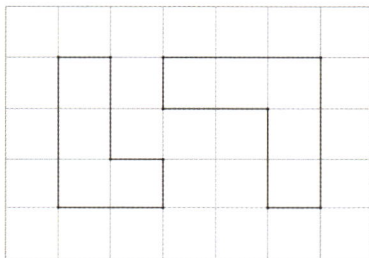

  o If two polygons have the same side lengths, but their orders can't be matched as you go around each polygon, the polygons can't be congruent. For example, rectangle $ABCD$ can't be congruent to quadrilateral $EFGH$. Even though they both have two sides of length 3 and two sides of length 5, they don't correspond in the same order. In $ABCD$, the order is 3, 5, 3, 5 or 5, 3, 5, 3; in $EFGH$, the order is 3, 3, 5, 5 or 3, 5, 5, 3 or 5, 5, 3, 3.

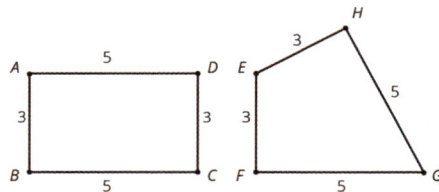

  o If two polygons have the same side lengths, in the same order, but different corresponding angles, the polygons can't be congruent. For example, parallelogram $JKLM$ can't be congruent to rectangle $ABCD$. Even though they have the same side lengths in the same order, the angles are different. All angles in $ABCD$ are right angles. In $JKLM$, angles J and L are less than 90 degrees and angles K and M are more than 90 degrees.

📝 **1.12.6 Practice Problems**

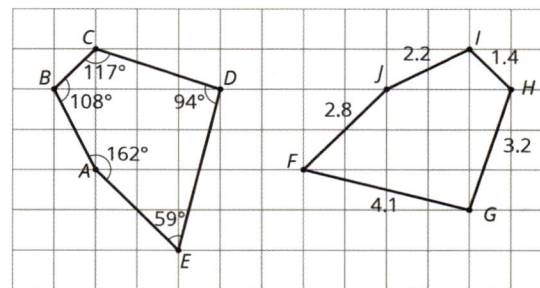

1.
  a. Show that the two pentagons are congruent.

  b. Find the side lengths of $ABCDE$ and the angle measures of $FGHIJ$.

2. For each pair of shapes, decide whether or not the two shapes are congruent. Explain your reasoning.

a.

b.

c.

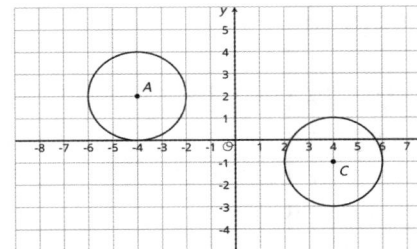

3.

a. Draw segment PQ.

b. When PQ is rotated 180° around point R, the resulting segment is the same as PQ. Where could point R be located?

Unit 1: Rigid Transformations and Congruence

MATH NATION

4. Here is trapezoid *ABCD*.

Using rigid transformations on the trapezoid, build a pattern. Describe some of the rigid transformations you used.

Let's find ways to test congruence of interesting figures.

1.13.1 Warm-Up: Not Just the Vertices

Trapezoids *ABCD* and *A'B'C'D'* are congruent.

- Draw and label the points on *A'B'C'D'* that correspond to *E* and *F*.

- Draw and label the points on *ABCD* that correspond to *G'* and *H'*.

- Draw and label at least three more pairs of corresponding points.

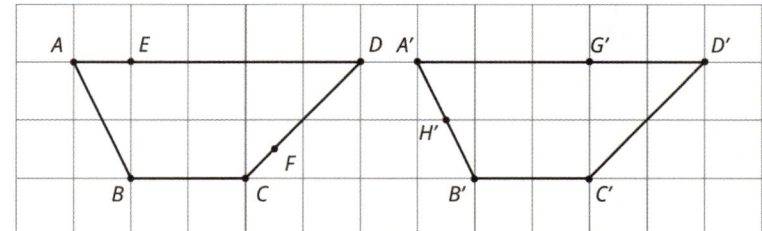

Are any of the ovals congruent to one another? Explain how you know.

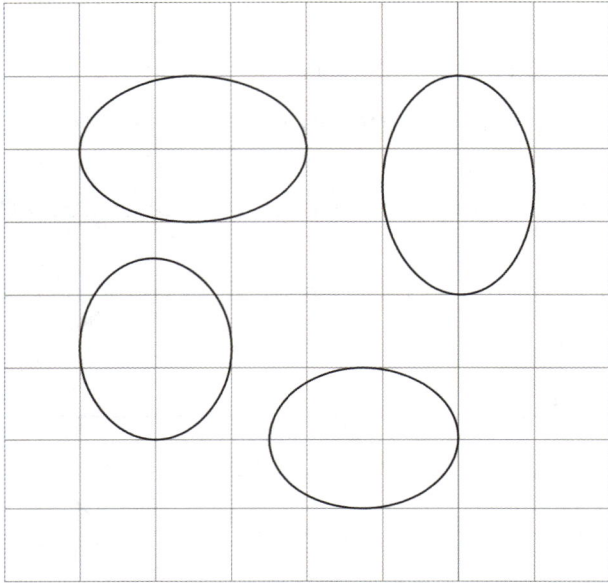

You can use 12 toothpicks to create a polygon with an area of five square toothpicks, like this:

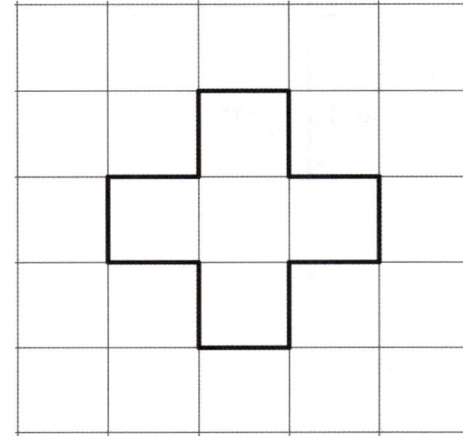

Can you use exactly 12 toothpicks to create a polygon with an area of four square toothpicks?

Unit 1: Rigid Transformations and Congruence

1.13.3 Exploration Activity: Corresponding Points in Congruent Figures

Here are two congruent shapes with some corresponding points labeled.

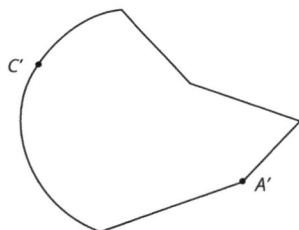

1. Draw the points corresponding to B, D, and E, and label them B', D', and E'.

2. Draw line segments AD and $A'D'$ and measure them. Do the same for segments BC and $B'C'$ and for segments AE and $A'E'$. What do you notice?

3. Do you think there could be a pair of corresponding segments with different lengths? Explain.

1.13.4 Exploration Activity: Astonished Faces

Are these faces congruent? Explain your reasoning.

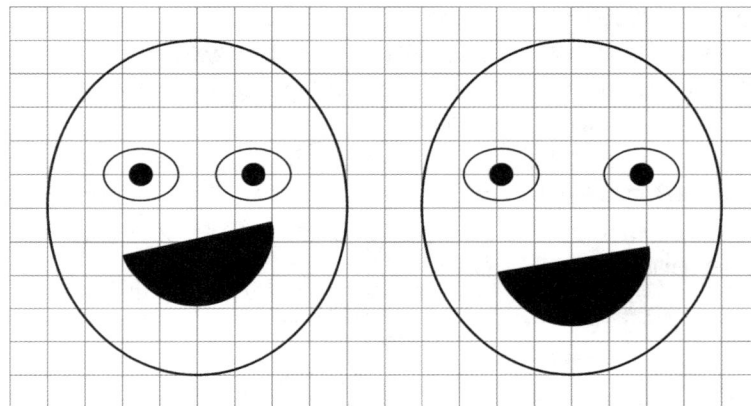

Lesson 13 Summary

To show two figures are congruent, you align one with the other by a sequence of rigid transformations. This is true even for figures with curved sides. Distances between corresponding points on congruent figures are always equal, even for curved shapes. For example, corresponding segments AB and $A'B'$ on these congruent ovals have the same length:

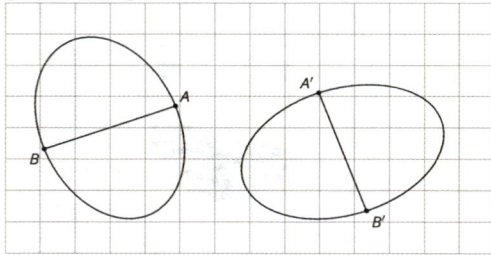

To show two figures are not congruent, you can find parts of the figures that should correspond but that have different measurements.

For example, these two ovals don't look congruent.

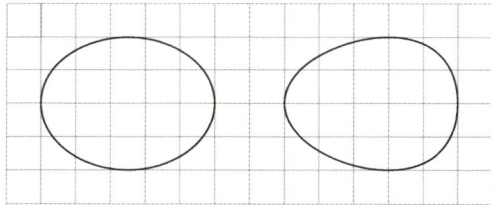

On both, the longest distance is 5 units across, and the longest distance from top to bottom is 4 units. The line segment from the highest to lowest point is in the middle of the left oval, but in the right oval, it's 2 units from the right end and 3 units from the left end. This proves they are not congruent.

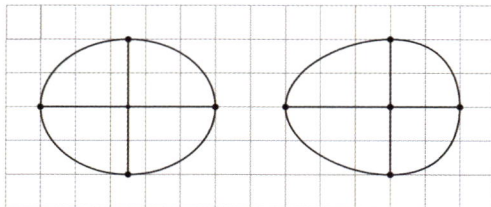

1. Which of these four figures are congruent to the top figure?

A   C

B   D

    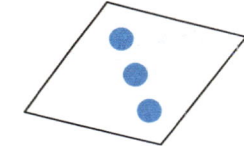

2. These two figures are congruent, with corresponding points marked.

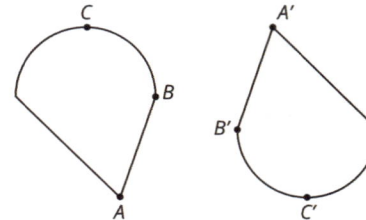

a. Are angles ABC and $A'B'C'$ congruent? Explain your reasoning.

b. Measure angles ABC and $A'B'C'$ to check your answer.

3. Here are two figures.

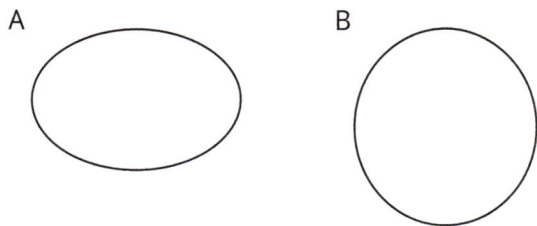

Show, using measurement, that these two figures are *not* congruent.

4. Each picture shows two polygons, one labeled Polygon A and one labeled Polygon B. Describe how to move Polygon A into the position of Polygon B using a transformation.

a.

b.

c.

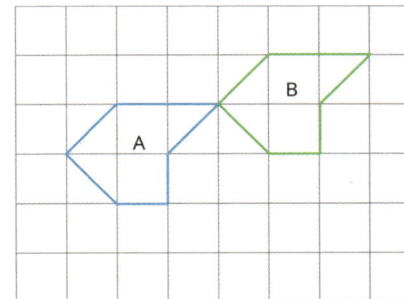

Let's explore why some angles are always equal.

1.14.1 Warm-Up: Angle Pairs

1. Find the measure of angle JGH. Explain or show your reasoning.

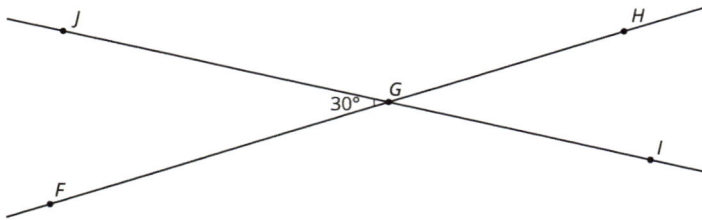

2. Find and label a second 30° degree angle in the diagram. Find and label an angle congruent to angle JGH.

1.14.2a Exploration Activity: Cutting Parallel Lines with a Transversal

Lines AC and DF are parallel. They are cut by **transversal** HJ.

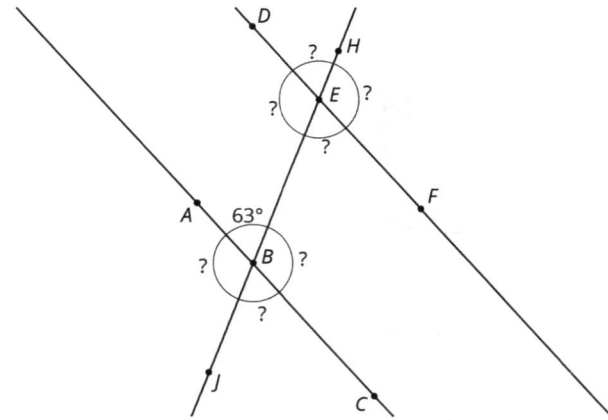

1. With your partner, find the seven unknown angle measures in the diagram. Explain your reasoning.

2. What do you notice about the angles with vertex B and the angles with vertex E?

3. Using what you noticed, find the measures of the four angles at point B in the second diagram. Lines AC and DF are parallel.

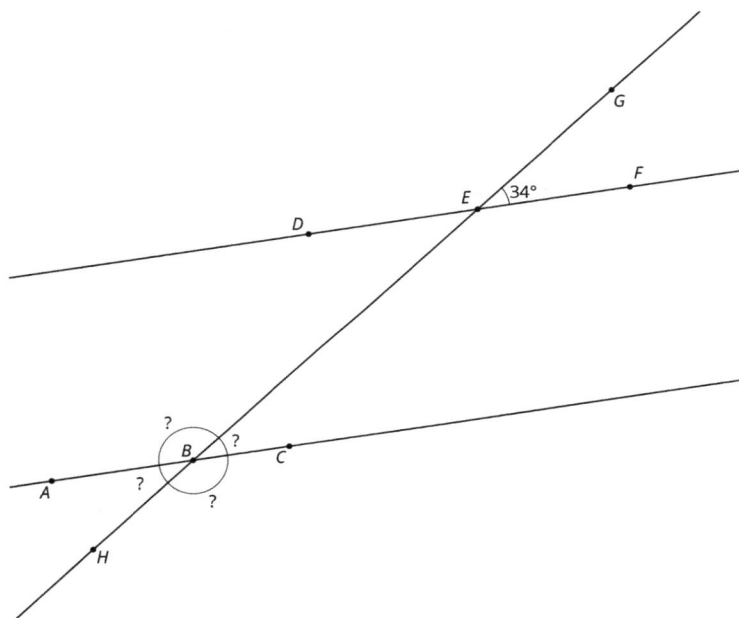

4. The next diagram resembles the first one, but the lines form slightly different angles. Work with your partner to find the six unknown angles with vertices at points B and E.

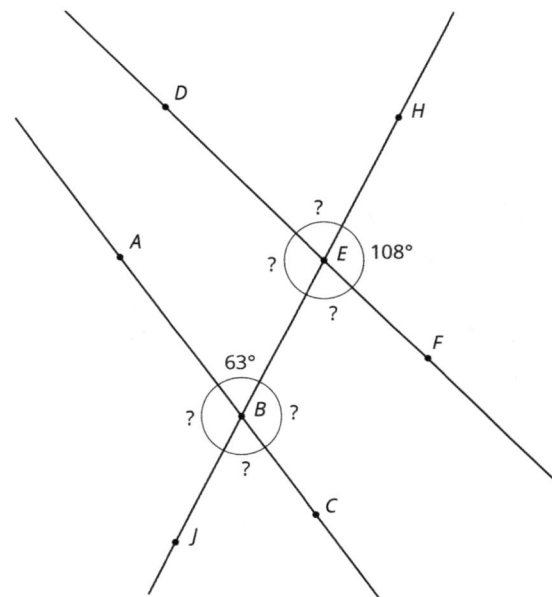

5. What do you notice about the angles in this diagram as compared to the earlier diagram? How are the two diagrams different? How are they the same?

1.14.2b Exploration Extension: Are you ready for more?

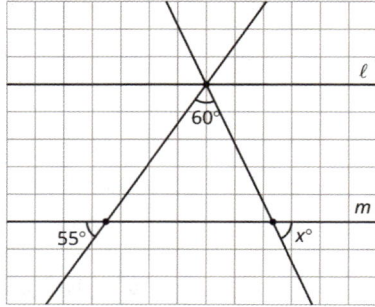

Parallel lines ℓ and m are cut by two transversals which intersect ℓ in the same point. Two angles are marked in the figure. Find the measure x of the third angle.

1.14.3 Exploration Activity: Alternate Interior Angles Are Congruent

1. Lines ℓ and k are parallel and t is a transversal. Point M is the midpoint of segment PQ.

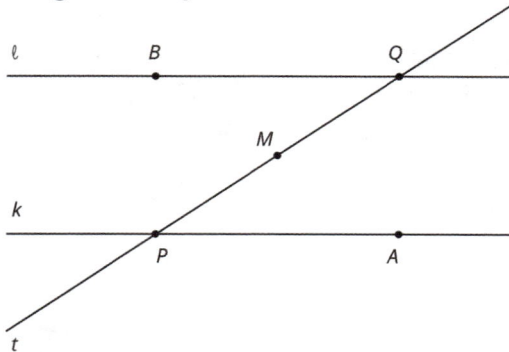

Find a rigid transformation showing that angles MPA and MQB are congruent.

2. In this picture, lines ℓ and k are no longer parallel. M is still the midpoint of segment PQ.

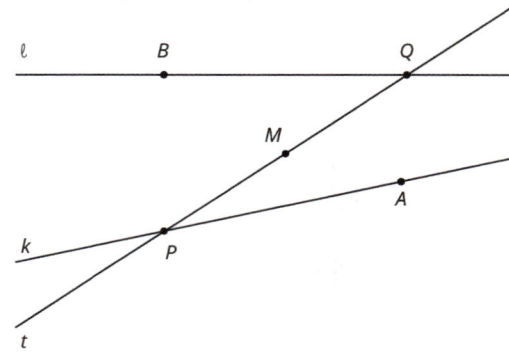

Does your argument in the earlier problem apply in this situation? Explain.

Lesson 14 Summary

When two lines intersect, vertical angles are equal and adjacent angles are supplementary, that is, their measures sum to 180°. For example, in this figure angles 1 and 3 are equal, angles 2 and 4 are equal, angles 1 and 4 are supplementary, and angles 2 and 3 are supplementary.

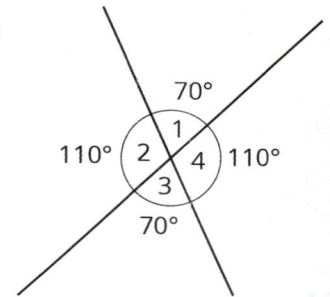

When two parallel lines are cut by another line, called a **transversal**, two pairs of **alternate interior angles** are created. ("Interior" means on the inside, or between, the two parallel lines.) For example, in this figure angles 3 and 5 are alternate interior angles and angles 4 and 6 are also alternate interior angles.

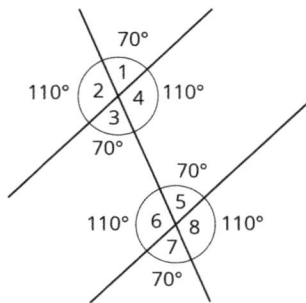

Alternate interior angles are equal because a 180° rotation around the midpoint of the segment that joins their vertices takes each angle to the other. Imagine a point *M* halfway between the two intersections—can you see how rotating 180° about *M* takes angle 3 to angle 5?

Using what we know about vertical angles, adjacent angles, and alternate interior angles, we can find the measures of any of the eight angles created by a transversal if we know just one of them. For example, starting with the fact that angle 1 is 70° we use vertical angles to see that angle 3 is 70°, then we use alternate interior angles to see that angle 5 is 70°, then we use the fact that angle 5 is supplementary to angle 8 to see that angle 8 is 110° since 180 − 70 = 110. It turns out that there are only two different measures. In this example, angles 1, 3, 5, and 7 measure 70°, and angles 2, 4, 6, and 8 measure 110°.

1. Use the diagram to find the measures of each angle. Explain your reasoning.

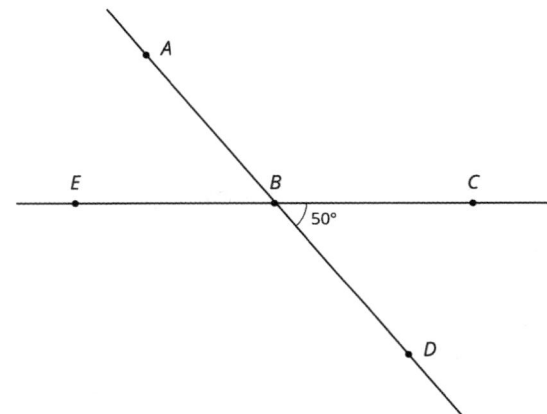

a. $m\angle ABC$

b. $m\angle EBD$

c. $m\angle ABE$

2. Lines k and ℓ are parallel, and the measure of angle ABC is 19 degrees.

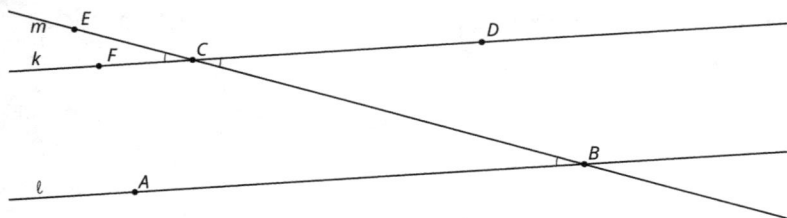

a. Explain why the measure of angle ECF is 19 degrees. If you get stuck, consider translating line ℓ by moving B to C.

b. What is the measure of angle BCD? Explain.

3. The diagram shows three lines with some marked angle measures.

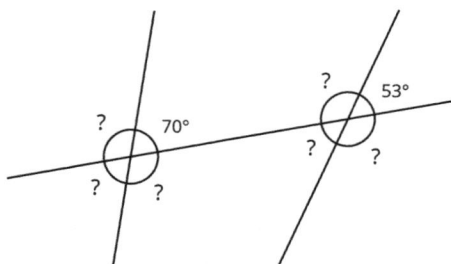

Find the missing angle measures marked with question marks.

4. The two figures are scaled copies of each other.

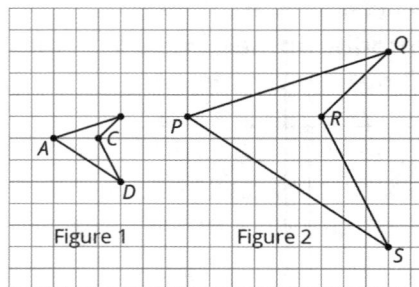

a. What are some ways that you can tell they are scaled copies?

b. What is the scale factor that takes Figure 1 to Figure 2?

c. What is the scale factor that takes Figure 2 to Figure 1?

Unit 1, Lesson 15: Adding the Angles in a Triangle

Let's explore angles in triangles.

🔔 1.15.1 Warm-Up: Can You Draw It?

1. Complete the table by drawing a triangle in each cell that has the properties listed for its column and row. If you think you cannot draw a triangle with those properties, write "impossible" in the cell.
2. Share your drawings with a partner. Discuss your thinking. If you disagree, work to reach an agreement.

	acute (all angles acute)	right (has a right angle)	obtuse (has an obtuse angle)
scalene (side lengths all different)			
isosceles (at least two side lengths are equal)			
equilateral (three side lengths equal)			

🔭 1.15.2 Exploration Activity: Find All Three

Your teacher will give you a card with a picture of a triangle.

1. The measurement of one of the angles is labeled. Mentally estimate the measures of the other two angles.

2. Find two other students with triangles congruent to yours but with a different angle labeled. Confirm that the triangles are congruent, that each card has a different angle labeled, and that the angle measures make sense.

3. Enter the three angle measures for your triangle on the table your teacher has posted.

🔭 1.15.3a Exploration Activity: Tear It Up

Your teacher will give you a page with three sets of angles and a blank space. Cut out each set of three angles. Can you make a triangle from each set that has these same three angles?

1.15.3b Exploration Extension: Are you ready for more?

1. Draw a quadrilateral. Cut it out, tear off its angles, and line them up. What do you notice?

2. Repeat this for several more quadrilaterals. Do you have a conjecture about the angles?

Lesson 15 Summary

A 180° angle is called a **straight angle** because when it is made with two rays, they point in opposite directions and form a straight line.

180°

If we experiment with angles in a triangle, we find that the sum of the measures of the three angles in each triangle is 180°— the same as a straight angle!

Through experimentation we find:

• If we add the three angles of a triangle physically by cutting them off and lining up the vertices and sides, then the three angles form a straight angle.

• If we have a line and two rays that form three angles added to make a straight angle, then there is a triangle with these three angles.

1.15.5 Practice Problems

1. In triangle ABC, the measure of angle A is 40°.

   a. Give possible measures for angles B and C if triangle ABC is isosceles.

   b. Give possible measures for angles B and C if triangle ABC is right.

2. For each set of angles, decide if there is a triangle whose angles have these measures in degrees:

   a. 60, 60, 60

   b. 90, 90, 45

   c. 30, 40, 50

   d. 90, 45, 45

   e. 120, 30, 30

   If you get stuck, consider making a line segment. Then use a protractor to measure angles with the first two angle measures.

Unit 1: Rigid Transformations and Congruence

3. Angle A in triangle ABC is obtuse. Can angle B or angle C be obtuse? Explain your reasoning.

4. For each pair of polygons, describe the transformation that could be applied to Polygon A to get Polygon B.

   a.

   b.

   c.

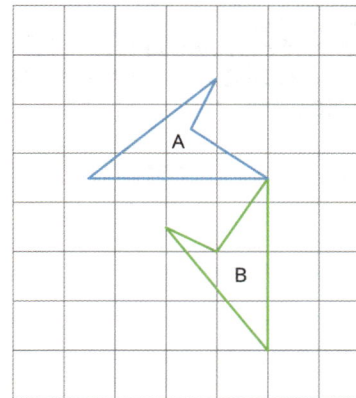

5. On the grid, draw a scaled copy of quadrilateral $ABCD$ using a scale factor of $\frac{1}{2}$.

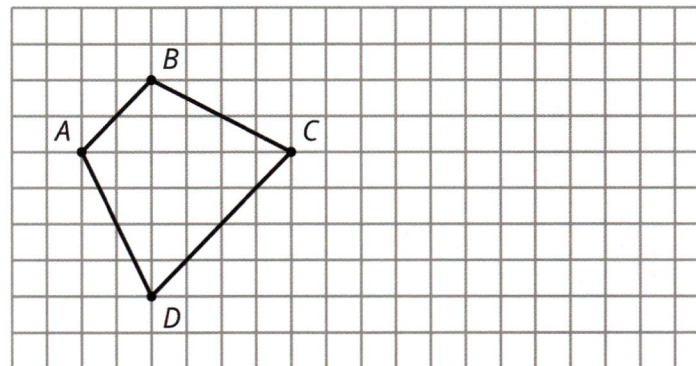

Unit 1, Lesson 16: Parallel Lines and the Angles in a Triangle

Let's see why the angles in a triangle add to 180 degrees.

1.16.1 Warm-Up: True or False: Computational Relationships

Is each equation true or false?

$62 - 28 = 60 - 30$

$3 \cdot -8 = (2 \cdot -8) - 8$

$\dfrac{16}{-2} + \dfrac{24}{-2} = \dfrac{40}{-2}$

1.16.2 Exploration Activity: Angle Plus Two

Here is triangle ABC.

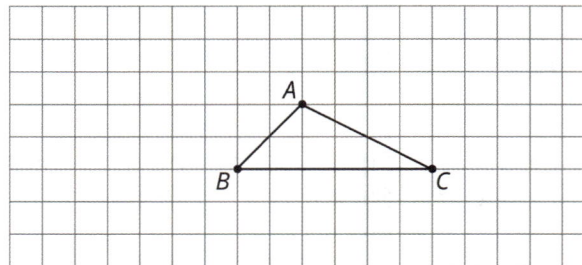

1. Rotate triangle ABC 180° around the midpoint of side AC. Label the new vertex D.

2. Rotate triangle ABC 180° around the midpoint of side AB. Label the new vertex E.

3. Look at angles EAB, BAC, and CAD. Without measuring, write what you think is the sum of the measures of these angles. Explain or show your reasoning.

4. Is the measure of angle EAB equal to the measure of any angle in triangle ABC? If so, which one? If not, how do you know?

5. Is the measure of angle CAD equal to the measure of any angle in triangle ABC? If so, which one? If not, how do you know?

6. What is the sum of the measures of angles ABC, BAC, and ACB?

![Exploration Activity icon]

1.16.3a Exploration Activity: Every Triangle in the World

Here is $\triangle ABC$. Line DE is parallel to line AC.

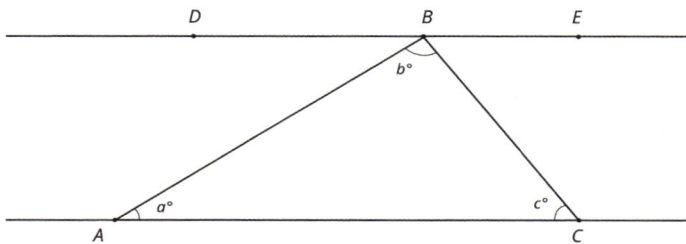

1. What is $m\angle DBA + b + m\angle CBE$? Explain how you know.

2. Use your answer to explain why $a + b + c = 180$.

3. Explain why your argument will work for *any* triangle: that is, explain why the sum of the angle measures in *any* triangle is 180°.

![Exploration Extension icon]

1.16.3b Exploration Extension: Are you ready for more?

1. Using a ruler, create a few quadrilaterals. Use a protractor to measure the four angles inside the quadrilateral. What is the sum of these four angle measures?

2. Come up with an explanation for why anything you notice must be true (hint: draw one diagonal in each quadrilateral).

Given that angle BAC measures 53 degrees, find as many other angle measures as you can.

1.16.4 Exploration Activity: Four Triangles Revisited

This diagram shows a square $BDFH$ that has been made by images of triangle ABC under rigid transformations.

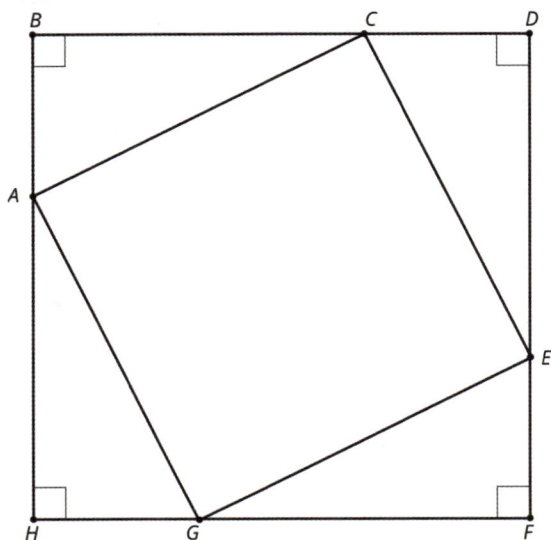

📖 Lesson 16 Summary

Using parallel lines and rotations, we can understand why the angles in a triangle always add to 180°. Here is triangle ABC. Line DE is parallel to AC and contains B.

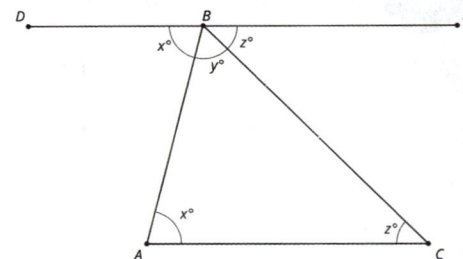

A 180 degree rotation of triangle ABC around the midpoint of AB interchanges angles A and DBA so they have the same measure: in the picture these angles are marked as $x°$. A 180 degree rotation of triangle ABC around the midpoint of BC interchanges angles C and CBE so they have the same measure: in the picture, these angles are marked as $z°$. Also, DBE is a straight line because 180 degree rotations take lines to parallel lines. So the three angles with vertex B make a line and they add up to 180° ($x + y + z = 180$). But x, y, z are the measures of the three angles in $\triangle ABC$ so the sum of the angles in a triangle is always 180°!

Unit 1: Rigid Transformations and Congruence

1. For each triangle, find the measure of the missing angle.

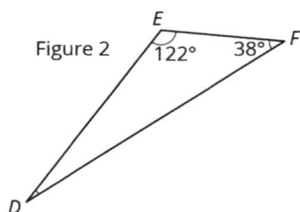

Figure 3

L

72° K

20°

J

Figure 4

I

G 56°

89°

H

C

Figure 1

128° B

28°

A

Figure 2

E

122° 38° F

D

3. In this diagram, lines AB and CD are parallel.

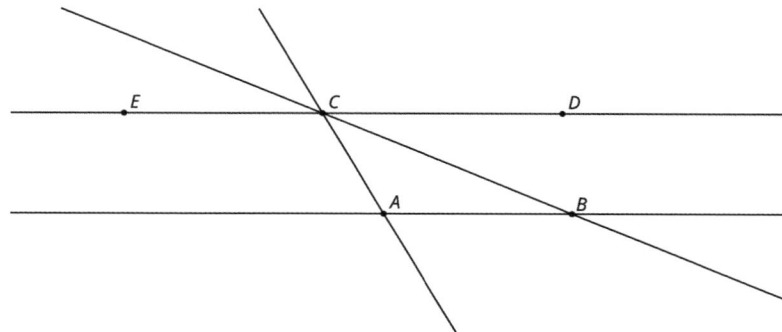

E   C   D

A   B

Angle ABC measures 35° and angle BAC measures 115°.

a. What is $m\angle ACE$?

b. What is $m\angle DCB$?

c. What is $m\angle ACB$?

2. Is there a triangle with *two* right angles? Explain your reasoning.

4. The two figures are congruent.

a. Label the points A', B', and C' that correspond to A, B, and C in the figure on the right.

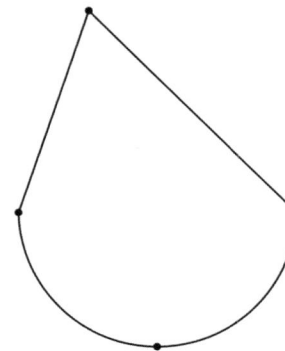

C

B

A

Continued on next page

b. If segment *AB* measures 2 cm, how long is segment *A′B′*? Explain.

c. The point *D* is shown in addition to *A* and *C*. How can you find the point *D′* that corresponds to *D*? Explain your reasoning.

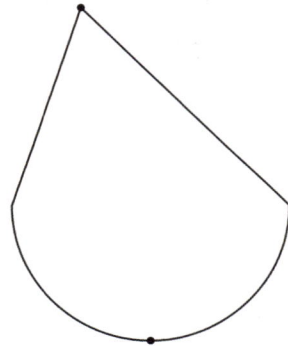

Let's make complex patterns using transformations.

1.17.1 Warm-Up: Deducing Angle Measures

Your teacher will give you some shapes.

1. How many copies of the equilateral triangle can you fit together around a single vertex, so that the triangles' edges have no gaps or overlaps? What is the measure of each angle in these triangles?

2. What are the measures of the angles in the

   a. square?

   b. hexagon?

   c. parallelogram?

   d. right triangle?

   e. octagon?

   f. pentagon?

1.17.2 Exploration Activity: Tessellate This

1. Design your own tessellation. You will need to decide which shapes you want to use and make copies. Remember that a tessellation is a repeating pattern that goes on forever to fill up the entire plane.

2. Find a partner and trade pictures. Describe a transformation of your partner's picture that takes the pattern to itself. How many different transformations can you find that take the pattern to itself? Consider translations, reflections, and rotations.

3. If there's time, color and decorate your tessellation.

1.17.3 Exploration Activity: Rotate That

1. Make a design with rotational symmetry.

2. Find a partner who has also made a design. Exchange designs and find a transformation of your partner's design that takes it to itself. Consider rotations, reflections, and translations.

3. If there's time, color and decorate your design.

THIS PAGE WAS INTENTIONALLY LEFT BLANK

Unit 2: Dilations, Similarity, and Introducing Slope

Section 1: Dilations

Section 2: Similarity

Adapted from Open Up Resources 6-8 Math (authored by Illustrative Mathematics).
See inside front cover for details.

Section 3: Slope

Section 4: Let's Put it to Work

Adapted from Open Up Resources 6-8 Math (authored by Illustrative Mathematics).
See inside front cover for details.

Unit 2, Lesson 1: Projecting and Scaling

Let's explore scaling.

2.1.1 Warm-Up: Number Talk: Remembering Fraction Division

Find each quotient. Write your answer as a fraction or a mixed number.

$6\frac{1}{4} \div 2$

$10\frac{1}{7} \div 5$

$8\frac{1}{2} \div 11$

2.1.2a Exploration Activity: Sorting Rectangles

Rectangles were made by cutting an $8\frac{1}{2}$-inch by 11-inch piece of paper in half, in half again, and so on, as illustrated in the diagram. Find the lengths of each rectangle and enter them in the appropriate table.

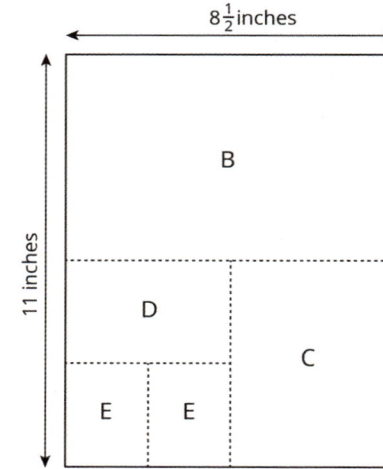

1. Some of the rectangles are scaled copies of the full sheet of paper (Rectangle A). Enter the measurements of those rectangles in the table.

rectangle	length of short side (inches)	length of long side (inches)
A	$8\frac{1}{2}$	11

Unit 2: Dilations, Similarity, and Introducing Slope

2. Some of the rectangles are *not* scaled copies of the full sheet of paper. Enter the measurements of those rectangles in the table.

rectangle	length of short side (inches)	length of long side (inches)

3. Look at the measurements for the rectangles that are scaled copies of the full sheet of paper. What do you notice about the measurements of these rectangles? Look at the measurements for the rectangles that are *not* scaled copies of the full sheet. What do you notice about these measurements?

4. Stack the rectangles that are scaled copies of the full sheet so that they all line up at a corner, as shown in the diagram. Do the same with the other set of rectangles. On each stack, draw a line from the bottom left corner to the top right corner of the biggest rectangle. What do you notice?

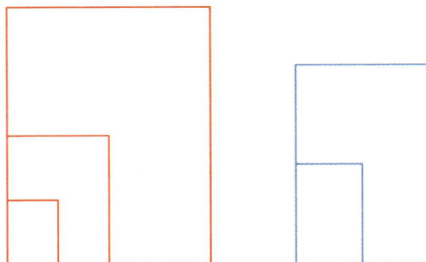

5. Stack *all* of the rectangles from largest to smallest so that they all line up at a corner. Compare the lines that you drew. Can you tell, from the drawn lines, which set each rectangle came from?

2.1.2b Exploration Extension: Are you ready for more?

In many countries, the standard paper size is not 8.5 inches by 11 inches (called "letter" size), but instead 210 millimeters by 297 millimeters (called "A4" size). Are these two rectangle sizes scaled copies of one another?

2.1.3 Exploration Activity: Scaled Rectangles

Here is a picture of Rectangle R, which has been evenly divided into smaller rectangles. Two of the smaller rectangles are labeled B and C.

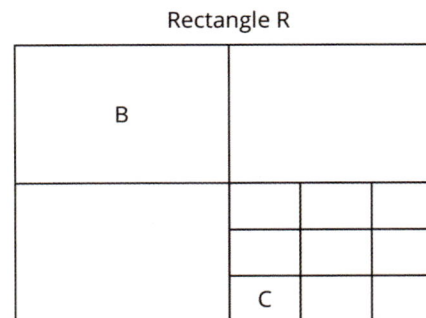

Rectangle R

1. Is B a scaled copy of R? If so, what is the scale factor?

2. Is C a scaled copy of B? If so, what is the scale factor?

3. Is C a scaled copy of R? If so, what is the scale factor?

Lesson 1 Summary

Scaled copies of rectangles have an interesting property. Can you see what it is?

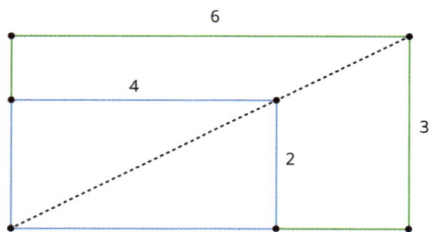

Here, the larger rectangle is a scaled copy of the smaller one (with a scale factor of $\frac{3}{2}$). Notice how the diagonal of the large rectangle contains the diagonal of the smaller rectangle. This is the case for any two scaled copies of a rectangle if we line them up as shown. If two rectangles are *not* scaled copies of one another, then the diagonals do not match up. In this unit, we will investigate how to make scaled copies of a figure.

2.1.5 Practice Problems

1. Rectangle A measures 12 cm by 3 cm. Rectangle B is a scaled copy of Rectangle A. Select **all** of the measurement pairs that could be the dimensions of Rectangle B.

   ☐ 6 cm by 1.5 cm
   ☐ 10 cm by 2 cm
   ☐ 13 cm by 4 cm
   ☐ 18 cm by 4.5 cm
   ☐ 80 cm by 20 cm

2. Rectangle A has length 12 and width 8. Rectangle B has length 15 and width 10. Rectangle C has length 30 and width 15.

   a. Is Rectangle A a scaled copy of Rectangle B? If so, what is the scale factor?

   b. Is Rectangle B a scaled copy of Rectangle A? If so, what is the scale factor?

   c. Explain how you know that Rectangle C is *not* a scaled copy of Rectangle B.

d. Is Rectangle A a scaled copy of Rectangle C? If so, what is the scale factor?

3. Here are three polygons.

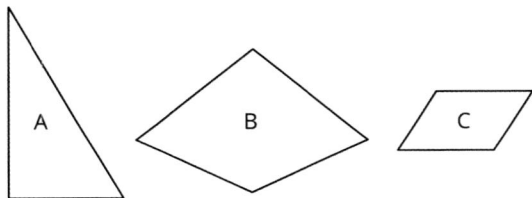

a. Draw a scaled copy of Polygon A with scale factor $\frac{1}{2}$.

b. Draw a scaled copy of Polygon B with scale factor 2.

c. Draw a scaled copy of Polygon C with scale factor $\frac{1}{4}$.

4. Which of these sets of angle measures could be the three angles in a triangle?

   A. 40°, 50°, 60°
   B. 50°, 60°, 70°
   C. 60°, 70°, 80°
   D. 70°, 80°, 90°

5. In the picture lines AB and CD are parallel. Find the measures of the following angles. Explain your reasoning.

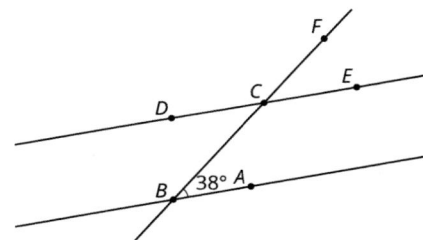

a. $\angle BCD$

b. $\angle ECF$

c. $\angle DCF$

Let's dilate figures on circular grids.

2.2.1 Warm-Up: Notice and Wonder: Concentric Circles

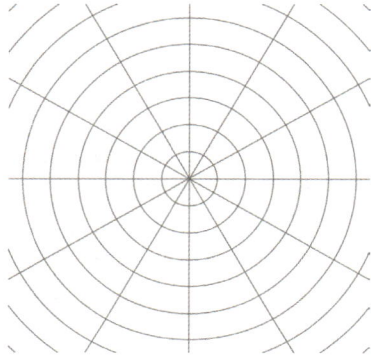

What do you notice? What do you wonder?

2.2.2 Exploration Activity: A Droplet on the Surface

The larger Circle d is a **dilation** of the smaller Circle c. P is the **center of dilation**.

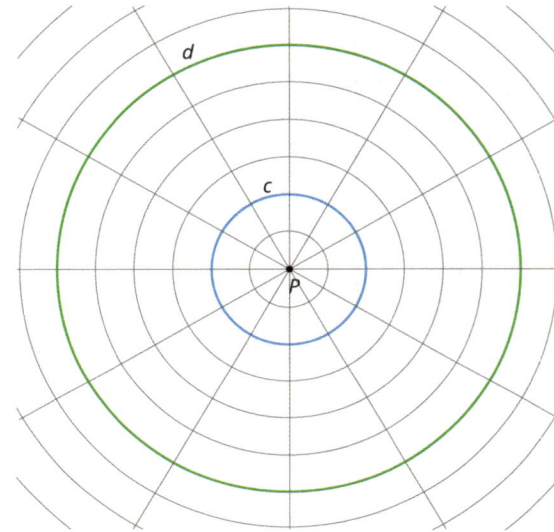

1. Draw four points *on* the smaller circle (not inside the circle!), and label them E, F, G, and H.

2. Draw the rays from P through each of those four points.

3. Label the points where the rays meet the larger circle E', F', G', and H'.

4. Complete the table. In the row labeled S, write the distance between P and the point on the smaller circle in grid units. In the row labeled L, write the distance between P and the corresponding point on the larger circle in grid units.

	E	F	G	H
S				
L				

5. The center of dilation is point P. What is the *scale factor* that takes the smaller circle to the larger circle? Explain your reasoning.

2.2.3a Exploration Activity: Quadrilateral on a Circular Grid

Here is a polygon $ABCD$.

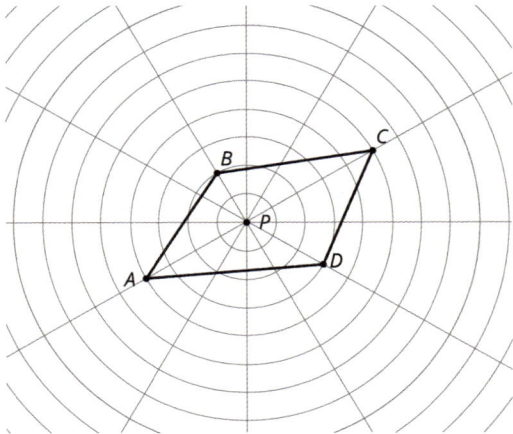

1. Dilate each vertex of polygon $ABCD$ using P as the center of dilation and a scale factor of 2. Label the image of A as A', and label the images of the remaining three vertices as B', C', and D'.
2. Draw segments between the dilated points to create polygon $A'B'C'D'$.
3. What are some things you notice about the new polygon?

4. Choose a few more points on the sides of the original polygon and transform them using the same dilation. What do you notice?

5. Dilate each vertex of polygon $ABCD$ using P as the center of dilation and a scale factor of $\frac{1}{2}$. Label the image of A as E, the image of B as F, the image of C as G, and the image of D as H.
6. What do you notice about polygon $EFGH$?

2.2.3b Exploration Extension: Are you ready for more?

Suppose P is a point not on line segment $\overline{WX}$. Let $\overline{YZ}$ be the dilation of line segment $\overline{WX}$ using P as the center with scale factor 2. Experiment using a circular grid to make predictions about whether each of the following statements must be true, might be true, or must be false.

1. $\overline{YZ}$ is twice as long as $\overline{WX}$.

2. $\overline{YZ}$ is five units longer than $\overline{WX}$.

3. The point P is on $\overline{YZ}$.

4. $\overline{YZ}$ and $\overline{WX}$ intersect.

2.2.4 Exploration Activity: A Quadrilateral and Concentric Circles

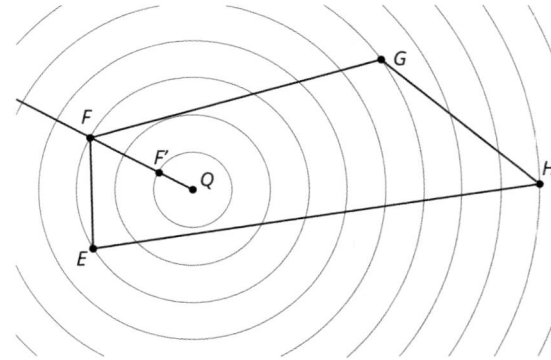

Dilate polygon $EFGH$ using Q as the center of dilation and a scale factor of $\frac{1}{3}$. The image of F is already shown on the diagram. (You may need to draw more rays from Q in order to find the images of other points.)

A circular grid like this one can be helpful for performing **dilations**.

The radius of the smallest circle is one unit, and the radius of each successive circle is one unit more than the previous one.

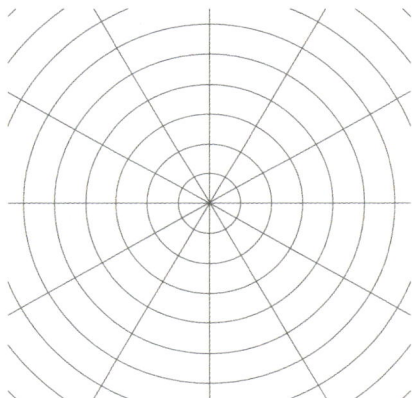

To perform a dilation, we need a **center of dilation**, a scale factor, and a point to dilate. In the picture, P is the center of dilation. With a scale factor of 2, each point stays on the same ray from P, but its distance from P doubles:

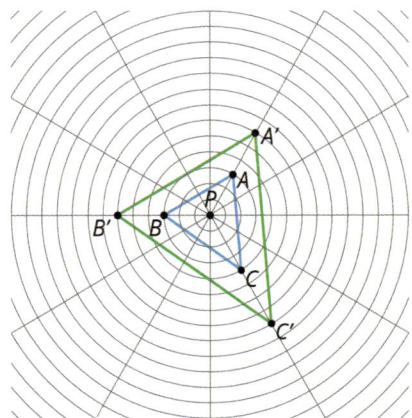

Since the circles on the grid are the same distance apart, segment PA' has twice the length of segment PA, and the same holds for the other points.

1. Here are Circles c and d. Point O is the center of dilation, and the dilation takes Circle c to Circle d.

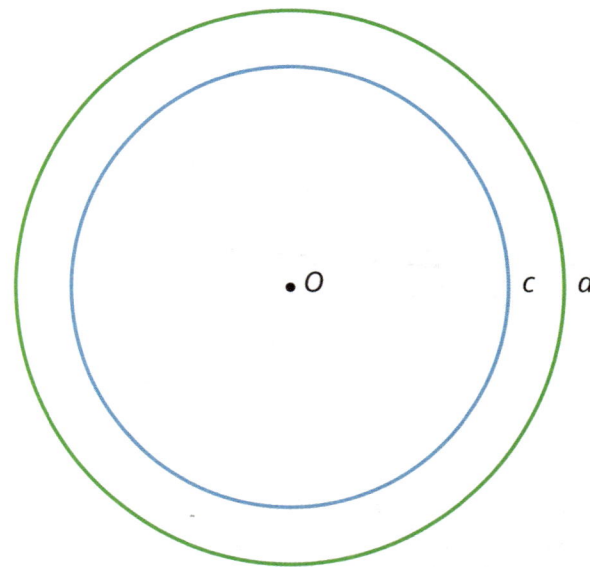

a. Plot a point on Circle c. Label the point P. Plot where P goes when the dilation is applied.

b. Plot a point on Circle d. Label the point Q. Plot a point that the dilation takes to Q.

2. Here is triangle ABC.

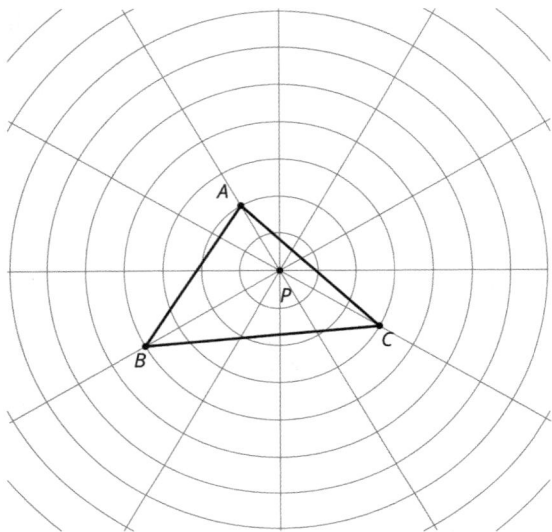

a. Dilate each vertex of triangle ABC using P as the center of dilation and a scale factor of 2. Draw the triangle connecting the three new points.

b. Dilate each vertex of triangle ABC using P as the center of dilation and a scale factor of $\frac{1}{2}$. Draw the triangle connecting the three new points.

c. Measure the longest side of each of the three triangles. What do you notice?

d. Measure the angles of each triangle. What do you notice?

3. Describe a rigid transformation that you could use to show the polygons are congruent.

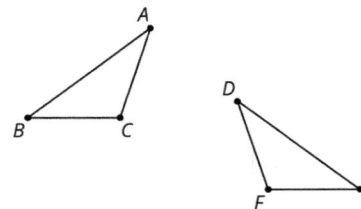

4. The line has been partitioned into three angles.

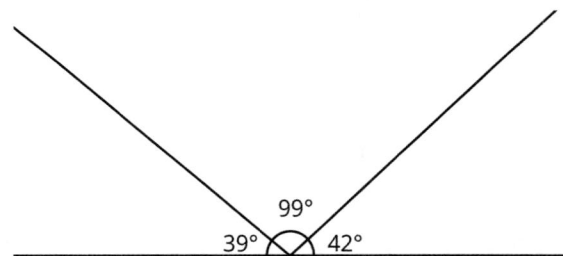

Is there a triangle with these three angle measures? Explain.

Unit 2, Lesson 3: Dilations with no Grid

Let's dilate figures not on grids.

🔔 2.3.1 Warm-Up: Points on a Ray

1. Find and label a point C on the ray whose distance from A is twice the distance from B to A.

2. Find and label a point D on the ray whose distance from A is half the distance from B to A.

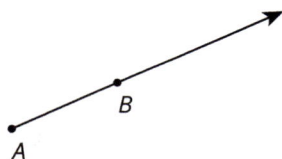

📡 2.3.2 Exploration Activity: Dilation Obstacle Course

Here is a diagram that shows nine points.

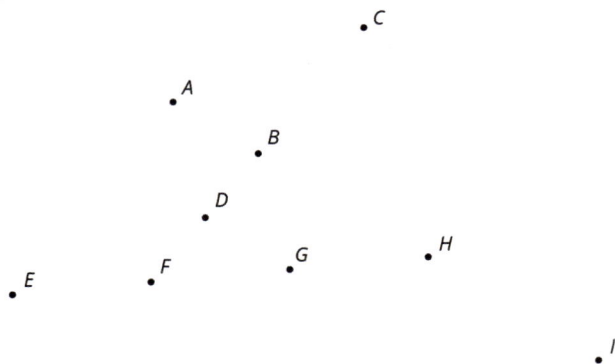

1. Dilate B using a scale factor of 5 and A as the center of dilation. Which point is its image?

2. Using H as the center of dilation, dilate G so that its image is E. What scale factor did you use?

3. Using H as the center of dilation, dilate E so that its image is G. What scale factor did you use?

4. To dilate F so that its image is B, what point on the diagram can you use as a center?

5. Dilate H using A as the center and a scale factor of $\frac{1}{3}$. Which point is its image?

6. Describe a dilation that uses a labeled point as its center and that would take F to H.

7. Using B as the center of dilation, dilate H so that its image is itself. What scale factor did you use?

2.3.3a Exploration Activity: Getting Perspective

1. Using one colored pencil, draw the images of points P and Q using C as the center of dilation and a scale factor of 4. Label the new points P' and Q'.

2. Using a different color, draw the images of points P and Q using C as the center of dilation and a scale factor of $\frac{1}{2}$. Label the new points P'' and Q''.

C · P ·

     Q ·

Pause here so your teacher can review your diagram. Your teacher will then give you a scale factor to use in the next part.

3. Now you'll make a perspective drawing. Here is a rectangle.

a. Choose a point *inside the shaded circular region* but *outside the rectangle* to use as the center of dilation. Label it C.

b. Using your center C and the scale factor you were given, draw the image under the dilation of each vertex of the rectangle, one at a time. Connect the dilated vertices to create the dilated rectangle.

c. Draw a segment that connects each of the original vertices with its image. This will make your diagram look like a cool three-dimensional drawing of a box! If there's time, you can shade the sides of the box to make it look more realistic.

d. Compare your drawing to other people's drawings. What is the same and what is different? How do the choices you made affect the final drawing? Was your dilated rectangle closer to C than to the original rectangle, or farther away? How is that decided?

2.3.3b Exploration Extension: Are you ready for more?

Here is line segment DE and its image $D'E'$ under a dilation.

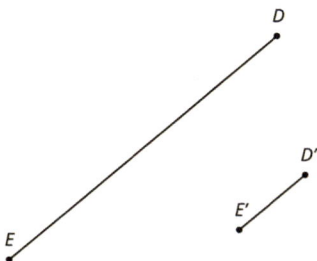

1. Use a ruler to find and draw the center of dilation. Label it F.
2. What is the scale factor of the dilation?

Lesson 3 Summary

If A is the center of dilation, how can we find which point is the dilation of B with scale factor 2?

Since the scale factor is larger than 1, the point must be farther away from A than B is, which makes C the point we are looking for. If we measure the distance between A and C, we would find that it is exactly twice the distance between A and B.

A dilation with scale factor less than 1 brings points closer. The point D is the dilation of B with center A and scale factor $\frac{1}{3}$.

2.3.5 Practice Problems

1. Segment AB measures 3 cm. Point O is the center of dilation. How long is the image of AB after a dilation with . . .

   a. Scale factor 5?

   b. Scale factor 3.7?

   c. Scale factor $\frac{1}{5}$?

   d. Scale factor s?

2. Here are points A and B. Plot the points for each dilation described.

   a. C is the image of B using A as the center of dilation and a scale factor of 2.

   b. D is the image of A using B as the center of dilation and a scale factor of 2.

   c. E is the image of B using A as the center of dilation and a scale factor of $\frac{1}{2}$.

   d. F is the image of A using B as the center of dilation and a scale factor of $\frac{1}{2}$.

3. Make a perspective drawing. Include in your work the center of dilation, the shape you dilate, and the scale factor you use.

5. The diagram shows two intersecting lines.

Find the missing angle measures.

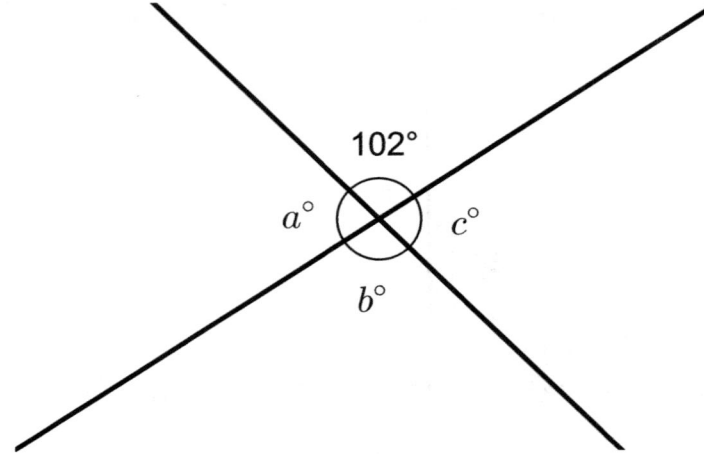

4. Triangle ABC is a scaled copy of triangle DEF. Side AB measures 12 cm and is the longest side of ABC. Side DE measures 8 cm and is the longest side of DEF.

   a. Triangle ABC is a scaled copy of triangle DEF with what scale factor?

   b. Triangle DEF is a scaled copy of triangle ABC with what scale factor?

6.

   a. Show that the two triangles are congruent.

   b. Find the side lengths of DEF and the angle measures of ABC.

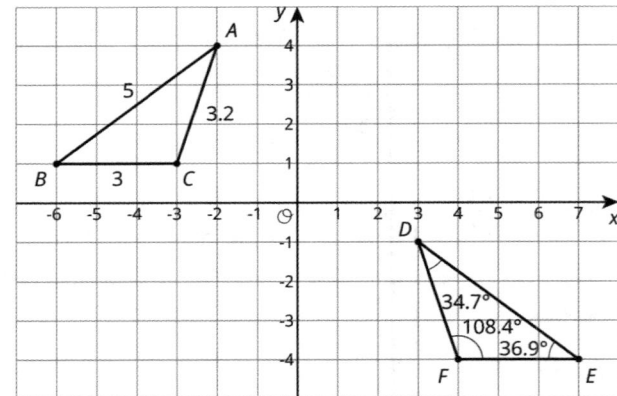

Unit 2: Dilations, Similarity, and Introducing Slope

MATH NATION

Unit 2, Lesson 4: Dilations on a Square Grid

Let's dilate figures on a rectangular grid.

2.4.1 Warm-Up: Estimating a Scale Factor

$\overset{\bullet}{A}$ $\quad\overset{\bullet}{B}$ $\quad\quad\overset{\bullet}{C}$

Point C is the dilation of point B with center of dilation A and scale factor s. Estimate s. Be prepared to explain your reasoning.

2.4.2 Exploration Activity: Dilations on a Grid

1. Find the dilation of quadrilateral $ABCD$ with center P and scale factor 2.

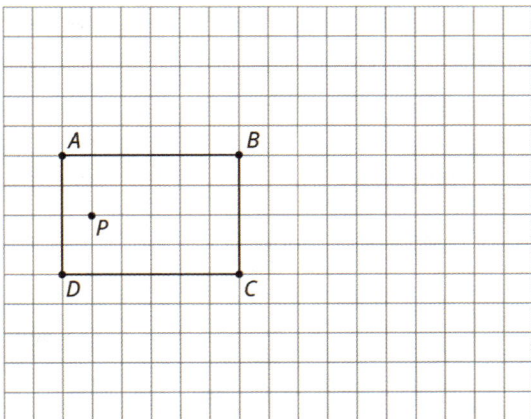

2. Find the dilation of triangle QRS with center T and scale factor 2.

3. Find the dilation of triangle QRS with center T and scale factor $\frac{1}{2}$.

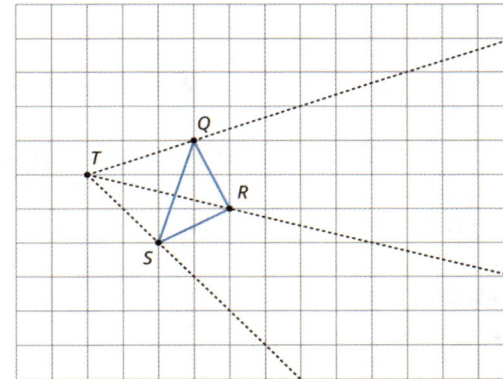

2.4.3a Exploration Activity: Card Sort: Matching Dilations on a Coordinate Grid

Your teacher will give you some cards. Each of Cards 1 through 6 shows a figure in the coordinate plane and describes a dilation.

Each of Cards A through E describes the image of the dilation for one of the numbered cards.

Match number cards with letter cards. One of the number cards will not have a match. For this card, you'll need to draw an image.

Square grids can be useful for showing dilations. The grid is helpful especially when the center of dilation and the point(s) being dilated lie at grid points. Rather than using a ruler to measure the distance between the points, we can count grid units.

2.4.3b Exploration Extension: Are you ready for more?

The image of a circle under dilation is a circle when the center of the dilation is the center of the circle. What happens if the center of dilation is a point on the circle? Using center of dilation (0,0) and scale factor 1.5, dilate the circle shown on the diagram. This diagram shows some points to try dilating.

For example, suppose we want to dilate point Q with center of dilation P and scale factor $\frac{3}{2}$. Since Q is 4 grid squares to the left and 2 grid squares down from P, the dilation will be 6 grid squares to the left and 3 grid squares down from P (can you see why?). The dilated image is marked as Q' in the picture.

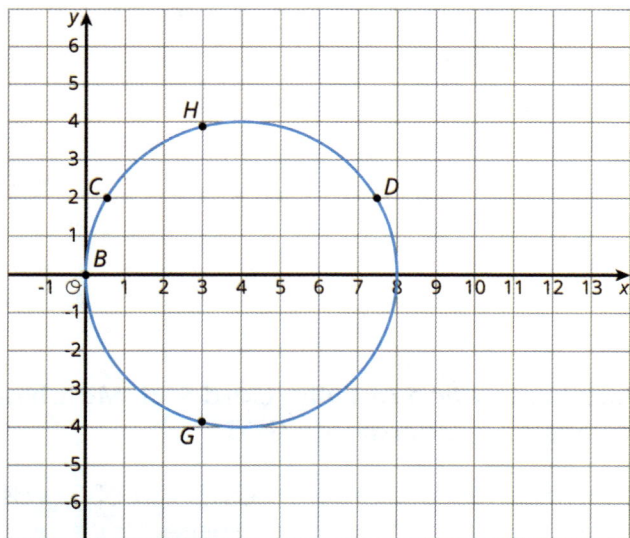

Sometimes the square grid comes with coordinates. The coordinate grid gives us a convenient way to *name* points, and sometimes the coordinates of the image can be found with just arithmetic.

For example, to make a dilation with center (0,0) and scale factor 2 of the triangle with coordinates $(-1,-2)$, $(3,1)$, and $(2,-1)$, we can just double the coordinates to get $(-2,-4)$, $(6,2)$, and $(4,-2)$.

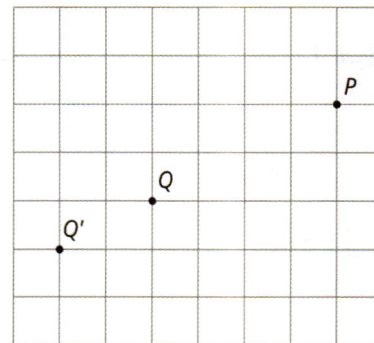

Unit 2: Dilations, Similarity, and Introducing Slope

1. Triangle *ABC* is dilated using *D* as the center of dilation with scale factor 2.

   The image is triangle *A'B'C'*. Clare says the two triangles are congruent, because their angle measures are the same. Do you agree? Explain how you know.

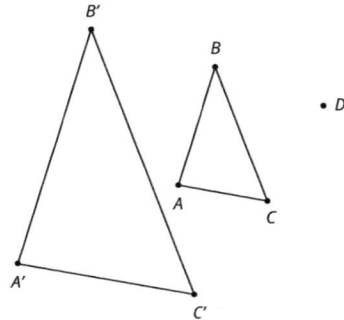

3. The diagram shows three lines with some marked angle measures.

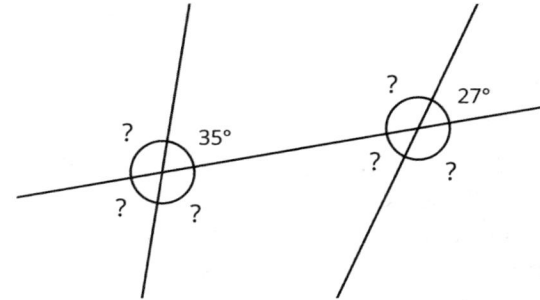

   Find the missing angle measures marked with question marks.

2. On graph paper, sketch the image of quadrilateral PQRS under the following dilations:

   o The dilation centered at *R* with scale factor 2.
   o The dilation centered at *O* with scale factor $\frac{1}{2}$.
   o The dilation centered at *S* with scale factor $\frac{1}{2}$.

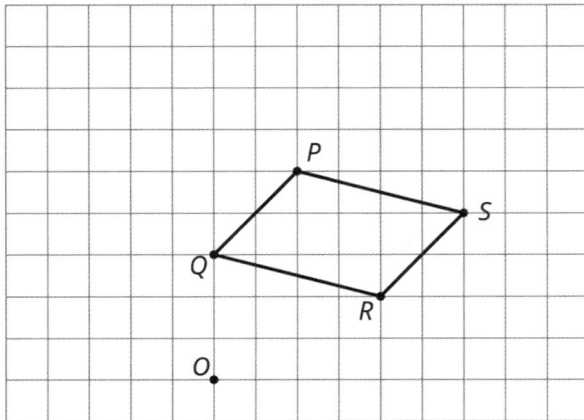

4. Describe a sequence of translations, rotations, and reflections that takes Polygon P to Polygon Q.

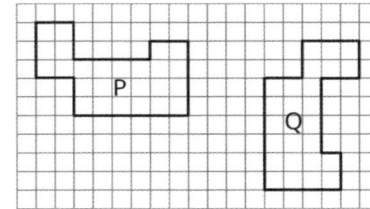

5. Point *B* has coordinates $(-2, -5)$. After a translation 4 units down, a reflection across the *y*-axis, and a translation 6 units up, what are the coordinates of the image?

Unit 2, Lesson 5: More Dilations

Let's look at dilations in the coordinate plane.

🔔 2.5.1 Warm-Up: Many Dilations of a Triangle

All of the triangles are dilations of Triangle D. The dilations use the same center P, but different scale factors. What do Triangles A, B, and C have in common? What do Triangles E, F, and G have in common? What does this tell us about the different scale factors used?

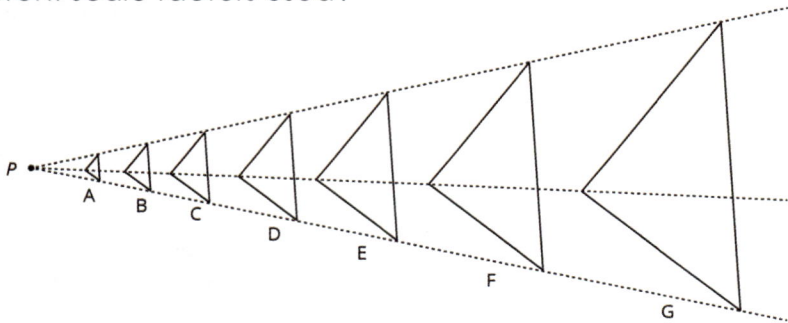

📣 2.5.2a Exploration Activity: Info Gap: Dilations

Your teacher will give you either a problem card or a data card. Do not show or read your card to your partner.

If your teacher gives you the *problem card*:

1. Silently read your card and think about what information you need to answer the question.
2. Ask your partner for the specific information that you need.
3. Explain to your partner how you are using the information to solve the problem.

4. Solve the problem and explain your reasoning to your partner.

If your teacher gives you the *data card*:

1. Silently read the information on your card.
2. Ask your partner "What specific information do you need?" and wait for your partner to *ask* for information. *Only* give information that is on your card. (Do not figure out anything for your partner!)
3. Before telling your partner the information, ask "Why do you need that information?"
4. After your partner solves the problem, ask them to explain their reasoning and listen to their explanation.

Pause here so your teacher can review your work. Ask your teacher for a new set of cards and repeat the activity, trading roles with your partner.

🧠 2.5.2b Exploration Extension: Are you ready for more?

Triangle EFG was created by dilating triangle ABC using a scale factor of 2 and center D. Triangle HIJ was created by dilating triangle ABC using a scale factor of $\frac{1}{2}$ and center D.

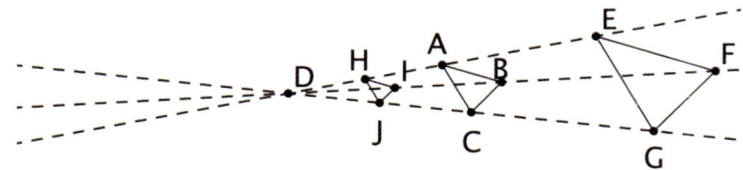

1. What would the image of triangle ABC look like under a dilation with scale factor 0?

Unit 2: Dilations, Similarity, and Introducing Slope

2. What would the image of the triangle look like under dilation with a scale factor of -1? If possible, draw it and label the vertices A', B', and C'. If it's not possible, explain why not.

3. If possible, describe what happens to a shape if it is dilated with a negative scale factor. If dilating with a negative scale factor is not possible, explain why not.

Lesson 5 Summary

One important use of coordinates is to communicate geometric information precisely. Let's consider a quadrilateral $ABCD$ in the coordinate plane. Performing a dilation of $ABCD$ requires three vital pieces of information:

1. The coordinates of A, B, C, and D
2. The coordinates of the center of dilation, P
3. The scale factor of the dilation

With this information, we can dilate the vertices A, B, C, and D and then draw the corresponding segments to find the dilation of $ABCD$. Without coordinates, describing the location of the new points would likely require sharing a picture of the polygon and the center of dilation.

2.5.4 Practice Problems

1. Quadrilateral $ABCD$ is dilated with center (0,0), taking B to B'. Draw $A'B'C'D'$.

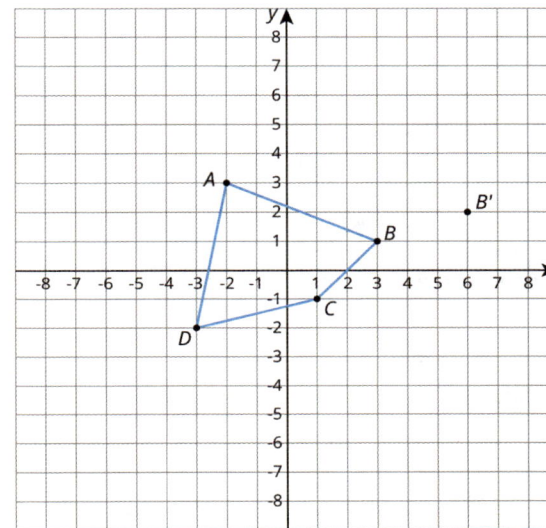

2. Triangles B and C have been built by dilating Triangle A.

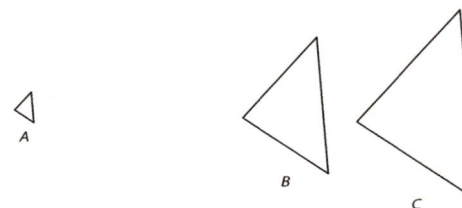

a. Find the center of dilation.

b. Triangle B is a dilation of A with approximately what scale factor?

c. Triangle A is a dilation of B with approximately what scale factor?

Continued on next page

d. Triangle B is a dilation of C with approximately what scale factor?

3. Here is a triangle.

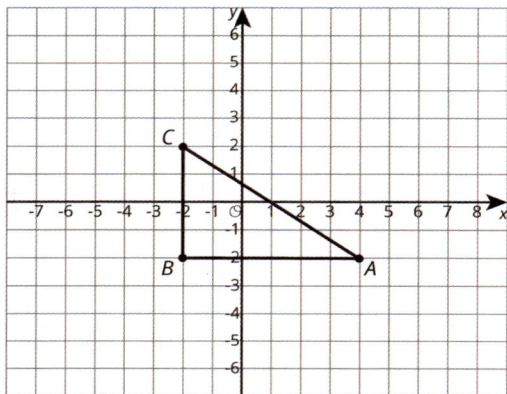

a. Draw the dilation of triangle ABC, with center $(0,0)$, and scale factor 2. Label this triangle $A'B'C'$.

b. Draw the dilation of triangle ABC, with center $(0,0)$, and scale factor $\frac{1}{2}$. Label this triangle $A''B''C''$.

c. Is $A''B''C''$ a dilation of triangle $A'B'C'$? If yes, what are the center of dilation and the scale factor?

4. Triangle ABC is a right triangle, and the measure of angle A is 28°. What are the measures of the other two angles?

Unit 2, Lesson 6: Similarity

Let's explore similar figures.

2.6.1 Warm-Up: Equivalent Expressions

Use what you know about operations and their properties to write three expressions equivalent to the expression shown.

$$10(2+3) - 8 \cdot 3$$

2.6.2a Exploration Activity: Similarity Transformations (Part 1)

1. Triangle EGH and triangle LME are **similar**. Find a sequence of translations, rotations, reflections, and dilations that shows this.

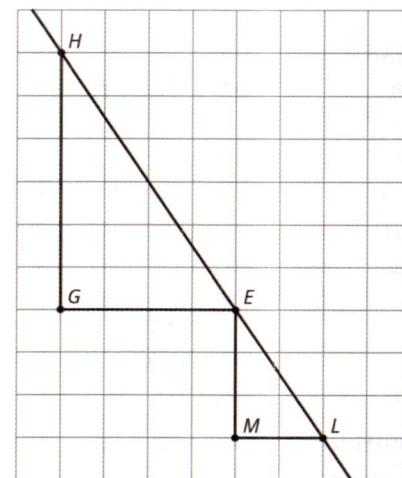

2. Hexagon *ABCDEF* and hexagon *HGLKJI* are similar. Find a sequence of translations, rotations, reflections, and dilations that shows this.

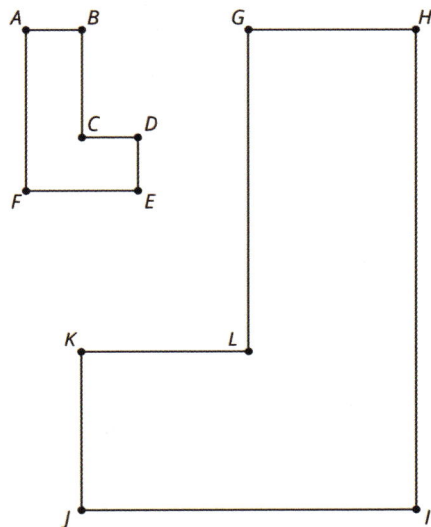

2.6.2b Exploration Extension: Are you ready for more?

The same sequence of transformations takes Triangle A to Triangle B, takes Triangle B to Triangle C, and so on. Describe a sequence of transformations with this property.

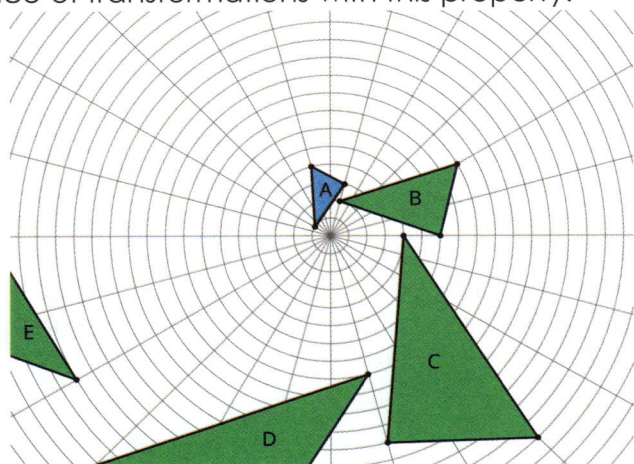

2.6.3 Exploration Activity: Similarity Transformations (Part 2)

Sketch figures similar to Figure A that use only the transformations listed to show similarity.

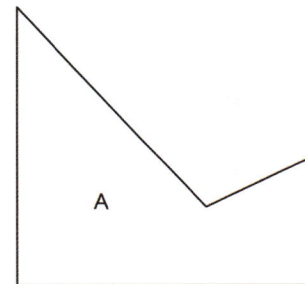

1. A translation and a reflection. Label your sketch Figure B. Pause here so that your teacher can check your work.

2. A reflection and a dilation with scale factor greater than 1. Label your sketch Figure C.

3. A rotation and a reflection. Label your sketch Figure D.

4. A dilation with scale factor less than 1 and a translation. Label your sketch Figure E.

2.6.4 Exploration Activity: Methods for Translations and Dilations

Your teacher will give you a set of five cards and your partner a different set of five cards. Using only the cards you were given, find at least one way to show that triangle *ABC* and triangle *DEF* are similar. Compare your method with your partner's method. What is the same about your methods? What is different?

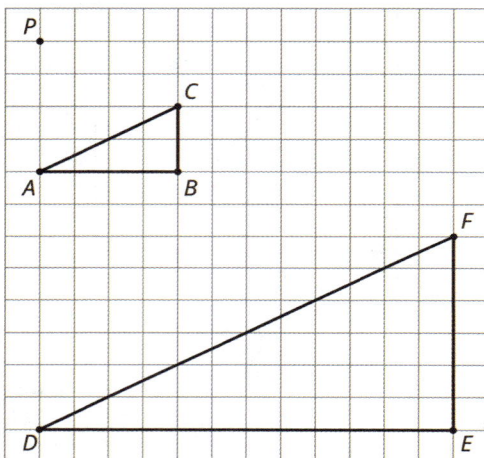

Lesson 6 Summary

Let's show that triangle *ABC* is similar to triangle *DEF*:

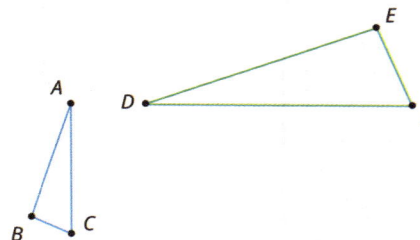

Two figures are **similar** if one figure can be transformed into the other by a sequence of translations, rotations, reflections, and dilations. There are many correct sequences of transformations, but we only need to describe one to show that two figures are similar.

One way to get from *ABC* to *DEF* follows these steps:

- step 1: reflect across line *f*
- step 2: rotate 90° counterclockwise around *D*
- step 3: dilate with center *D* and scale factor 2

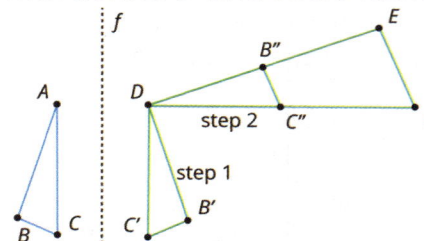

Another way would be to dilate triangle *ABC* by a scale factor of 2 with center of dilation *A*, then translate *A* to *D*, then reflect over a vertical line through *D*, and finally rotate it so it matches up with triangle *DEF*. What steps would you choose to show the two triangles are similar?

Unit 2: Dilations, Similarity, and Introducing Slope

1. Each diagram has a pair of figures, one larger than the other. For each pair, show that the two figures are similar by identifying a sequence of translations, rotations, reflections, and dilations that takes the smaller figure to the larger one.

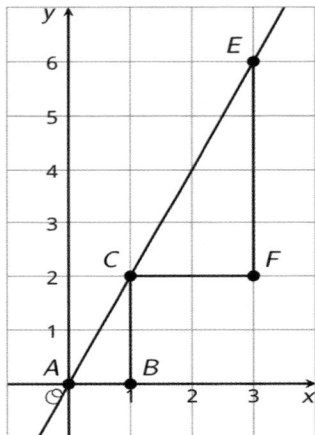

2. Here are two similar polygons.

   Measure the side lengths and angles of each polygon. What do you notice?

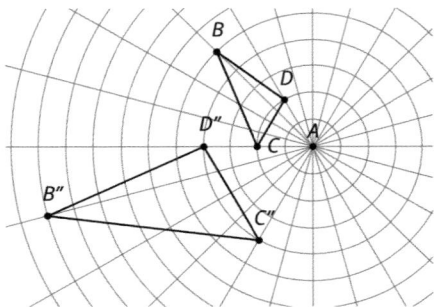

3. Each figure shows a pair of similar triangles, one contained in the other. For each pair, describe a point and a scale factor to use for a dilation moving the larger triangle to the smaller one. Use a measurement tool to find the scale factor.

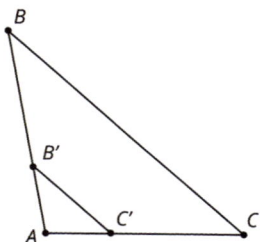

Let's look at sides and angles of similar polygons.

2.7.1 Warm-Up: All, Some, None: Congruence and Similarity

Choose whether each of the statements is true in *all* cases, in *some* cases, or in *no* cases.

1. If two figures are congruent, then they are similar.

2. If two figures are similar, then they are congruent.

3. If an angle is dilated with the center of dilation at its vertex, the angle measure may change.

2.7.2a Exploration Activity: Are They Similar?

1. Let's look at a square and a rhombus.

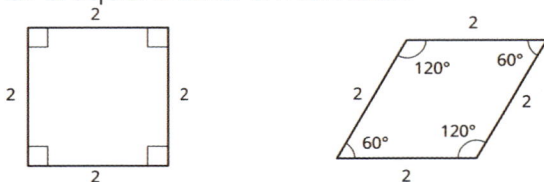

Priya says, "These polygons are similar because their side lengths are all the same." Clare says, "These polygons are not similar because the angles are different." Do you agree with either Priya or Clare? Explain your reasoning.

2. Now, let's look at rectangles $ABCD$ and $EFGH$.

Jada says, "These rectangles are similar because all of the side lengths differ by 2." Lin says, "These rectangles are similar. I can dilate AD and BC using a scale factor of 2 and AB and CD using a scale factor of 1.5 to make the rectangles congruent. Then I can use a translation to line up the rectangles." Do you agree with either Jada or Lin? Explain your reasoning.

2.7.2b Exploration Extension: Are you ready for more?

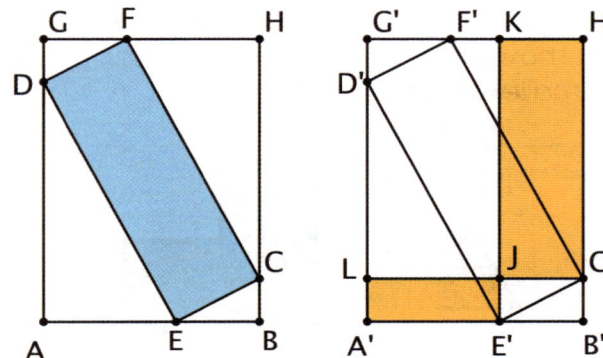

Points A through H are translated to the right to create points A' through H'. All of the following are rectangles: $GHBA$, $FCED$, $KH'C'J$, and $LJE'A'$. Which is greater, the area of blue rectangle $DFCE$ or the total area of yellow rectangles $KH'C'J$ and $LJE'A'$?

2.7.3a Exploration Activity: Find Someone Similar

Your teacher will give you a card. Find someone else in the room who has a card with a polygon that is similar but not congruent to yours. When you have found your partner, work with them to explain how you know that the two polygons are similar.

2.7.3b Exploration Extension: Are you ready for more?

On the left is an equilateral triangle where dashed lines have been added, showing how you can partition an equilateral triangle into smaller similar triangles.

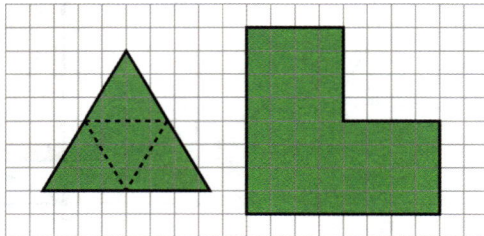

Find a way to do this for the figure on the right, partitioning it into smaller figures which are each similar to that original shape. What's the fewest number of pieces you can use? The most?

Lesson 7 Summary

When two polygons are similar:

- Every angle and side in one polygon has a corresponding part in the other polygon.
- All pairs of corresponding angles have the same measure.
- Corresponding sides are related by a single scale factor. Each side length in one figure is multiplied by the scale factor to get the corresponding side length in the other figure.

Consider the two rectangles shown here. Are they similar?

It looks like rectangles $ABCD$ and $EFGH$ could be similar, if you match the long edges and match the short edges. All the corresponding angles are congruent because they are all right angles. Calculating the scale factor between the sides is where we see that "looks like" isn't enough to make them similar. To scale the long side AB to the long side EF, the scale factor must be $\frac{3}{4}$, because $4 \cdot \frac{3}{4} = 3$. But the scale factor to match AD to EH has to be $\frac{2}{3}$, because $3 \cdot \frac{2}{3} = 2$. So, the rectangles are not similar because the scale factors for all the parts must be the same.

Here is an example that shows how sides can correspond (with a scale factor of 1), but the quadrilaterals are not similar because the angles don't have the same measure:

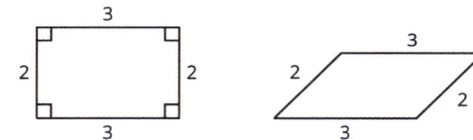

2.7.5 Practice Problems

1. Triangle DEF is a dilation of triangle ABC with scale factor 2. In triangle ABC, the largest angle measures 82°. What is the largest angle measure in triangle DEF?

    A. 41°

    B. 82°

    C. 123°

    D. 164°

2. Draw two polygons that are similar but could be mistaken for not being similar. Explain why they are similar.

3. Draw two polygons that are *not* similar but could be mistaken for being similar. Explain why they are not similar.

4. These two triangles are similar. Find side lengths a and b. Note: the two figures are not drawn to scale.

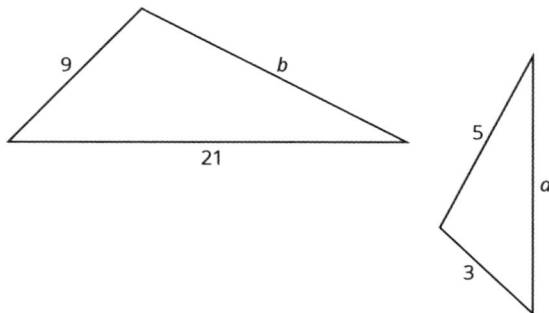

5. Jada claims that $B'C'D'$ is a dilation of BCD using A as the center of dilation.

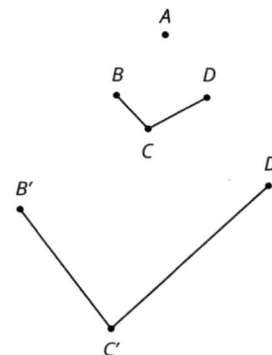

What are some ways you can convince Jada that her claim is not true?

6.
   a. Draw a horizontal line segment AB.
   b. Rotate segment AB 90° counterclockwise around point A. Label any new points.
   c. Rotate segment AB 90° clockwise around point B. Label any new points.
   d. Describe a transformation on segment AB you could use to finish building a square.

Unit 2, Lesson 8: Similar Triangles

Let's look at similar triangles.

2.8.1 Warm-Up: Equivalent Expressions

Create three different expressions that are each equal to 20. Each expression should include only these three numbers: 4, −2, and 10.

2.8.2a Exploration Activity: Making Pasta Angles and Triangles

Your teacher will give you some dried pasta and a set of angles.

1. Create a triangle using three pieces of pasta and angle A. Your triangle *must* include the angle you were given, but you are otherwise free to make any triangle you like. Tape your pasta triangle to a sheet of paper so it won't move.

   a. After you have created your triangle, measure each side length with a ruler and record the length on the paper next to the side. Then measure the angles to the nearest 5 degrees using a protractor and record these measurements on your paper.

   b. Find two others in the room who have the same angle A and compare your triangles. What is the same? What is different? Are the triangles congruent? Similar?

   c. How did you decide if they were or were not congruent or similar?

2. Now use more pasta and angles A, B, and C to create another triangle. Tape this pasta triangle on a separate sheet of paper.

   a. After you have created your triangle, measure each side length with a ruler and record the length on the paper next to the side. Then measure the angles to the nearest 5 degrees using a protractor and record these measurements on your paper.

   b. Find two others in the room who used your same angles and compare your triangles. What is the same? What is different? Are the triangles congruent? Similar?

   c. How did you decide if they were or were not congruent or similar?

Unit 2: Dilations, Similarity, and Introducing Slope

3. Here is triangle PQR. Break a new piece of pasta, different in length than segment PQ.

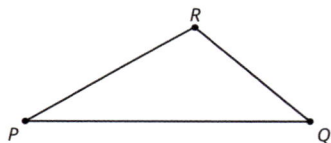

- ○ Tape the piece of pasta so that it lays on top of line PQ with one end of the pasta at P (if it does not fit on the page, break it further). Label the other end of the piece of pasta S.
- ○ Tape a full piece of pasta, with one end at S, making an angle congruent to $\angle PQR$.
- ○ Tape a full piece of pasta on top of line PR with one end of the pasta at P. Call the point where the two full pieces of pasta meet T.

a. Is your new pasta triangle PST similar to $\triangle PQR$? Explain your reasoning.

b. If your broken piece of pasta were a different length, would the pasta triangle still be similar to $\triangle PQR$? Explain your reasoning.

2.8.2b Exploration Extension: Are you ready for more?

Quadrilaterals $ABCD$ and $EFGH$ have four angles measuring 240°, 40°, 40°, and 40°. Do $ABCD$ and $EFGH$ have to be similar?

2.8.3a Exploration Activity: Similar Figures in a Regular Pentagon

1. This diagram has several triangles that are similar to triangle DJI.

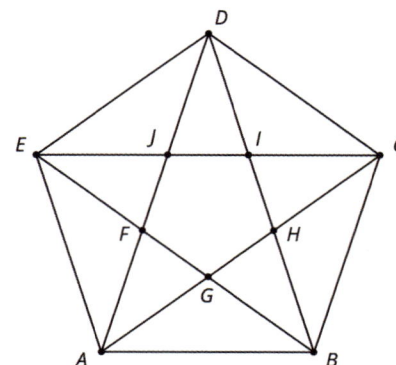

a. Three different scale factors were used to make triangles similar to DJI. In the diagram, find at least one triangle of each size that is similar to DJI.

b. Explain how you know each of these three triangles is similar to DJI.

2. Find a triangle in the diagram that is not similar to DJI.

⚙ 2.8.3b Exploration Extension: Are you ready for more?

Figure out how to draw some more lines in the pentagon diagram to make more triangles similar to DJI.

📕 Lesson 8 Summary

We learned earlier that two polygons are similar when there is a sequence of translations, rotations, reflections, and dilations taking one polygon to the other. When the polygons are triangles, we only need to check that that both triangles have two corresponding angles to show they are similar—can you tell why?

Here is an example. Triangle ABC and triangle DEF each have a 30 degree angle and a 45 degree angle.

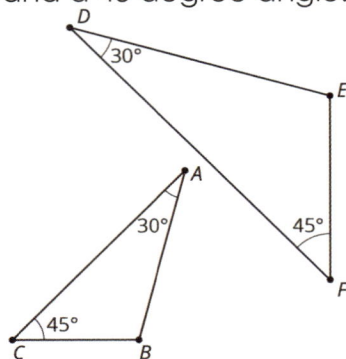

We can translate A to D and then rotate so that the two 30 degree angles are aligned, giving this picture:

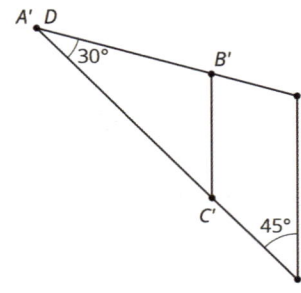

Now a dilation with center D and appropriate scale factor will move C' to F. This dilation also moves B' to E, showing that triangles ABC and DEF are similar.

✏ 2.8.5 Practice Problems

1. In each pair, some of the angles of two triangles in degrees are given. Use the information to decide if the triangles are similar or not. Explain how you know.

   a. Triangle A: 53, 71, ___; Triangle B: 53, 71, ___

   b. Triangle C: 90, 37, ___; Triangle D: 90, 53, ___

   c. Triangle E: 63, 45, ___; Triangle F: 14, 71, ____

MATH NATION

d. Triangle G: 121, ___, ___; Triangle H: 70, ___, ___

2.

a. Draw two equilateral triangles that are not congruent.

b. Measure the side lengths and angles of your triangles. Are the two triangles similar?

c. Do you think two equilateral triangles will be similar *always*, *sometimes*, or *never*? Explain your reasoning.

3. In the figure, line BC is parallel to line DE.

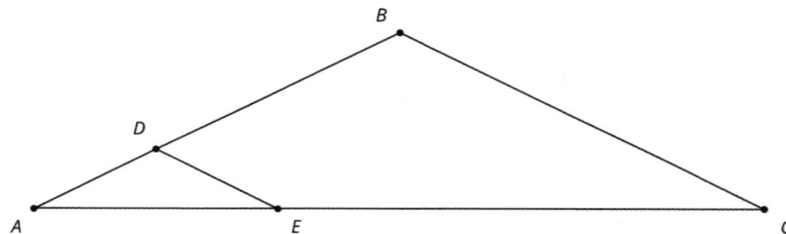

Explain why $\triangle ABC$ is similar to $\triangle ADE$.

4. The quadrilateral $PQRS$ in the diagram is a parallelogram. Let $P'Q'R'S'$ be the image of $PQRS$ after applying a dilation centered at a point O (not shown) with scale factor 3.

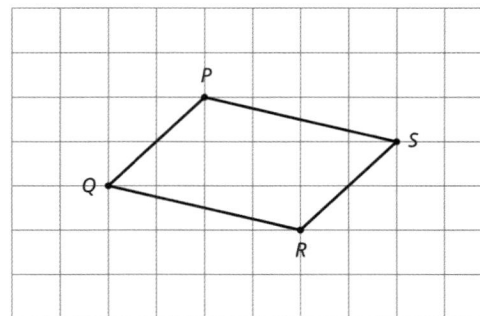

Which of the following is true?

A. $P'Q' = PQ$

B. $P'Q' = 3PQ$

C. $PQ = 3P'Q'$

D. Cannot be determined from the information given

5. Describe a sequence of transformations for which Quadrilateral P is the image of Quadrilateral Q.

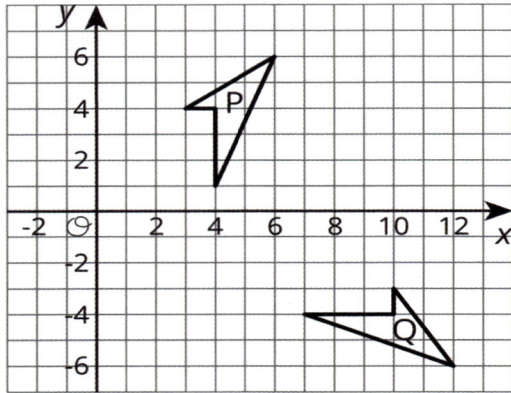

Let's find missing side lengths in triangles.

2.9.1 Warm-Up: Two-three-four and Four-five-six

Triangle A has side lengths 2, 3, and 4. Triangle B has side lengths 4, 5, and 6. Is Triangle A similar to Triangle B?

2.9.2a Exploration Activity: Quotients of Sides Within Similar Triangles

Your teacher will assign you one of the three columns in the second table.

Triangle ABC is similar to triangles DEF, GHI, and JKL. The scale factors for the dilations that show triangle ABC is similar to each triangle are in the table.

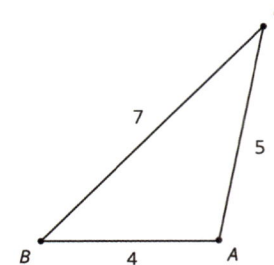

triangle	scale factor	length of short side	length of medium side	length of long side
ABC	1	4	5	7
DEF	2			
GHI	3			
JKL	$\frac{1}{2}$			

triangle	(long side) ÷ (short side)	(long side) ÷ (medium side)	(medium side) ÷ (short side)
ABC	$\frac{7}{4}$ or 1.75		
DEF			
GHI			
JKL			

1. Find the side lengths of triangles *DEF*, *GHI*, and *JKL*. Record them in the first table.

2. For all four triangles, find the quotient of the triangle side lengths assigned to you and record them in the second table. What do you notice about the quotients?

3. Compare your results with your partner's and complete your table.

Triangles *ABC* and *DEF* are similar. Explain why $\frac{AB}{BC} = \frac{DE}{EF}$.

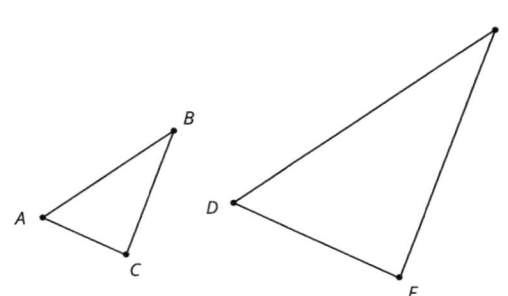

Triangles ABC, EFD, and GHI are all similar. The side lengths of the triangles all have the same units. Find the unknown side lengths.

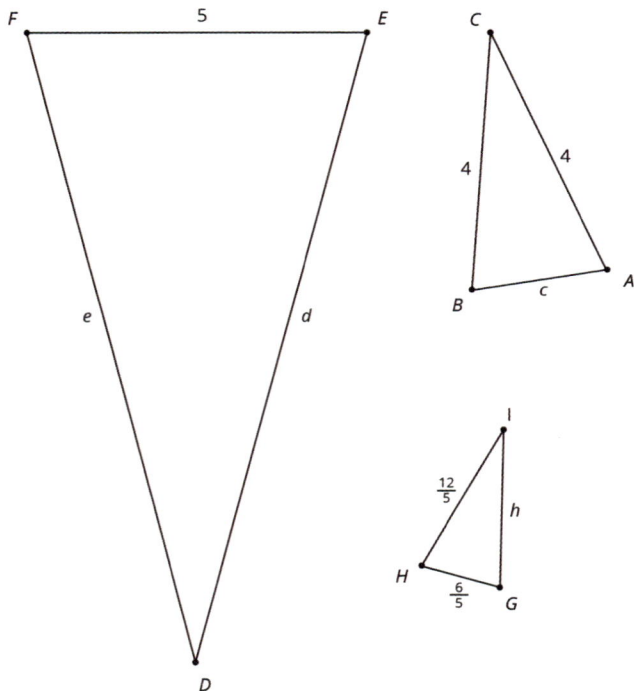

Lesson 9 Summary

If two polygons are similar, then the side lengths in one polygon are multiplied by the same scale factor to give the corresponding side lengths in the other polygon. For these triangles the scale factor is 2:

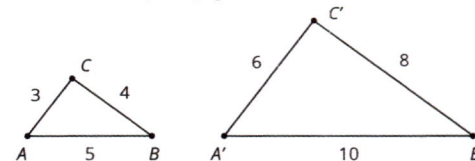

Here is a table that shows relationships between the short and medium length sides of the small and large triangle.

	small triangle	large triangle
medium side	4	8
short side	3	6
(medium side) ÷ (short side)	$\dfrac{4}{3}$	$\dfrac{8}{6} = \dfrac{4}{3}$

The lengths of the medium side and the short side are in a ratio of $4 : 3$. This means that the medium side in each triangle is $\frac{4}{3}$ as long as the short side.

This is true for all similar polygons; the ratio between two sides in one polygon is the same as the ratio of the corresponding sides in a similar polygon.

We can use these facts to calculate missing lengths in similar polygons. For example, triangles $A'B'C'$ and ABC shown here are similar. Let's find the length of segment $B'C'$.

In triangle ABC, side BC is twice as long as side AB, so this must be true for any triangle that is similar to triangle ABC. Since $A'B'$ is 1.2 units long and $2 \cdot 1.2 = 2.4$, the length of side $B'C'$ is 2.4 units.

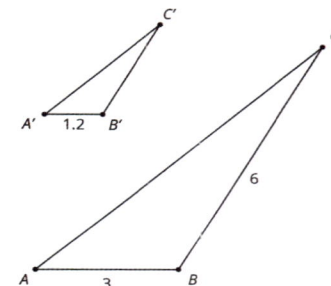

1. These two triangles are similar.

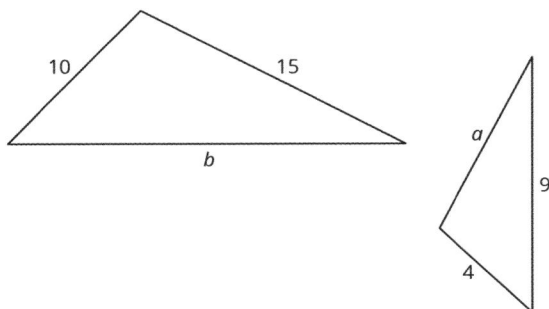

What are a and b? Note: the two figures are not drawn to scale.

2. Here is triangle ABC. Triangle XYZ is similar to ABC with scale factor $\frac{1}{4}$.

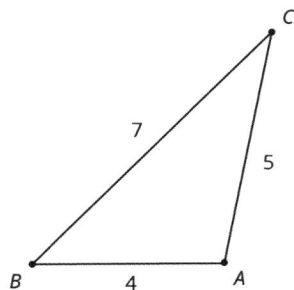

a. Draw what triangle XYZ might look like.

b. How do the angle measures of triangle XYZ compare to triangle ABC? Explain how you know.

c. What are the side lengths of triangle XYZ?

d. For triangle XYZ, calculate (long side) ÷ (medium side), and compare to triangle ABC.

3. The two triangles shown are similar. Find the value of $\frac{d}{c}$.

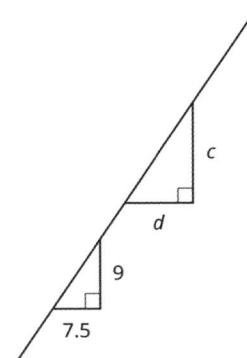

4. The diagram shows two nested triangles that share a vertex. Find a center and a scale factor for a dilation that would move the larger triangle to the smaller triangle.

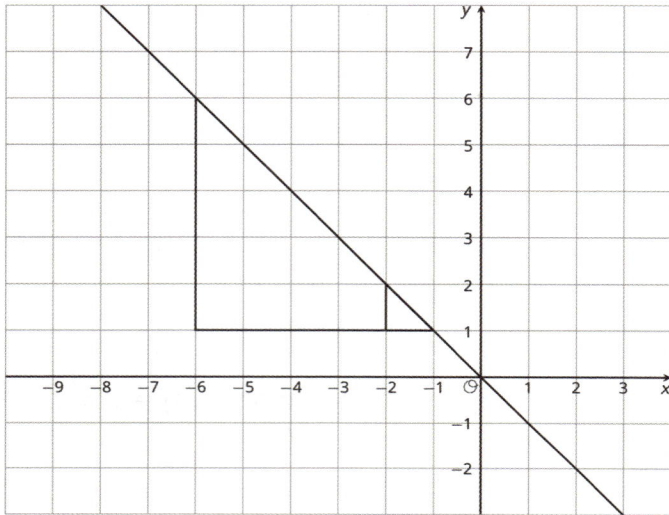

Let's learn about the slope of a line.

2.10.1 Warm-Up: Equal Quotients

Write some numbers that are equal to $15 \div 12$.

2.10.2 Exploration Activity: Similar Triangles on the Same Line

1. The figure shows three right triangles, each with its longest side on the same line.

   Your teacher will assign you two triangles. Explain why the two triangles are similar.

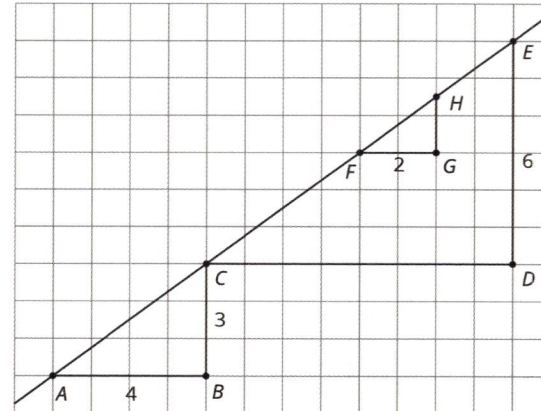

2. Complete the table.

triangle	vertical side	horizontal side	(vertical side) ÷ (horizontal side)
ABC			
CDE			
FGH			

2.10.3a Exploration Activity: Multiple Lines with the Same Slope

1. Draw two lines with **slope** 3. What do you notice about the two lines?

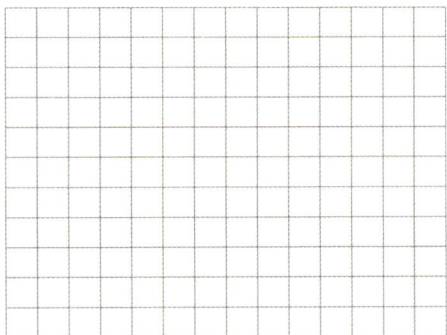

2. Draw two lines with slope $\frac{1}{2}$. What do you notice about the two lines?

2.10.3b Exploration Extension: Are you ready for more?

As we learn more about lines, we will occasionally have to consider perfectly vertical lines as a special case and treat them differently. Think about applying what you have learned in the last couple of activities to the case of vertical lines. What is the same? What is different?

2.10.4 Exploration Activity: Different Slopes of Different Lines

Here are several lines.

A   B   C

D   E   F

1. Match each line shown with a slope from this list: $\frac{1}{3}$, 2, 1, 0.25, $\frac{3}{2}$, $\frac{1}{2}$.

2. One of the given slopes does not have a line to match. Draw a line with this slope on the empty grid (F).

Lesson 10 Summary

Here is a line drawn on a grid. There are also four right triangles drawn. Do you notice anything the triangles have in common?

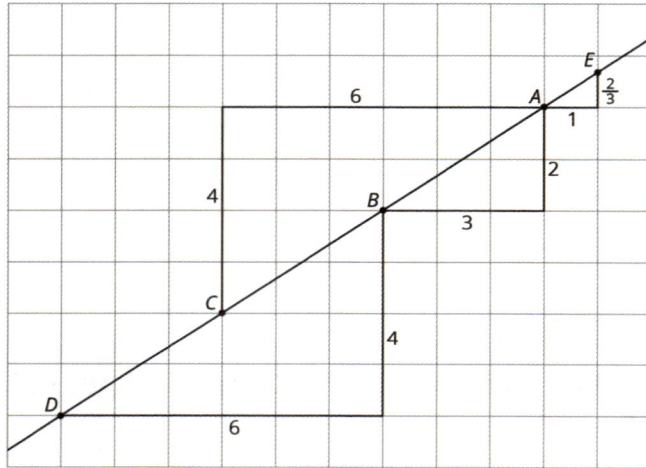

These four triangles are all examples of *slope triangles*. One side of a slope triangle is on the line, one side is vertical, and another side is horizontal. The **slope** of the line is the quotient of the length of the vertical side and the length of the horizontal side of the slope triangle. This number is the same for *all* slope triangles for the same line because all slope triangles for the same line are similar.

In this example, the slope of the line is $\frac{2}{3}$, which is what all four triangles have in common. Here is how the slope is calculated using the slope triangles:

- Points A and B give $2 \div 3 = \frac{2}{3}$
- Points D and B give $4 \div 6 = \frac{2}{3}$
- Points A and C give $4 \div 6 = \frac{2}{3}$
- Points A and E give $\frac{2}{3} \div 1 = \frac{2}{3}$

2.10.6 Practice Problems

1. Of the three lines in the graph, one has slope 1, one has slope 2, and one has slope $\frac{1}{5}$. Label each line with its slope.

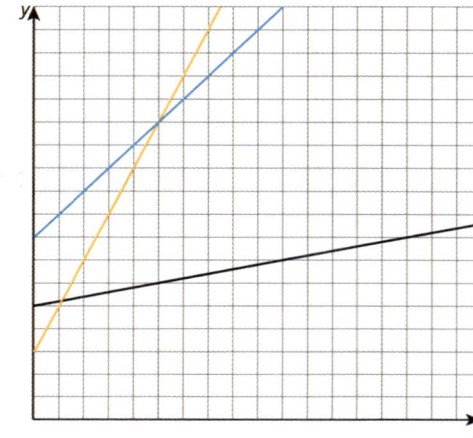

2. Draw three lines with slope 2, and three lines with slope $\frac{1}{3}$. What do you notice?

Unit 2: Dilations, Similarity, and Introducing Slope

3. The figure shows two right triangles, each with its longest side on the same line.

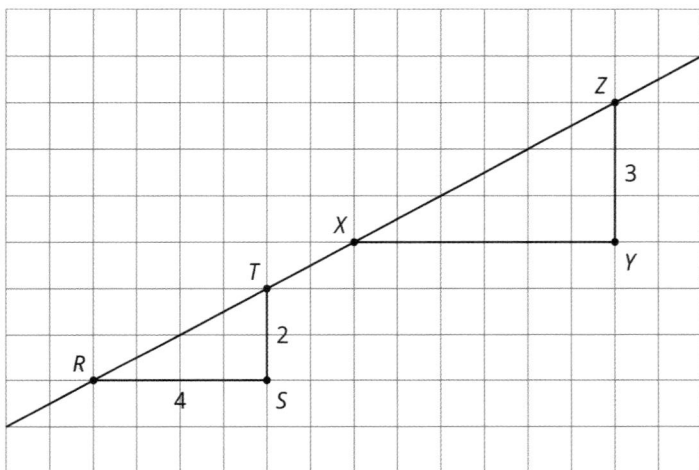

a. Explain how you know the two triangles are similar.

b. How long is *XY*?

c. For each triangle, calculate (vertical side) ÷ (horizontal side).

d. What is the slope of the line? Explain how you know.

4. Triangle *A* has side lengths 3, 4, and 5. Triangle *B* has side lengths 6, 7, and 8.

a. Explain how you know that Triangle *B* is *not* similar to Triangle *A*.

b. Give possible side lengths for Triangle *B* so that it is similar to Triangle *A*.

Let's explore the relationship between points on a line and the slope of the line.

2.11.1 Warm-Up: Coordinates and Lengths in the Coordinate Plane

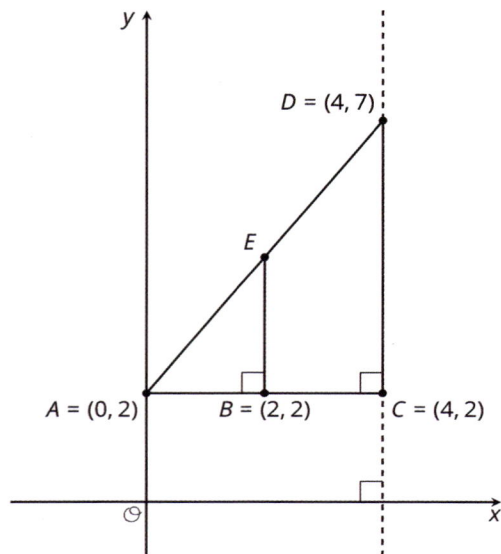

Find each of the following and explain your reasoning:

1. The length of segment BE.

2. The coordinates of E.

2.11.2 Exploration Activity: What We Mean by an Equation of a Line

Line j is shown in the coordinate plane.

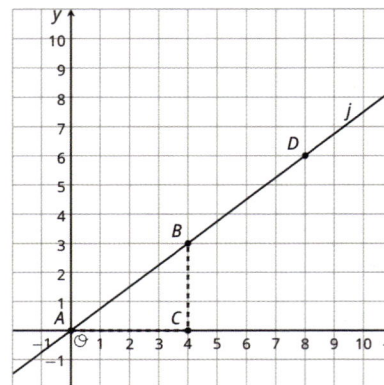

1. What are the coordinates of B and D?

2. Is point $(20,15)$ on line j? Explain how you know.

3. Is point $(100,75)$ on line j? Explain how you know.

4. Is point $(90,68)$ on line j? Explain how you know.

5. Suppose you know the x- and y-coordinates of a point. Write a rule that would allow you to test whether the point is on line j.

2.11.3a Exploration Activity: Writing Relationships from Slope Triangles

Here are two diagrams:

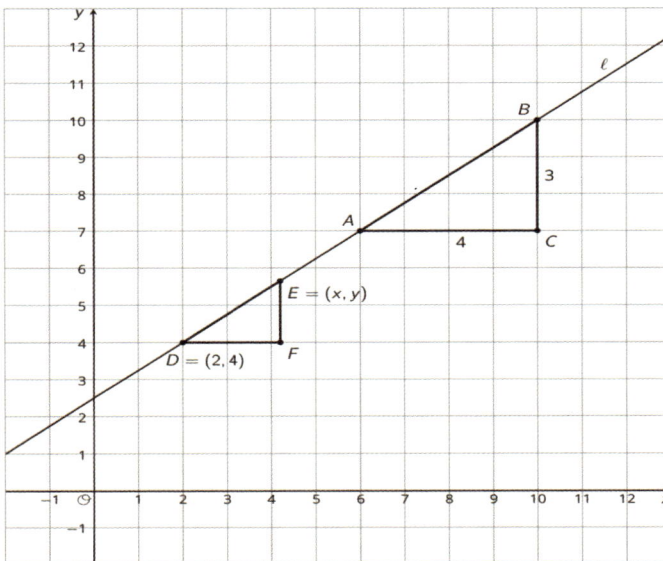

1. Complete each diagram so that all vertical and horizontal segments have expressions for their lengths.

2. Use what you know about similar triangles to find an equation for the quotient of the vertical and horizontal side lengths of △ DFE in each diagram.

2.11.3b Exploration Extension: Are you ready for more?

1. Find the area of the shaded region by summing the areas of the shaded triangles.

2. Find the area of the shaded region by subtracting the area of the unshaded region from the large triangle.

3. What is going on here?

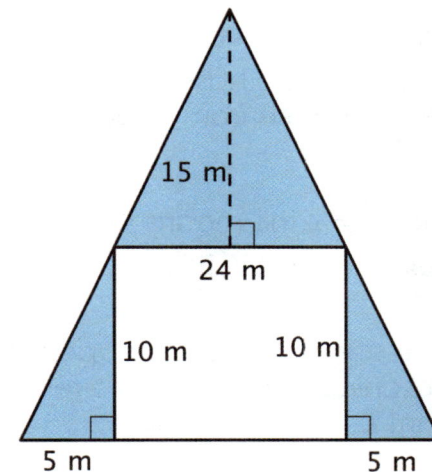

Here are the points A, C, and E on the same line. Triangles ABC and ADE are slope triangles for the line so we know they are similar triangles. Let's use their similarity to better understand the relationship between x and y, which make up the coordinates of point E.

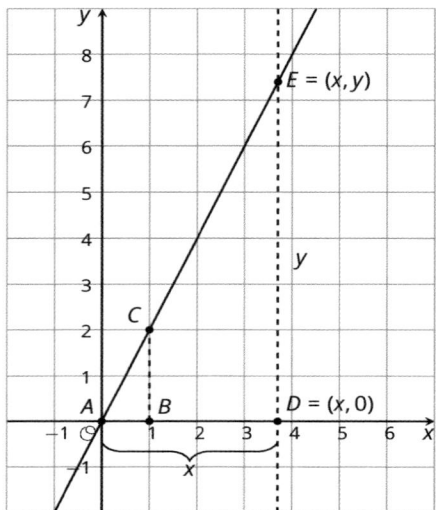

The slope for triangle ABC is $\frac{2}{1}$ since the vertical side has length 2 and the horizontal side has length 1. The slope we find for triangle ADE is $\frac{y}{x}$ because the vertical side has length y and the horizontal side has length x. These two slopes must be equal since they are from slope triangles for the same line, and so:
$$\frac{2}{1} = \frac{y}{x}$$

Since $\frac{2}{1} = 2$ this means that the value of y is twice the value of x, or that $y = 2x$. This equation is true for any point (x, y) on the line!

Here are two different slope triangles. We can use the same reasoning to describe the relationship between x and y for this point E.

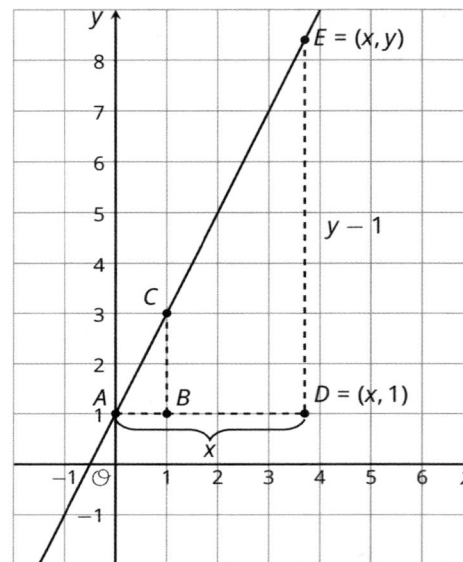

The slope for triangle ABC is $\frac{2}{1}$ since the vertical side has length 2 and the horizontal side has length 1. For triangle ADE, the horizontal side has length x. The vertical side has length $y - 1$ because the distance from (x, y) to the x-axis is y but the vertical side of the triangle stops 1 unit short of the x-axis. So the slope we find for triangle ADE is $\frac{y-1}{x}$. The slopes for the two slope triangles are equal, meaning: $\frac{2}{1} = \frac{y-1}{x}$

Since $y - 1$ is twice x, another way to write this equation is $y - 1 = 2x$. This equation is true for any point (x, y) on the line!

Unit 2: Dilations, Similarity, and Introducing Slope

MATH NATION

2.11.5 Practice Problems

1. For each pair of points, find the slope of the line that passes through both points. If you get stuck, try plotting the points on graph paper and drawing the line through them with a ruler.

   a. (1,1) and (7,5)

   b. (1,1) and (5,7)

   c. (2,5) and (−1,2)

   d. (2,5) and (−7,−4)

2. Line ℓ is shown in the coordinate plane.

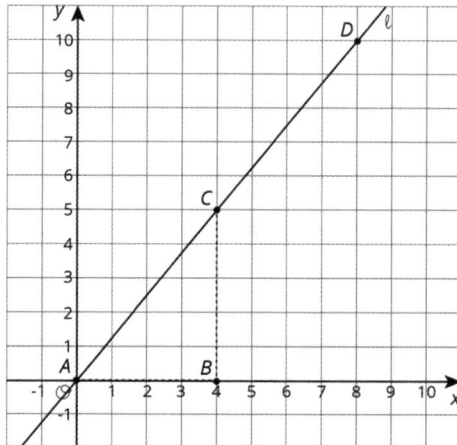

   a. What are the coordinates of B and D?

b. Is the point (16,20) on line ℓ? Explain how you know.

c. Is the point (20,24) on line ℓ? Explain how you know.

d. Is the point (80,100) on line ℓ? Explain how you know.

e. Write a rule that would allow you to test whether (x, y) is on line ℓ.

3. Consider the graphed line.

   Mai uses Triangle A and says the slope of this line is $\frac{6}{4}$. Elena uses Triangle B and says no, the slope of this line is 1.5. Do you agree with either of them? Explain.

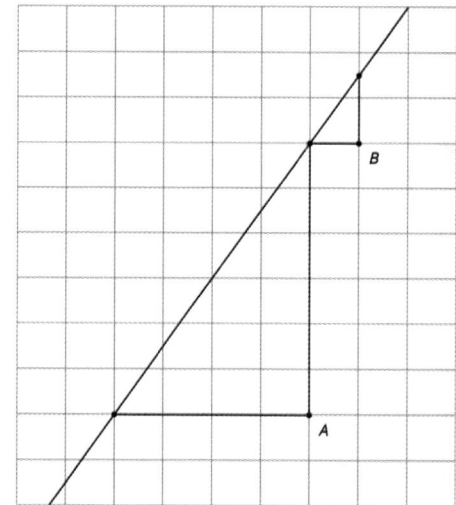

4. A rectangle has length 6 and height 4.

Which of these would tell you that quadrilateral $ABCD$ is definitely *not* similar to this rectangle? Select **all** that apply.

- ☐ $AB = BC$
- ☐ $m\angle ABC = 105°$
- ☐ $AB = 8$
- ☐ $BC = 8$
- ☐ $BC = 2 \cdot AB$
- ☐ $2 \cdot AB = 3 \cdot BC$

Unit 2, Lesson 12: Using Equations for Lines

Let's write equations for lines.

2.12.1 Warm-Up: Missing center

A dilation with scale factor 2 sends A to B. Where is the center of the dilation?

$\cdot B$

$\cdot A$

Unit 2: Dilations, Similarity, and Introducing Slope

Here is a line.

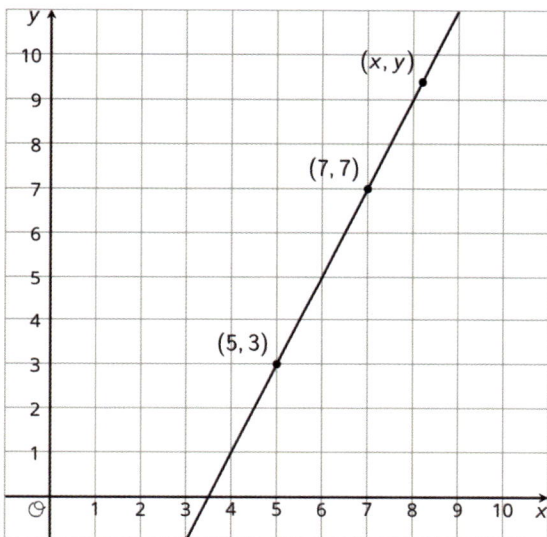

1. Using what you know about similar triangles, find an equation for the line in the diagram.

2. What is the slope of this line? Does it appear in your equation?

3. Is (9,11) also on the line? How do you know?

4. Is (100,193) also on the line?

⚙️ **2.12.2b Exploration Extension: Are you ready for more?**

There are many different ways to write down an equation for a line like the one in the problem. Does $\frac{y-3}{x-6} = 2$ represent the line? What about $\frac{y-6}{x-4} = 5$? What about $\frac{y+5}{x-1} = 2$? Explain your reasoning.

📢 **2.12.3 Exploration Activity: Dilations and Slope Triangles**

Here is triangle ABC.

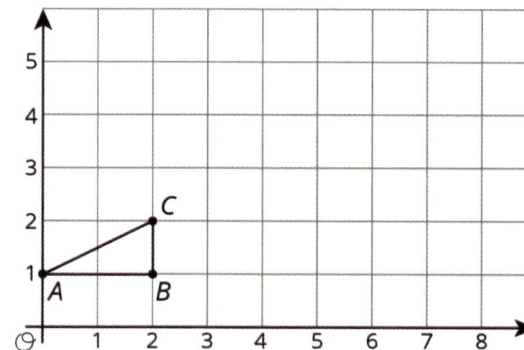

1. Draw the dilation of triangle ABC with center $(0,1)$ and scale factor 2.

2. Draw the dilation of triangle ABC with center $(0,1)$ and scale factor 2.5.

3. Where is C mapped by the dilation with center $(0,1)$ and scale factor s?

4. For which scale factor does the dilation with center $(0,1)$ send C to $(9,5.5)$? Explain how you know.

Lesson 12 Summary

We can use what we know about slope to decide if a point lies on a line. Here is a line with a few points labeled.

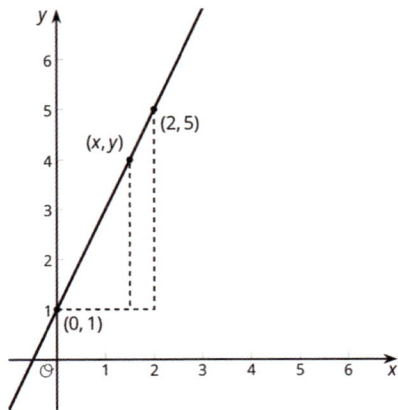

The slope triangle with vertices $(0,1)$ and $(2,5)$ gives a slope of $\frac{5-1}{2-0} = 2$. The slope triangle with vertices $(0,1)$ and (x,y) gives a slope of $\frac{y-1}{x}$. Since these slopes are the same, $\frac{y-1}{x} = 2$ is an equation for the line. So, if we want to check whether or not the point $(11,23)$ lies on this line, we can check that $\frac{23-1}{11} = 2$. Since $(11,23)$ is a solution to the equation, it is on the line!

2.12.5 Practice Problems

1. Select **all** the points that are on the line through $(0,5)$ and $(2,8)$.

   ☐ $(4,11)$
   ☐ $(5,10)$
   ☐ $(6,14)$
   ☐ $(30,50)$
   ☐ $(40,60)$

2. All three points displayed are on the line. Find an equation relating x and y.

3. Here is triangle ABC.

   a. Draw the dilation of triangle ABC with center $(2,0)$ and scale factor 2.

   b. Draw the dilation of triangle ABC with center $(2,0)$ and scale factor 3.

c. Draw the dilation of triangle ABC with center $(2,0)$ and scale factor $\frac{1}{2}$.

d. What are the coordinates of the image of point C when triangle ABC is dilated with center $(2,0)$ and scale factor s?

e. Write an equation for the line containing all possible images of point C.

4. Here are some line segments.

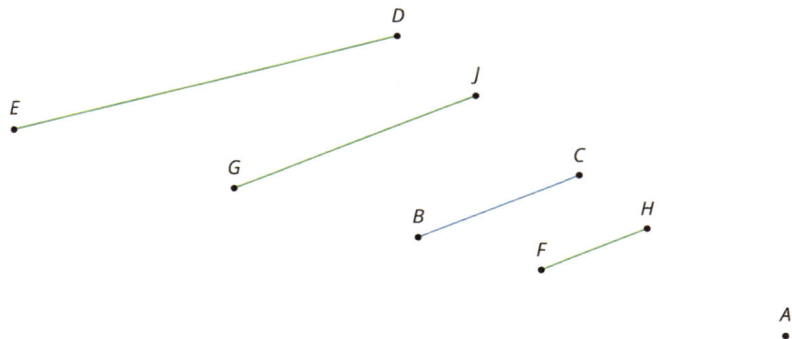

a. Which segment is a dilation of $\overline{BC}$ using A as the center of dilation and a scale factor of $\frac{2}{3}$?

b. Which segment is a dilation of $\overline{BC}$ using A as the center of dilation and a scale factor of $\frac{3}{2}$?

c. Which segment is not a dilation of $\overline{BC}$, and how do you know?

Unit 2, Lesson 13: The Shadow Knows

Let's use shadows to find the heights of an object.

What do you notice? What do you wonder?

2.13.2 Exploration Activity: Objects and Shadows

Here are some measurements that were taken when the photo was taken. It was impossible to directly measure the height of the lamppost, so that cell is blank.

	height (inches)	shadow length (inches)
younger boy	43	29
man	72	48
older boy	51	34
lamppost		114

1. What relationships do you notice between an object's height and the length of its shadow?

2. Make a conjecture about the height of the lamppost and explain your thinking.

2.13.3 Exploration Activity: Justifying the Relationship

Explain *why* the relationship between the height of these objects and the length of their shadows is approximately proportional.

2.13.4 Exploration Activity: The Height of a Tall Object

1. Head outside. Make sure that it is a sunny day and you take a measuring device (like a tape measure or meter stick) as well as a pencil and some paper.

2. Choose an object whose height is too large to measure directly. Your teacher may assign you an object.

3. Use what you have learned to figure out the height of the object! Explain or show your reasoning.

Unit 3: Linear Relationships

Section 1: Proportional Relationships

☐ *I can use the constant of proportionality to compare the pace of different animals.*

☐ *I can graph a proportional relationship from a story.*

☐ *I can graph a proportional relationship from an equation.*

☐ *I can tell when two graphs are of the same proportional relationship even if the scales are different.*

☐ *I can scale and label a coordinate axes in order to graph a proportional relationship.*

☐ *I can compare proportional relationships represented in different ways.*

Section 2: Representing Linear Relationships

☐ *I can find the rate of change of a linear relationship by figuring out the slope of the line representing the relationship.*

☐ *I can interpret the vertical intercept of a graph of a real-world situation.*

☐ *I can match graphs to the real-world situations they represent by identifying the slope and the vertical intercept.*

☐ *I can write an equation for the relationship between the total volume in a graduated cylinder and the number of objects added to the graduated cylinder.*

☐ *I can use patterns to write a linear equation to represent a situation.*

Adapted from Open Up Resources 6-8 Math (authored by Illustrative Mathematics).
See inside front cover for details.

Adapted from Open Up Resources 6-8 Math (authored by Illustrative Mathematics).
See inside front cover for details.

MATH NATION

Unit 3, Lesson 1: Understanding Proportional Relationships

Let's study some graphs.

🔔 3.1.1 Warm-Up: Notice and Wonder: Two Graphs

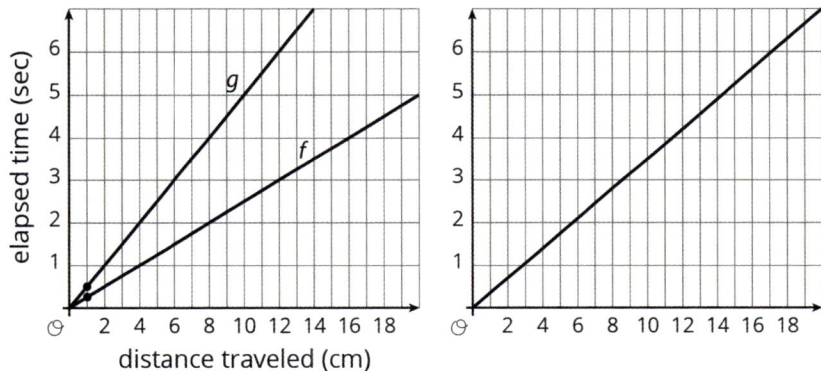

What do you notice? What do you wonder?

🔭 3.1.2a Exploration Activity: Moving Through Representations

A ladybug and ant move at constant speeds. The diagrams with tick marks show their positions at different times. Each tick mark represents 1 centimeter.

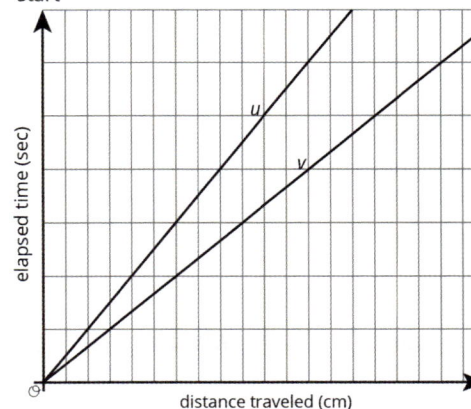

1. Lines u and v also show the positions of the two bugs. Which line shows the ladybug's movement? Which line shows the ant's movement? Explain your reasoning.

2. How long does it take the ladybug to travel 12 cm? The ant?

3. Scale the vertical and horizontal axes by labeling each grid line with a number. You will need to use the time and distance information shown in the tick-mark diagrams.

4. Mark and label the point on line u and the point on line v that represent the time and position of each bug after travelling 1 cm.

🔴 3.1.2b Exploration Extension: Are you ready for more?

1. How fast is each bug traveling?

2. Will there ever be a time when the purple bug (ant) is twice as far away from the start as the red bug (ladybug)? Explain or show your reasoning.

🔭 3.1.3 Exploration Activity: Moving Twice as Fast

Refer to the tick-mark diagrams and graph in the earlier activity when needed.

1. Imagine a bug that is moving twice as fast as the ladybug. On each tick-mark diagram, mark the position of this bug.

2. Plot this bug's positions on the coordinate axes with lines u and v, and connect them with a line.

3. Write an equation for each of the three lines.

📗 Lesson 1 Summary

Graphing is a way to help us make sense of relationships. But the graph of a line on a coordinate axes without scale or labels isn't very helpful. For example, let's say we know that on longer bike rides Kiran can ride 4 miles every 16 minutes and Mai can ride 4 miles every 12 minutes. Here are the graphs of these relationships:

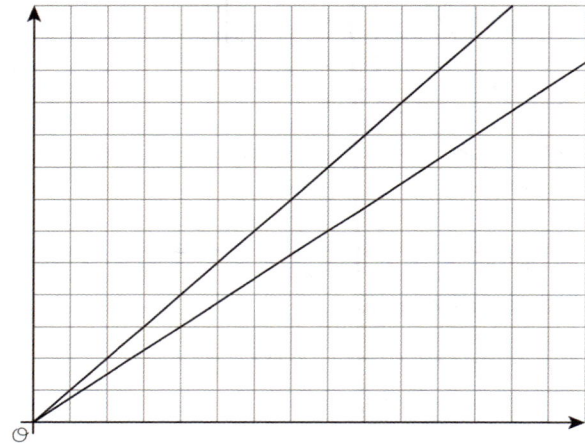

Without labels we can't even tell which line is Kiran and which is Mai! Without labels and a scale on the axes, we can't use these graphs to answer questions like:

1. Which graph goes with which rider?
2. Who rides faster?
3. If Kiran and Mai start a bike trip at the same time, how far are they after 24 minutes?
4. How long will it take each of them to reach the end of the 12 mile bike path?

Here are the same graphs, but now with labels and scale:

Revisiting the questions from earlier:

1. Which graph goes with each rider? If Kiran rides 4 miles in 16 minutes, then the point (4,16) is on his graph. If he rides for 1 mile, it will take 4 minutes. 10 miles will take 40 minutes. So the upper graph represents Kiran's ride. Mai's points for the same distances are (1,3), (4,12), and (10,30), so hers is the lower graph. (A letter next to each line would help us remember which is which!)

2. Who rides faster? Mai rides faster because she can ride the same distance as Kiran in a shorter time.

3. If Kiran and Mai start a bike trip at the same time, how far are they after 20 minutes? The points on the graphs at height 20 are 5 miles for Kiran and a little less than 7 miles for Mai.

4. How long will it take each of them to reach the end of the 12 mile bike path? The points on the graphs at a horizontal distance of 12 are 36 minutes for Mai and 48 minutes for Kiran. (Kiran's time after 12 miles is almost off the grid!)

1. Priya jogs at a constant speed. The relationship between her distance and time is shown on the graph. Diego bikes at a constant speed twice as fast as Priya. Sketch a graph showing the relationship between Diego's distance and time.

2. A you-pick blueberry farm offers 5 lbs of blueberries for $16.50.

   Sketch a graph of the relationship between cost and pounds of blueberries.

   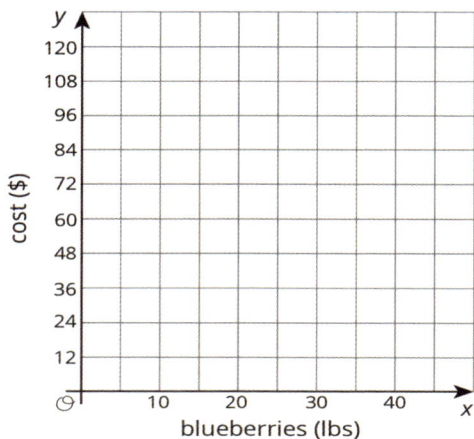

3. A line contains the points $(-4,1)$ and $(4,6)$. Decide whether or not each of these points is also on the line:

   a. $(0,3.5)$

   b. $(12,11)$

   c. $(80,50)$

   d. $(-1,2.875)$

4. The points $(2,-4)$, (x,y), A, and B all lie on the line. Find an equation relating x and y.

   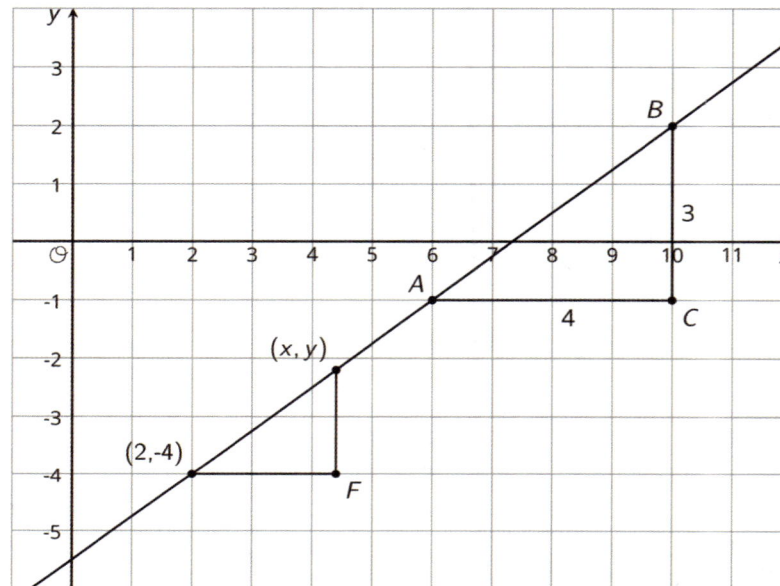

MATH NATION

Unit 3, Lesson 2: Graphs of Proportional Relationships

Let's think about scale.

🔔 3.2.1 Warm-Up: An Unknown Situation

Here is a graph that could represent a variety of different situations.

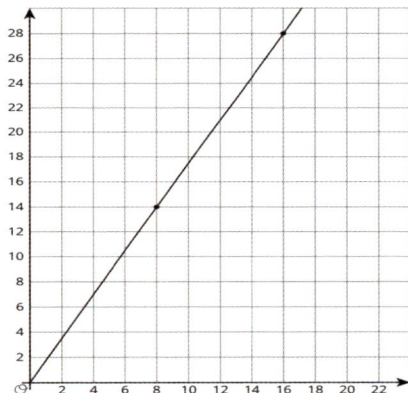

1. Write an equation for the graph.

2. Sketch a new graph of this relationship.

🔭 3.2.2 Exploration Activity: Card Sort: Proportional Relationships

You teacher will give you 12 graphs of proportional relationships.

1. Sort the graphs into groups based on what proportional relationship they represent.

2. Write an equation for each *different* proportional relationship you find.

🔭 3.2.3a Exploration Activity: Different Scales

Two large water tanks are filling with water. Tank A is not filled at a constant rate, and the relationship between its volume of water and time is graphed on each set of axes. Tank B is filled at a constant rate of $\frac{1}{2}$ liters per minute. The relationship between its volume of water and time can be described by the equation $v = \frac{1}{2}t$, where t is the time in minutes and v is the total volume in liters of water in the tank.

volume (liters) vs. time (minutes)

1. Sketch and label a graph of the relationship between the volume of water, v, and time, t, for Tank B on each of the axes.

2. Answer the following questions and say which graph you used to find your answer.
   a. After 30 seconds, which tank has the most water?

   b. At approximately what times do both tanks have the same amount of water?

   c. At approximately what times do both tanks contain 1 liter of water? 20 liters?

A giant tortoise travels at 0.17 miles per hour and an arctic hare travels at 37 miles per hour.

1. Draw separate graphs that show the relationship between time elapsed, in hours, and distance traveled, in miles, for both the tortoise and the hare.

2. Would it be helpful to try to put both graphs on the same pair of axes? Why or why not?

3. The tortoise and the hare start out together and after half an hour the hare stops to take a rest. How long does it take the tortoise to catch up?

The scales we choose when graphing a relationship often depend on what information we want to know. For example, say two water tanks are filled at different constant rates. The relationship between time in minutes, t, and volume in liters, v, of tank A is given by $v = 2.2t$. For tank B the relationship is $v = 2.75t$.

These equations tell us that tank A is being filled at a constant rate of 2.2 liters per minute and tank B is being filled at a constant rate of 2.75 liters per minute.

If we want to use graphs to see at what times the two tanks will have 110 liters of water, then using an axis scale from 0 to 10, as shown here, isn't very helpful.

If we use a vertical scale that goes to 150 liters, a bit beyond the 110 we are looking for, and a horizontal scale that goes to 100 minutes, we get a much more useful set of axes for answering our question.

Now we can see that the two tanks will reach 110 liters 10 minutes apart—tank B after 40 minutes of filling and tank A after 50 minutes of filling.

It is important to note that both of these graphs are correct, but one uses a range of values that helps answer the question. In order to always pick a helpful scale, we should consider the situation and the questions asked about it.

3.2.5 Practice Problems

1. The tortoise and the hare are having a race. After the hare runs 16 miles the tortoise has only run 4 miles.

   The relationship between the distance, x, the tortoise "runs" in miles for every, y, miles the hare runs is $y = 4x$. Graph this relationship.

2. The table shows a proportional relationship between the weight on a spring scale and the distance the spring has stretched.

   a. Complete the table.

   b. Describe the scales you could use on the x and y axes of a coordinate grid that would show all the distances and weights in the table.

distance (cm)	weight (newtons)
20	28
55	
	140
1	

3. Find a sequence of rotations, reflections, translations, and dilations showing that one figure is similar to the other. Be specific: give the amount and direction of a translation, a line of reflection, the center and angle of a rotation, and the center and scale factor of a dilation.

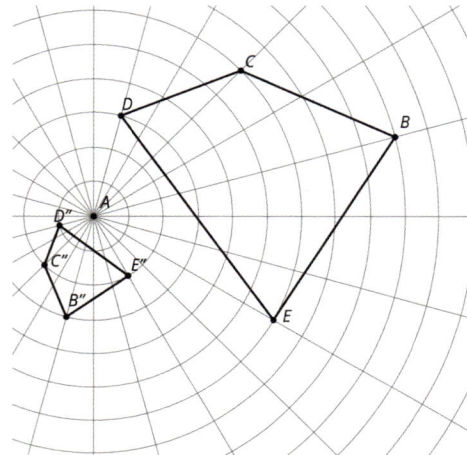

4. Consider the following dialogue:

   Andre said, "I found two figures that are congruent, so they can't be similar."

   Diego said, "No, they are similar! The scale factor is 1."

   Who is correct? Use the definition of similarity to explain your answer.

Let's graph proportional relationships.

🔔 3.3.1 Warm-Up: Number Talk: Multiplication

Find the value of each product mentally.

$15 \cdot 2$

$15 \cdot 0.5$

$15 \cdot 0.25$

$15 \cdot (2.25)$

3.3.2 Exploration Activity: Representations of Proportional Relationships

1. Here are two ways to represent a situation.

   Description: Jada and Noah counted the number of steps they took to walk a set distance. To walk the same distance,

   o Jada took 8 steps
   o Noah took 10 steps

   Then they found that when Noah took 15 steps, Jada took 12 steps.

   Equation: Let x represent the number of steps Jada takes and let y represent the number of steps Noah takes. $y = \frac{5}{4}x$

   a. Create a table that represents this situation with at least 3 pairs of values.

   b. Graph this relationship and label the axes.

   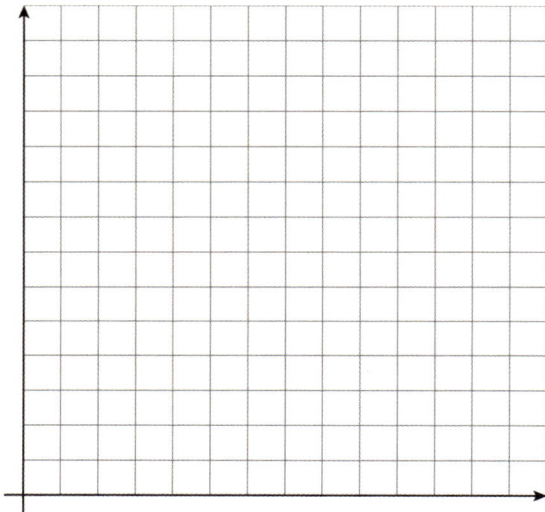

c. How can you see or calculate the constant of proportionality in each representation? What does it mean?

d. Explain how you can tell that the equation, description, graph, and table all represent the same situation.

2. Here are two ways to represent a situation.

   Description: The Origami Club is doing a car wash fundraiser to raise money for a trip. They charge the same price for every car. After 11 cars, they raised a total of $93.50. After 23 cars, they raised a total of $195.50.

   Table:

number of cars	amount raised in dollars
11	93.50
23	195.50

   a. Write an equation that represents this situation. (Use c to represent number of cars and use m to represent amount raised in dollars.)

Continued on next page

b. Create a graph that represents this situation.

c. How can you see or calculate the constant of proportionality in each representation? What does it mean?

d. Explain how you can tell that the equation, description, graph, and table all represent the same situation.

3.3.3a Exploration Activity: Info Gap: Proportional Relationships

Your teacher will give you either a problem card or a data card. Do not show or read your card to your partner.

If your teacher gives you the *problem card*:

1. Silently read your card and think about what information you need to answer the question.
2. Ask your partner for the specific information that you need.
3. Explain to your partner how you are using the information to solve the problem.
4. Solve the problem and explain your reasoning to your partner.

If your teacher gives you the *data card*:

1. Silently read the information on your card.
2. Ask your partner "What specific information do you need?" and wait for your partner to *ask* for information. *Only* give information that is on your card. (Do not figure out anything for your partner!)
3. Before telling your partner the information, ask "Why do you need that information?"
4. After your partner solves the problem, ask them to explain their reasoning and listen to their explanation.

Pause here so your teacher can review your work. Ask your teacher for a new set of cards and repeat the activity, trading roles with your partner.

3.3.3b Exploration Extension: Are you ready for more?

Ten people can dig five holes in three hours. If n people digging at the same rate dig m holes in d hours:

1. Is n proportional to m when $d = 3$?

2. Is n proportional to d when $m = 5$?

3. Is m proportional to d when $n = 10$?

Lesson 3 Summary

Proportional relationships can be represented in multiple ways. Which representation we choose depends on the purpose. And when we create representations we can choose helpful values by paying attention to the context. For example, a stew recipe calls for 3 carrots for every 2 potatoes. One way to represent this is using an equation. If there are p potatoes and c carrots, then $c = \frac{3}{2}p$.

Suppose we want to make a large batch of this recipe for a family gathering, using 150 potatoes. To find the number of carrots we could just use the equation: $\frac{3}{2} \cdot 150 = 225$ carrots.

Now suppose the recipe is used in a restaurant that makes the stew in large batches of different sizes depending on how busy a day it is, using up to 300 potatoes at at time. Then we might make a graph to show how many carrots are needed for different amounts of potatoes. We set up a pair of coordinate axes with a scale from 0 to 300 along the horizontal axis and 0 to 450 on the vertical axis, because $450 = \frac{3}{2} \cdot 300$. Then we can read how many carrots are needed for any number of potatoes up to 300.

Or if the recipe is used in a food factory that produces very large quantities and the potatoes come in bags of 150, we might just make a table of values showing the number of carrots needed for different multiplies of 150.

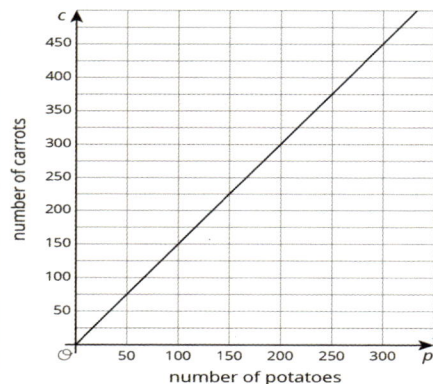

number of potatoes	number of carrots
150	225
300	450
450	675
600	900

No matter the representation or the scale used, the constant of proportionality, $\frac{3}{2}$, is evident in each. In the equation it is the number we multiply p by; in the graph, it is the slope; and in the table, it is the number we multiply values in the left column to get numbers in the right column. We can think of the constant of proportionality as a **rate of change** of c with respect to p. In this case the rate of change is $\frac{3}{2}$ carrots per potato.

3.3.5 Practice Problems

1. Here is a graph of the proportional relationship between calories and grams of fish:

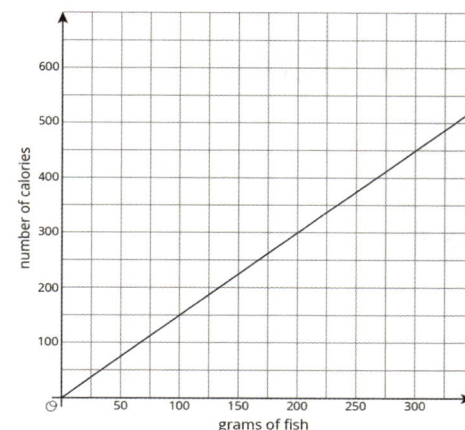

   a. Write an equation that reflects this relationship using x to represent the amount of fish in grams and y to represent the number of calories.

   b. Use your equation to complete the table:

grams of fish	number of calories
1000	
	2001
1	

2. Students are selling raffle tickets for a school fundraiser. They collect $24 for every 10 raffle tickets they sell.

   a. Suppose M is the amount of money the students collect for selling R raffle tickets. Write an equation that reflects the relationship between M and R.

   b. Label and scale the axes and graph this situation with M on the vertical axis and R on the horizontal axis. Make sure the scale is large enough to see how much they would raise if they sell 1000 tickets.

3. Describe how you can tell whether a line's slope is greater than 1, equal to 1, or less than 1.

4. A line is represented by the equation $\frac{y}{x-2} = \frac{3}{11}$. What are the coordinates of some points that lie on the line? Graph the line on graph paper.

Unit 3: Linear Relationships

Unit 3, Lesson 4: Comparing Proportional Relationships

Let's compare proportional relationships.

3.4.1 Warm-Up: What's the Relationship?

The equation $y = 4.2x$ could represent a variety of different situations.

1. Write a description of a situation represented by this equation. Decide what quantities x and y represent in your situation.

2. Make a table and a graph that represent the situation.

3.4.2a Exploration Activity: Comparing Two Different Representations

1. Elena babysits her neighbor's children. Her earnings are given by the equation $y = 8.40x$, where x represents the number of hours she worked and y represents the amount of money she earned. Jada earns $7 per hour mowing her neighbors' lawns.

   a. Who makes more money after working 12 hours? How much more do they make? Explain how you know.

   b. What is the rate of change for each situation and what does it mean?

   c. How long would it take each person to earn $150? Explain or show your reasoning.

2. Clare and Han have summer jobs stuffing envelopes for two different companies.

   Clare's earnings can be seen in the table.

number of envelopes	money in dollars
400	40
900	90

   Han earns $15 for every 300 envelopes he finishes.

   a. Who would make more money after stuffing 1500 envelopes? How much more money would they make? Explain how you know.

   b. What is the rate of change for each situation and what does it mean?

   c. Who gets paid more in their job? Explain or show your reasoning.

3. Tyler plans to start a lemonade stand and is trying to perfect his recipe for lemonade. He wants to make sure the recipe doesn't use too much lemonade mix (lemon juice and sugar) but still tastes good.

   Lemonade Recipe 1 is given by the equation $y = 4x$ where x represents the amount of lemonade mix in cups and y represents the amount of water in cups.

   Lemonade Recipe 2 is given in the table.

lemonade mix (cups)	water (cups)
10	50
13	65
21	105

   a. If Tyler had 16 cups of lemonade mix, how many cups of water would he need for each recipe? Explain how you know.

   b. What is the rate of change for each situation and what does it mean?

   c. Tyler has a 5-gallon jug (which holds 80 cups) to use for his lemonade stand and 16 cups of lemonade mix. Which lemonade recipe should he use? Explain or show your reasoning.

Unit 3: Linear Relationships

MATH NATION

🔴 3.4.2b Exploration Extension: Are you ready for more?

Han and Clare are still stuffing envelopes. Han can stuff 20 envelopes in a minute, and Clare can stuff 10 envelopes in a minute. They start working together on a pile of 1,000 envelopes.

1. How long does it take them to finish the pile?

2. Who earns more money?

📗 Lesson 4 Summary

When two proportional relationships are represented in different ways, we compare them by finding a common piece of information.

For example, Clare's earnings are represented by the equation $y = 14.5x$, where y is her earnings in dollars for working x hours.

The table shows some information about Jada's pay.

Who is paid at a higher rate per hour? How much more does that person have after 20 hours?

time worked (hours)	earnings (dollars)
7	92.75
4.5	59.63
37	490.25

In Clare's equation we see that the constant of proportionality relating her earnings to time worked is 14.50. This means that she earns $14.50 per hour.

We can calculate Jada's constant of proportionality by dividing a value in the earnings column by a value in the same row in the time worked column. Using the last row, the constant of proportionality for Jada is 13.25, since $490.25 \div 37 = 13.25$. An equation representing Jada's earnings is $y = 13.25x$. This means she earns $13.25 per hour.

So Clare is paid at a higher rate than Jada. Clare earns $1.25 more per hour than Jada, which means that after 20 hours of work, she has $20 \cdot \$1.25 = \$25$ more than Jada.

🔴 3.4.4 Practice Problems

1. A contractor must haul a large amount of dirt to a work site. She collected information from two hauling companies. EZ Excavation gives its prices in a table. Happy Hauling Service gives its prices in a graph.

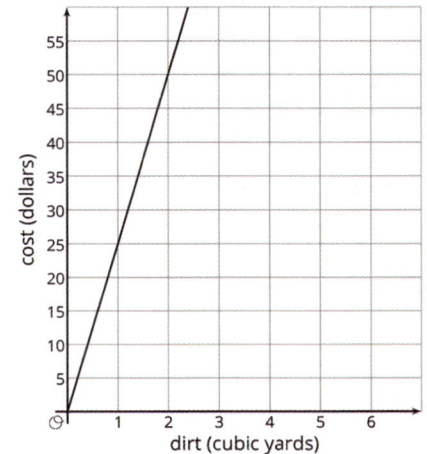

dirt (cubic yards)	cost (dollars)
8	196
20	490
26	637

a. How much would each hauling company charge to haul 40 cubic yards of dirt? Explain or show your reasoning.

Continued on next page

b. Calculate the rate of change for each relationship. What do they mean for each company?

c. If the contractor has 40 cubic yards of dirt to haul and a budget of $1000, which hauling company should she hire? Explain or show your reasoning.

2. Andre and Priya are tracking the number of steps they walk. Andre records that he can walk 6000 steps in 50 minutes. Priya writes the equation $y = 118x$, where y is the number of steps and x is the number of minutes she walks, to describe her step rate. This week, Andre and Priya each walk for a total of 5 hours. Who walks more steps? How many more?

3. Find the coordinates of point D in each diagram:

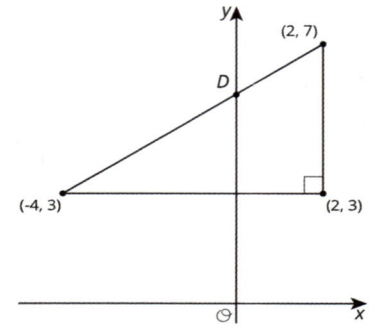

4. Select **all** the pairs of points so that the line between those points has slope $\frac{2}{3}$.

☐ (0,0) and (2,3)

☐ (0,0) and (3,2)

☐ (1,5) and (4,7)

☐ (−2,−2) and (4,2)

☐ (20,30) and (−20,−30)

Unit 3: Linear Relationships

Unit 3, Lesson 5: Introduction to Linear Relationships

Let's explore some relationships between two variables.

3.5.1 Warm-Up: Number Talk: Fraction Division

Find the value of $2\frac{5}{8} \div \frac{1}{2}$.

3.5.2 Exploration Activity: Stacking Cups

We have two stacks of styrofoam cups. One stack has 6 cups, and its height is 15 cm. The other one has 12 cups, and its height is 23 cm. How many cups are needed for a stack with a height of 50 cm?

3.5.3 Exploration Activity: Connecting Slope to Rate of Change

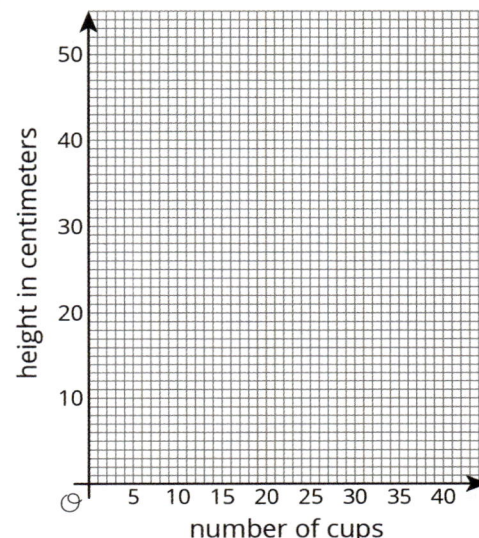

1. If you didn't create your own graph of the situation before, do so now.

2. What are some ways you can tell that the number of cups is not proportional to the height of the stack?

3. What is the **slope** of the line in your graph? What does the slope mean in this situation?

4. At what point does your line intersect the vertical axis? What do the coordinates of this point tell you about the cups?

5. How much height does each cup after the first add to the stack?

Andre starts babysitting and charges $10 for traveling to and from the job, and $15 per hour. For every additional hour he works he charges another $15. If we graph Andre's earnings based on how long he works, we have a line that starts at $10 on the vertical axis and then increases by $15 each hour. A **linear relationship** is any relationship between two quantities where one quantity has a constant **rate of change** with respect to the other.

We can figure out the rate of change using the graph. Because the rate of change is constant, we can take any two points on the graph and divide the amount of vertical change by the amount of horizontal change. For example, take the points (2,40) and (6,100). They mean that Andre earns $40 for working 2 hours and $100 for working 6 hours. The rate of change is $\frac{100-40}{6-2} = 15$ dollars per hour. Andre's earnings go up $15 for each hour of babysitting. Notice that this is the same way we calculate the **slope** of the line. That's why the graph is a line, and why we call this a linear relationship. The rate of change of a linear relationship is the same as the slope of its graph.

With proportional relationships we are used to graphs that contain the point (0,0). But proportional relationships are just one type of linear relationship. In the following lessons, we will continue to explore the other type of linear relationship where the quantities are not both 0 at the same time.

1. A restaurant offers delivery for their pizzas. The total cost is a delivery fee added to the price of the pizzas. One customer pays $25 to have 2 pizzas delivered. Another customer pays $58 for 5 pizzas. How many pizzas are delivered to a customer who pays $80?

2. To paint a house, a painting company charges a flat rate of $500 for supplies, plus $50 for each hour of labor.

   a. How much would the painting company charge to paint a house that needs 20 hours of labor? A house that needs 50 hours?

b. Draw a line representing the relationship between x, the number of hours it takes the painting company to finish the house, and y, the total cost of painting the house. Label the two points from the earlier question on your graph.

c. Find the slope of the line. What is the meaning of the slope in this context?

3. Tyler and Elena are on the cross-country team.

   Tyler's distances and times for a training run are shown on the graph.

distance (miles)

Elena's distances and times for a training run are given by the equation $y = 8.5x$, where x represents distance in miles and y represents time in minutes.

a. Who ran farther in 10 minutes? How much farther? Explain how you know.

b. Calculate each runner's pace in minutes per mile.

c. Who ran faster during the training run? Explain or show your reasoning.

4. Write an equation for the line that passes through $(2,5)$ and $(6,7)$.

Unit 3, Lesson 6: More Linear Relationships

Let's explore some more relationships between two variables.

🔔 3.6.1 Warm-Up: Growing

Look for a growing pattern. Describe the pattern you see.

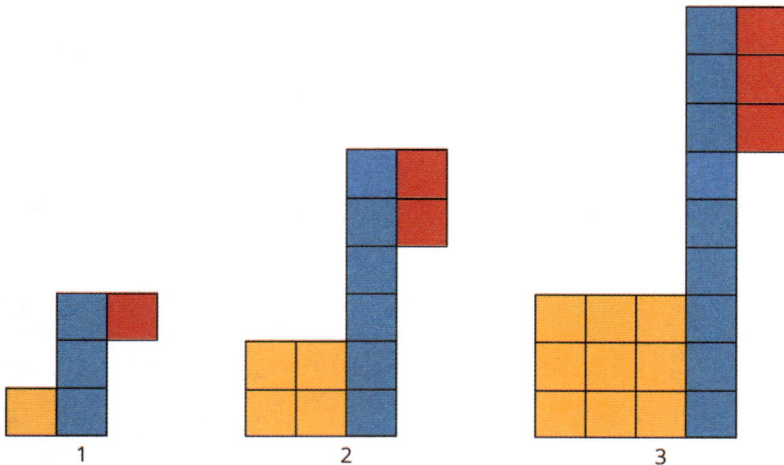

1. If your pattern continues growing in the same way, how many tiles of each color will be in the 4th and 5th diagram? The 10th diagram?

2. How many tiles of each color will be in the nth diagram? Be prepared to explain how your reasoning.

📢 3.6.2 Exploration Activity: Slopes, Vertical Intercepts, and Graphs

Your teacher will give you 6 cards describing different situations and 6 cards with graphs.

1. Match each situation to a graph.

2. Pick one proportional relationship and one non-proportional relationship and answer the following questions about them.

   a. How can you find the slope from the graph? Explain or show your reasoning.

   b. Explain what the slope means in the situation.

   c. Find the point where the line crosses the vertical axis. What does that point tell you about the situation?

3.6.3a Exploration Activity: Summer Reading

Lin has a summer reading assignment. After reading the first 30 pages of the book, she plans to read 40 pages each day until she finishes. Lin makes the graph shown here to track how many total pages she'll read over the next few days.

After day 1, Lin reaches page 70, which matches the point (1,70) she made on her graph. After day 4, Lin reaches page 190, which does not match the point (4,160) she made on her graph. Lin is not sure what went wrong since she knows she followed her reading plan.

1. Sketch a line showing Lin's original plan on the axes.

2. What does the **vertical intercept** mean in this situation? How do the vertical intercepts of the two lines compare?

3. What does the slope mean in this situation? How do the slopes of the two lines compare?

3.6.3b Exploration Extension: Are you ready for more?

Jada's grandparents started a savings account for her in 2010. The table shows the amount in the account each year.

year	amount in dollars
2010	600
2012	750
2014	900
2016	1050

If this relationship is graphed with the year on the horizontal axis and the amount in dollars on the vertical axis, what is the vertical intercept? What does it mean in this context?

At the start of summer break, Jada and Lin decide to save some of the money they earn helping out their neighbors to use during the school year. Jada starts by putting $20 into a savings jar in her room and plans to save $10 a week. Lin starts by putting $10 into a savings jar in her room plans to save $20 a week. Here are graphs of how much money they will save after 10 weeks if they each follow their plans:

The value where a line intersects the vertical axis is called the **vertical intercept**. When the vertical axis is labeled with a variable like y, this value is also often called the *y-intercept*. Jada's graph has a vertical intercept of $20 while Lin's graph has a vertical intercept of $10. These values reflect the amount of money they each started with. At 1 week they will have saved the same amount, $30. But after week 1, Lin is saving more money per week (so she has a larger rate of change), so she will end up saving more money over the summer if they each follow their plans.

1. Explain what the slope and intercept mean in each situation.

   a. A graph represents the perimeter, y, in units, for an equilateral triangle with side length x units. The slope of the line is 3 and the y-intercept is 0.

   b. The amount of money, y, in a cash box after x tickets are purchased for carnival games. The slope of the line is $\frac{1}{4}$ and the y-intercept is 8.

   c. The number of chapters read, y, after x days. The slope of the line is $\frac{5}{4}$ and the y-intercept is 2.

   d. The graph shows the cost in dollars, y, of a muffin delivery and the number of muffins, x, ordered. The slope of the line is 2 and the y-intercept is 3.

MATH NATION

2. The graph shows the relationship between the number of cups of flour and the number of cups of sugar in Lin's favorite brownie recipe.

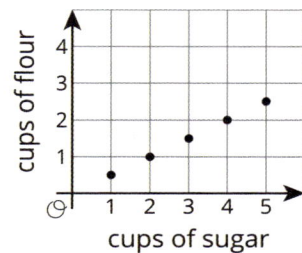

The table shows the amounts of flour and sugar needed for Noah's favorite brownie recipe.

amount of sugar (cups)	amount of flour (cups)
$\dfrac{3}{2}$	1
3	2
$4\dfrac{1}{2}$	3

a. Noah and Lin buy a 12-cup bag of sugar and divide it evenly to make their recipes. If they each use all their sugar, how much flour do they each need?

b. Noah and Lin buy a 10-cup bag of flour and divide it evenly to make their recipes. If they each use all their flour, how much sugar do they each need?

3. Customers at the gym pay a membership fee to join and then a fee for each class they attend. Here is a graph that represents the situation.

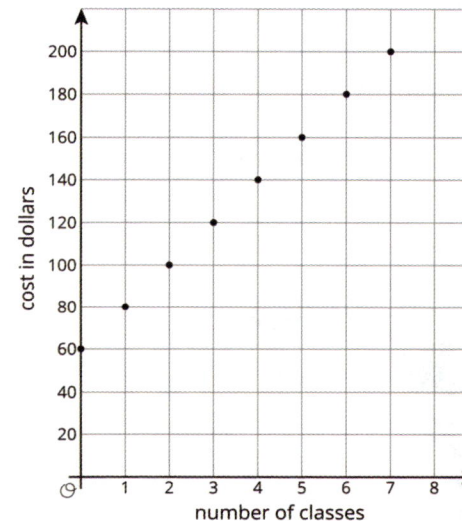

a. What does the slope of the line shown by the points mean in this situation?

b. What does the vertical intercept mean in this situation?

Unit 3, Lesson 7: Representations of Linear Relationships

Let's write equations from real situations.

🔔 3.7.1 Warm-Up: Estimation: Which Holds More?

Which glass will hold the most water? The least?

A   B   C

🔭 3.7.2a Exploration Activity: Rising Water Levels

1. Record data from your teacher's demonstration in the table. (You may not need all the rows.)

number of objects	volume in ml

2. What is the volume, V, in the cylinder after you add x objects? Explain your reasoning.

3. If you wanted to make the water reach the highest mark on the cylinder, how many objects would you need?

4. Plot and label points that show your measurements from the experiment.

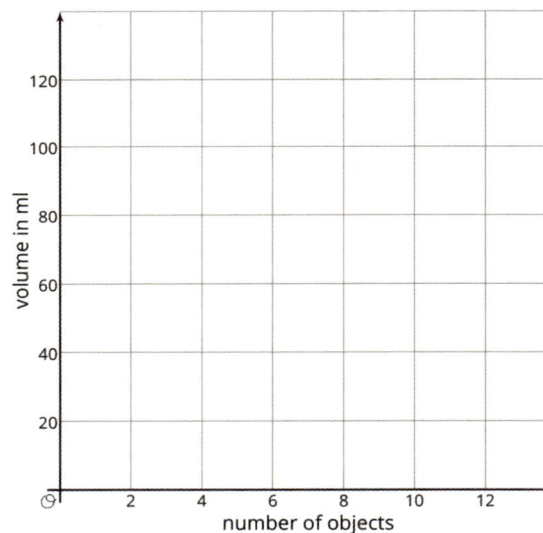

5. The points should fall on a line. Use a ruler to graph this line.

6. Compute the slope of the line. What does the slope mean in this situation?

7. What is the vertical intercept? What does vertical intercept mean in this situation?

3.7.2b Exploration Extension: Are you ready for more?

A situation is represented by the equation $y = 5 + \frac{1}{2}x$.

1. Invent a story for this situation.

2. Graph the equation.

3. What do the $\frac{1}{2}$ and the 5 represent in your situation?

4. Where do you see the $\frac{1}{2}$ and 5 on the graph?

3.7.3 Exploration Activity: Calculate the Slope

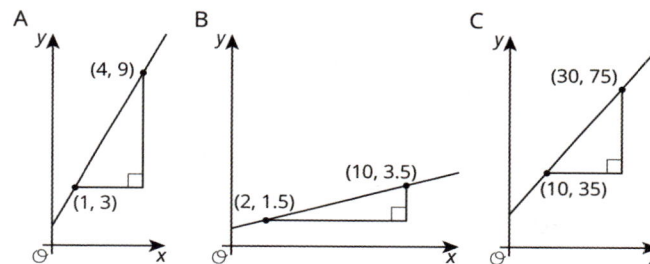

1. For each graph, record:

	vertical change	horizontal change	slope
A			
B			
C			

2. Describe a procedure for finding the slope between any two points on a line.

3. Write an expression for the slope of the line in the graph using the letters $u, v, s,$ and t.

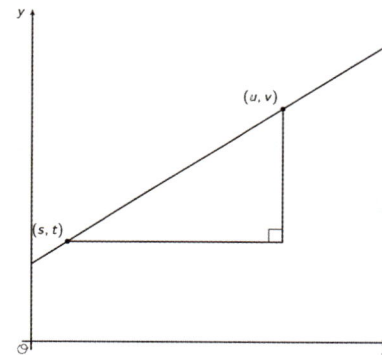

Lesson 7 Summary

Let's say we have a glass cylinder filled with 50 ml of water and a bunch of marbles that are 3 ml in volume. If we drop marbles into the cylinder one at a time, we can watch the height of the water increase by the same amount, 3 ml, for each one added. This constant rate of change means there is a linear relationship between the number of marbles and the height of the water. Add one marble, the water height goes up 3 ml. Add 2 marbles, the water height goes up 6 ml. Add x marbles, the water height goes up $3x$ ml.

Reasoning this way, we can calculate that the height, y, of the water for x marbles is $y = 3x + 50$. Any linear relationships can be expressed in the form $y = mx + b$ using just the rate of change, m, and the initial amount, b. The 3 represents the rate of change, or slope of the graph, and the 50 represents the initial amount, or vertical intercept of the graph. We'll learn about some more ways to think about this equation in future lessons.

Now what if we didn't have a description to use to figure out the slope and the vertical intercept? That's okay so long as we can find some points on the line! For the line graphed here, two of the points on the line are (3,3) and (9,5) and we can use these points to draw in a slope triangle as shown:

The slope of this line is the quotient of the length of the vertical side of the slope triangle and the length of the horizontal side of the slope triangle. So the slope, m, is $\frac{\text{vertical change}}{\text{horizontal change}} = \frac{2}{6} = \frac{1}{3}$.

We can also see from the graph that the vertical intercept, b, is 2. Putting these together, we can say that the equation for this line is $y = \frac{1}{3}x + 2$.

3.7.5 Practice Problems

1. Here are recipes for two different banana cakes. Information for the first recipe is shown in the table.

sugar (cups)	flour (cups)
$\frac{1}{2}$	$\frac{3}{4}$
$2\frac{1}{2}$	$3\frac{3}{4}$
3	$4\frac{1}{2}$

The relationship between cups of flour, y, and cups of sugar, x, in the second recipe is $y = \frac{7}{4}x$

a. If you used 4 cups of sugar, how much flour does each recipe need?

b. What is the constant of proportionality for each situation and what does it mean?

2. Show that the two figures are similar by identifying a sequence of translations, rotations, reflections, and dilations that takes the larger figure to the smaller one.

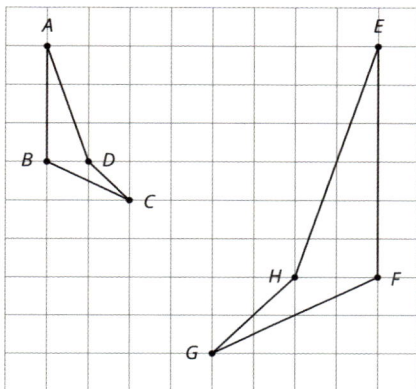

3. Create a graph that shows three linear relationships with different y-intercepts using the following slopes, and write an equation for each line.

Slopes:

○ $\frac{1}{5}$

○ $\frac{3}{5}$

○ $\frac{6}{5}$

4. The graph shows the height in inches, h, of a bamboo plant t months after it has been planted.

a. Write an equation that describes the relationship between h and t.

b. After how many months will the bamboo plant be 66 inches tall? Explain or show your reasoning.

Unit 3, Lesson 8: Translating to $y = mx + b$

Let's see what happens to the equations of translated lines.

3.8.1 Warm-Up: Lines that Are Translations

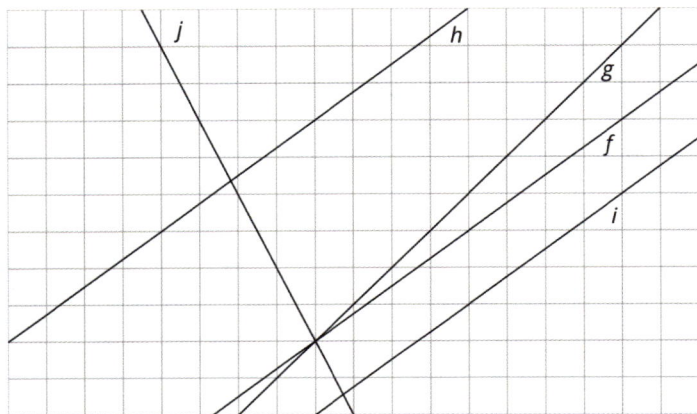

The diagram shows several lines. You can only see part of the lines, but they actually continue forever in both directions.

1. Which lines are images of line f under a translation?

2. For each line that is a translation of f, draw an arrow on the grid that shows the vertical translation distance.

3.8.2 Exploration Activity: Increased Savings

1. Diego earns $10 per hour babysitting. Assume that he has no money saved before he starts babysitting and plans to save all of his earnings. Graph how much money, y, he has after x hours of babysitting.

2. Now imagine that Diego started with $30 saved before he starts babysitting. On the same set of axes, graph how much money, y, he would have after x hours of babysitting.

3. Compare the second line with the first line. How much *more* money does Diego have after 1 hour of babysitting? 2 hours? 5 hours? x hours?

4. Write an equation for each line.

Unit 3: Linear Relationships

3.8.3a Exploration Activity: Translating a Line

This graph shows two lines. Line a goes through the origin $(0,0)$. Line h is the image of line a under a translation.

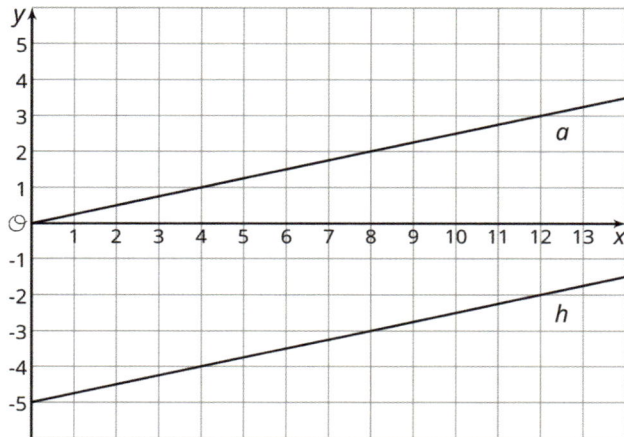

1. Select all of the equations whose graph is the line h.

   ☐ $y = \frac{1}{4}x - 5$

   ☐ $y = \frac{1}{4}x + 5$

   ☐ $\frac{1}{4}x - 5 = y$

   ☐ $y = -5 + \frac{1}{4}x$

   ☐ $-5 + \frac{1}{4}x = y$

   ☐ $y = 5 - \frac{1}{4}x$

2. Your teacher will give you 12 cards. There are 4 pairs of lines, A–D, showing the graph, a, of a proportional relationship and the image, h, of a under a translation. Match each line h with an equation and either a table or description. For the line with no matching equation, write one on the blank card.

3.8.3b Exploration Extension: Are you ready for more?

A student says that the graph of the equation $y = 3(x + 8)$ is the same as the graph of $y = 3x$, only translated upwards by 8 units. Do you agree? Why or why not?

Lesson 8 Summary

During an early winter storm, the snow fell at a rate of $\frac{1}{2}$ inches per hour. We can see the rate of change, $\frac{1}{2}$, in both the equation that represents this storm, $y = \frac{1}{2}x$, and in the slope of the line representing this storm.

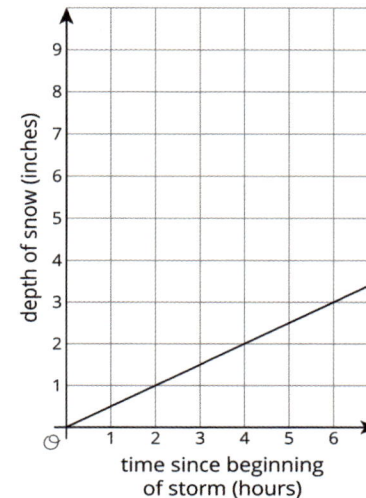

In addition to being a linear relationship between the time since the beginning of the storm and the depth of the snow, we can also call this as a proportional relationship since the depth of snow was 0 at the beginning of the storm.

During a mid-winter storm, the snow again fell at a rate of $\frac{1}{2}$ inches per hour, but this time there was already 5 inches of snow on the ground. We can graph this storm on the same axes as the first storm by taking all the points on the graph of the first storm and translating them up 5 inches.

2 hours after each storm begins, 1 inch of new snow has fallen. For the first storm, this means there is now 1 inch of snow on the ground. For the second storm, this means there are now 6 inches of snow on the ground. Unlike the first storm, the second is not a proportional relationship since the line representing the second storm has a vertical intercept of 5. The equation representing the storm, $y = \frac{1}{2}x + 5$, is of the form $y = mx + b$, where m is the rate of change, also the slope of the graph, and b is the initial amount, also the vertical intercept of the graph.

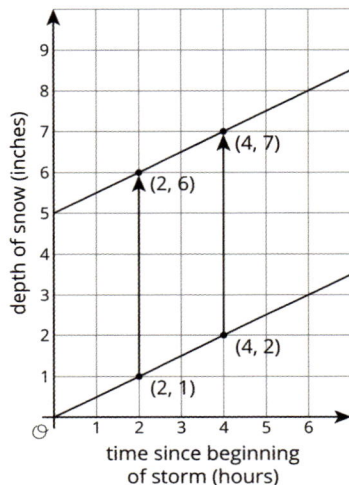

3.8.5 Practice Problems

1. Select **all** equations that have graphs with the same y-intercept.

   ☐ $y = 3x - 8$

   ☐ $y = 3x - 9$

   ☐ $y = 3x + 8$

   ☐ $y = 5x - 8$

   ☐ $y = 2x - 8$

   ☐ $y = \frac{1}{3}x - 8$

2. Create a graph showing the equations $y = \frac{1}{4}x$ and $y = \frac{1}{4}x - 5$. Explain how the graphs are the same and how they are different.

3. A cable company charges $70 per month for cable service to existing customers.

   a. Find a linear equation representing the relationship between x, the number of months of service, and y, the total amount paid in dollars by an existing customer.

   b. For new customers, there is an additional one-time $100 service fee. Repeat the previous problem for new customers.

   c. When the two equations are graphed in the coordinate plane, how are they related to each other geometrically?

Unit 3: Linear Relationships

4. Match each graph to a situation.

A

B

C

D

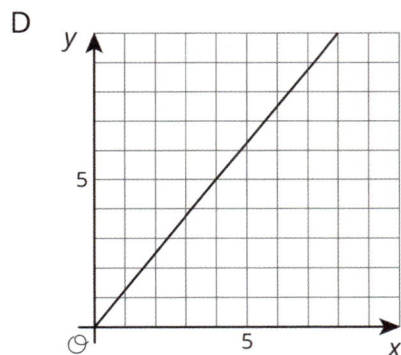

I. The graph represents the perimeter, y, in units, for an equilateral triangle with side length of x units. The slope of the line is 3.

II. The amount of money, y, in a cash box after x tickets are purchased for carnival games. The slope of the line is $\frac{1}{4}$.

III. The number of chapters read, y, after x days. The slope of the line is $\frac{5}{4}$.

IV. The graph shows the cost in dollars, y, of a muffin delivery and the number of muffins, x, ordered. The slope of the line is 2.

5. A mountain road is 5 miles long and gains elevation at a constant rate. After 2 miles, the elevation is 5,500 feet above sea level. After 4 miles, the elevation is 6,200 feet above sea level.

a. Find the elevation of the road at the point where the road begins.

b. Describe where you would see the point in part a. on a graph where y represents the elevation in feet and x represents the distance along the road in miles.

Let's find out what a negative slope means.

3.9.1 Warm-Up: Which One Doesn't Belong: Odd Line Out

Which line doesn't belong?

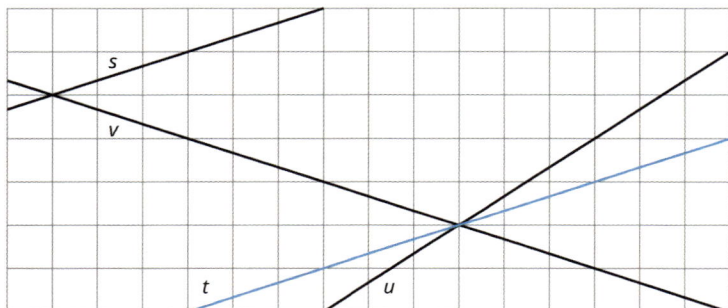

3.9.2 Exploration Activity: Stand Clear of the Closing Doors, Please

Noah put $40 on his fare card. Every time he rides public transportation, $2.50 is subtracted from the amount available on his card.

1. How much money, in dollars, is available on his card after he takes
   a. 0 rides?

   b. 1 ride?

   c. 2 rides?

   d. x rides?

2. Graph the relationship between amount of money on the card and number of rides.

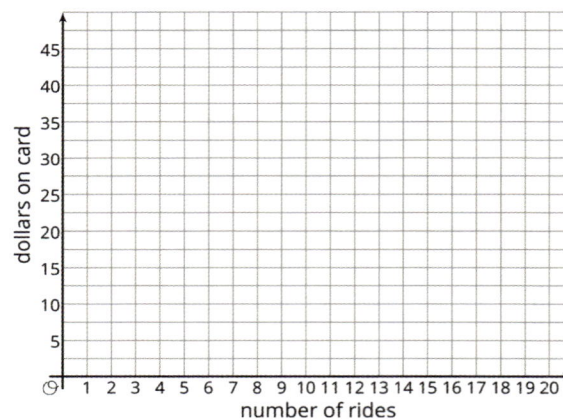

3. How many rides can Noah take before the card runs out of money? Where do you see this number of rides on your graph?

3.9.3a Exploration Activity: Travel Habits in July

Here is a graph that shows the amount on Han's fare card for every day of last July.

1. Describe what happened with the amount on Han's fare card in July.

2. Plot and label 3 different points on the line.

3. Write an equation that represents the amount on the card in July, y, after x days.

4. What value makes sense for the slope of the line that represents the amounts on Han's fare card in July?

3.9.3b Exploration Extension: Are you ready for more?

Let's say you have taken out a loan and are paying it back. Which of the following graphs have positive slope and which have negative slope?

1. Amount paid on the vertical axis and time since payments started on the horizontal axis.

2. Amount owed on the vertical axis and time remaining until the loan is paid off on the horizontal axis.

3. Amount paid on the vertical axis and time remaining until the loan is paid off on the horizontal axis.

3.9.4 Exploration Activity: Payback Plan

Elena borrowed some money from her brother. She pays him back by giving him the same amount every week. The graph shows how much she owes after each week.

Answer and explain your reasoning for each question.

1. What is the slope of the line?

2. Explain how you know whether the slope is positive or negative.

3. What does the slope represent in this situation?

4. How much did Elena borrow?

5. How much time will it take for Elena to pay back all the money she borrowed?

Lesson 9 Summary

At the end of winter in Maine, the snow on the ground was 30 inches deep. Then there was a particularly warm day and the snow melted at the rate of 1 inch per hour. The graph shows the relationship between the time since the snow started to melt and the depth of the snow.

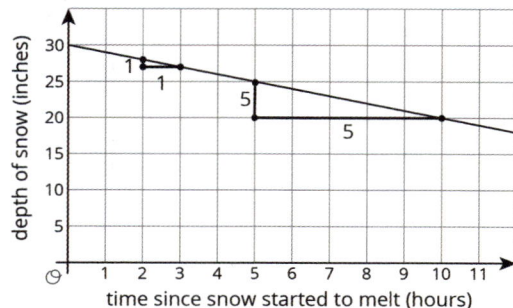

The slope of the graph is -1 since the rate of change is -1 inch per hour. That is, the depth goes *down* 1 inch per hour. The vertical intercept is 30 since the snow was 30 inches deep when the warmth started to melt the snow. The two slope triangles show how the rate of change is constant. It just also happens to be negative in this case since after each hour that passes, there is 1 inch *less* snow.

Graphs with negative slope often describe situations where some quantity is decreasing over time, like the depth of snow on warm days or the amount of money on a fare card being used to take rides on buses.

Slopes can be positive, negative, or even zero! A slope of 0 means there is no change in the y-value even though the x-value may be changing. For example, Elena won a contest where the prize was a special pass that gives her free bus rides for a year. Her fare card had $5 on it when she won the prize. Here is a graph of the amount of money on her fare card after winning the prize:

The vertical intercept is 5, since the graph starts when she has $5 on her fare card. The slope of the graph is 0 since she doesn't use her fare card for the next year, meaning the amount on her fare card doesn't change for a year. In fact, all graphs of linear relationships with slopes equal to 0 are horizontal—a rate of change of 0 means that, from one point to the next, the y-values remain the same.

Unit 3: Linear Relationships

1. Suppose that during its flight, the elevation, e, (in feet) of a certain airplane and its time, t, in minutes since takeoff, are related by a linear equation. Consider the graph of this equation, with time represented on the horizontal axis and elevation on the vertical axis. For each situation, decide if the slope is positive, zero, or negative.

   a. The plane is cruising at an altitude of 37,000 feet above sea level.

   b. The plane is descending at rate of 1,000 feet per minute.

   c. The plane is ascending at a rate of 2,000 feet per minute.

2. A group of hikers park their car at a trail head and hike into the forest to a campsite. The next morning, they head out on a hike from their campsite walking at a steady rate. The graph shows their distance in miles, d, from the car on the day of their hike after h hours.

   a. How far is the campsite from their car? Explain how you know.

   b. Write an equation that describes the relationship between d and h.

   c. After how many hours will the hikers be 16 miles from their car? Explain or show your reasoning.

3. Elena's aunt pays her $1 for each call she makes to let people know about her aunt's new business. The table shows how much money Diego receives for washing windows for his neighbors.

number of windows	number of dollars
27	30
45	50
81	90

Select **all** the statements about the situation that are true.

☐ Elena makes more money for making 10 calls than Diego makes for washing 10 windows.

☐ Diego makes more money for washing each window than Elena makes for making each call.

☐ Elena makes the same amount of money for 20 calls as Diego makes for 18 windows.

☐ Diego needs to wash 35 windows to make as much money as Elena makes for 40 calls.

☐ The equation $y = \frac{9}{10}x$, where y is number of dollars and x is number of windows, represents Diego's situation.

☐ The equation $y = x$, where y is the number of dollars and x is the number of calls, represents Elena's situation.

4. Each square on a grid represents 1 unit on each side. Match the numbers with the slopes of the lines.

I. $-\frac{1}{4}$

II. $\frac{1}{4}$

III. 4

A

B

C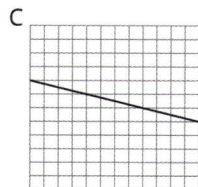

Unit 3, Lesson 10: Calculating Slope

Let's calculate slope from two points.

3.10.1 Warm-Up: Integer Operations Review

Find values for a and b that make each side have the same value.

1. $\frac{a}{b} = -2$

2. $\frac{a}{b} = 2$

3. $a - b = -2$

Unit 3: Linear Relationships

3.10.2a Exploration Activity: Toward a More General Slope Formula

1. Plot the points (1,11) and (8,2), and use a ruler to draw the line that passes through them.

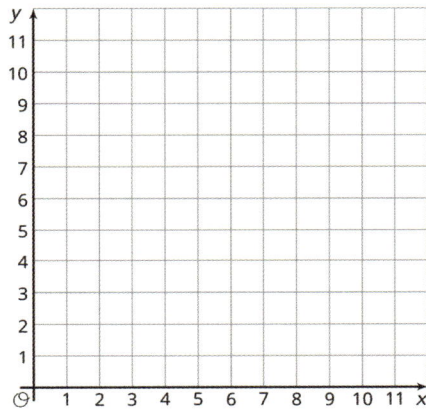

2. Without calculating, do you expect the slope of the line through (1,11) and (8,2) to be positive or negative? How can you tell?

3. Calculate the slope of this line.

3.10.2b Exploration Extension: Are you ready for more?

Find the value of k so that the line passing through each pair of points has the given slope.

1. $(k, 2)$ and $(11,14)$, slope = 2

2. $(1, k)$ and $(4,1)$, slope = -2

3. $(3,5)$ and $(k, 9)$, slope = $\frac{1}{2}$

4. $(-1,4)$ and $(-3, k)$, slope = $\frac{-1}{2}$

5. $(\frac{-15}{2}, \frac{3}{16})$ and $(\frac{-13}{22}, k)$, slope = 0

3.10.3 Exploration Activity: Making Designs

Your teacher will give you either a design or a blank graph. Do not show your card to your partner.

If your teacher gives you the design:

1. Look at the design silently and think about how you could communicate what your partner should draw. Think about ways that you can describe what a line looks like, such as its slope or points that it goes through.
2. Describe each line, one at a time, and give your partner time to draw them.
3. Once your partner thinks they have drawn all the lines you described, only then should you show them the design.

If your teacher gives you the blank graph:

1. Listen carefully as your partner describes each line, and draw each line based on their description.
2. You are not allowed to ask for more information about a line than what your partner tells you.
3. Do not show your drawing to your partner until you have finished drawing all the lines they describe.

When finished, place the drawing next to the card with the design so that you and your partner can both see them. How is the drawing the same as the design? How is it different? Discuss any miscommunication that might have caused the drawing to look different from the design.

Pause here so your teacher can review your work. When your teacher gives you a new set of cards, switch roles for the second problem.

Lesson 10 Summary

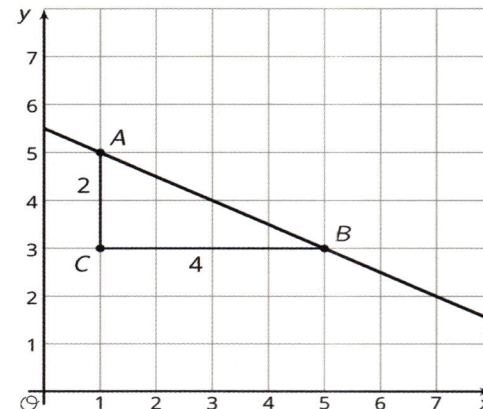

We learned earlier that one way to find the slope of a line is by drawing a slope triangle. For example, using the slope triangle shown here, the slope of the line is $-\frac{2}{4}$, or $-\frac{1}{2}$ (we know the slope is negative because the line is decreasing from left to right).

But slope triangles are only one way to calculate the slope of a line. Let's compute the slope of this line a different way using just the points $A = (1,5)$ and $B = (5,3)$. Since we know the slope is the vertical change divided by the horizontal change, we can calculate the change in the y-values and then the change in the x-values. Between points A and B, the y-value change is $3 - 5 = -2$ and the x-value change is $5 - 1 = 4$. This means the slope is $-\frac{2}{4}$, or $-\frac{1}{2}$, which is the same as what we found using the slope triangle.

Notice that in each of the calculations, we subtracted the value from point A from the value from point B. If we had done it the other way around, then the y-value change would have been $5 - 3 = 2$ and the x-value change would have been $1 - 5 = -4$, which still gives us a slope of $-\frac{1}{2}$. But what if we were to mix up the orders? If that had happened, we would think the slope of the line is *positive* $\frac{1}{2}$ since we would either have calculated $\frac{-2}{-4}$ or $\frac{2}{4}$. Since we already have a graph of the line and can see it has a negative slope, this is clearly incorrect. It we don't have a graph to check our calculation, we could think about how the point on the left, (1,5), is higher than the point on the right, (5,3), meaning the slope of the line must be negative.

Unit 3: Linear Relationships

1. For each graph, calculate the slope of the line.

A

(2, 6)
(8, 4)

B

(-5, 7)
(1, 1)

C
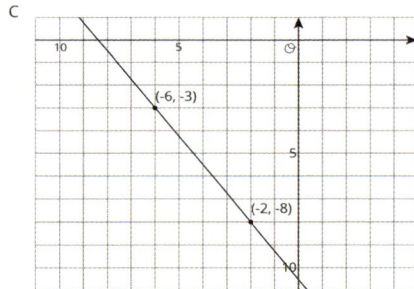
(-6, -3)
(-2, -8)

2. Match each pair of points to the slope of the line that joins them.

A. 4

B. -3

C. $-\frac{5}{2}$

D. $\frac{6}{7}$

I. $(9,10)$ and $(7,2)$

II. $(-8,-11)$ and $(-1,-5)$

III. $(5,-6)$ and $(2,3)$

IV. $(6,3)$ and $(5,-1)$

V. $(4,7)$ and $(6,2)$

3. Draw a line with the given slope through the given point. What other point lies on that line?

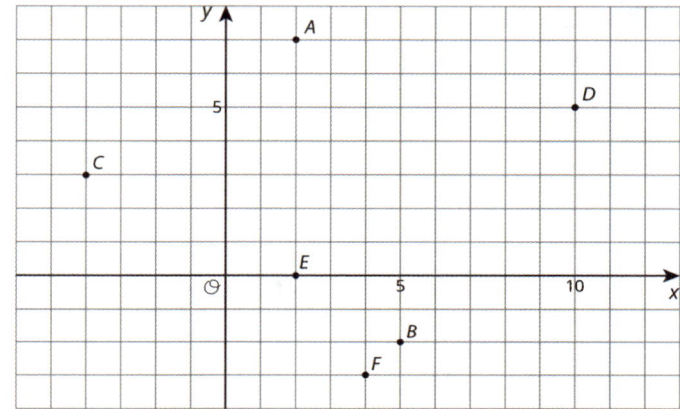

a. Point A, slope = -3

b. Point A, slope = $\frac{-1}{4}$

c. Point C, slope = $\frac{-1}{2}$

d. Point E, slope = $\frac{-2}{3}$

4. Make a sketch of a linear relationship with a slope of 4 and a negative y-intercept. Show how you know the slope is 4 and write an equation for the line.

Let's write equations for vertical and horizontal lines.

3.11.1 Warm-Up: Which One Doesn't Belong: Pairs of Lines

Which one doesn't belong?

A

B

C

D

3.11.2a Exploration Activity: All the Same

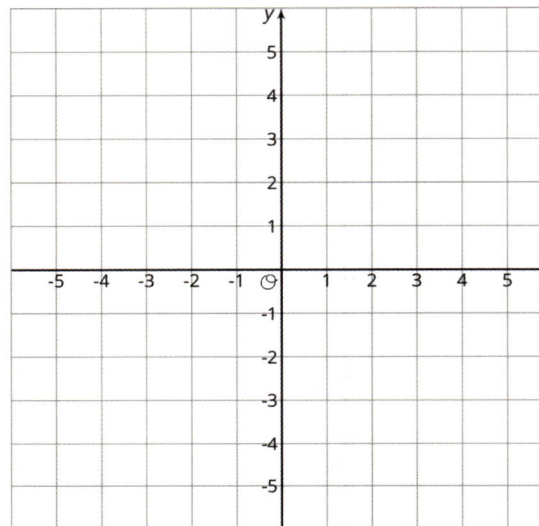

1. Plot at least 10 points whose y-coordinate is -4. What do you notice about them?

2. Which equation makes the most sense to represent all of the points with y-coordinate -4? Explain how you know.

   A. $x = -4$

   B. $y = -4x$

   C. $y = -4$

   D. $x + y = -4$

3. Plot at least 10 points whose x-coordinate is 3. What do you notice about them?

4. Which equation makes the most sense to represent all of the points with x-coordinate 3? Explain how you know.

   A. $x = 3$

   B. $y = 3x$

   C. $y = 3$

   D. $x + y = 3$

5. Graph the equation $x = -2$.

6. Graph the equation $y = 5$.

3.11.2b Exploration Extension: Are you ready for more?

1. Draw the rectangle with vertices (2,1), (5,1), (5,3), (2,3).

2. For each of the four sides of the rectangle, write an equation for a line containing the side.

3. A rectangle has sides on the graphs of $x = -1$, $x = 3$, $y = -1$, $y = 1$. Find the coordinates of each vertex.

3.11.3 Exploration Activity: Same Perimeter

1. There are many possible rectangles whose perimeter is 50 units. Complete the table with lengths, ℓ, and widths, w, of at least 10 such rectangles.

ℓ									
w									

2. The graph shows one rectangle whose perimeter is 50 units, and has its lower left vertex at the origin and two sides on the axes. On the same graph, draw more rectangles with perimeter 50 units using the values from your table. Make sure that each rectangle has a lower left vertex at the origin and two sides on the axes.

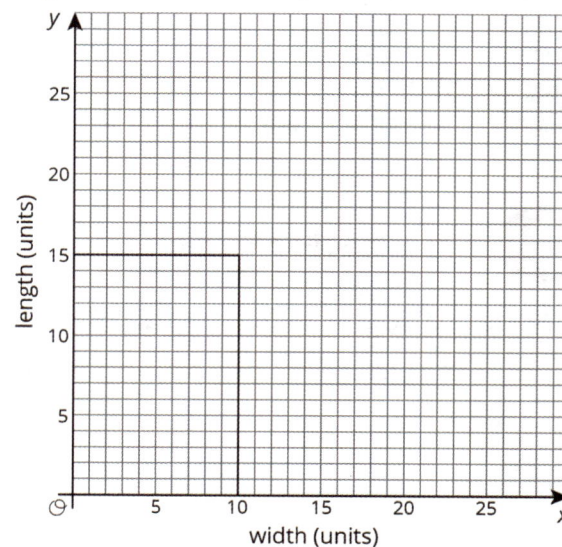

3. Each rectangle has a vertex that lies in the first quadrant. These vertices lie on a line. Draw in this line and write an equation for it.

4. What is the the slope of this line? How does the slope describe how the width changes as the length changes (or vice versa)?

Lesson 11 Summary

Horizontal lines in the coordinate plane represent situations where the y value doesn't change at all while the x value changes. For example, the horizontal line that goes through the point $(0,13)$ can be described in words as "for all points on the line, the y value is always 13." An equation that says the same thing is $y = 13$.

Vertical lines represent situations where the x value doesn't change at all while the y value changes. The equation $x = -4$ describes a vertical line through the point $(-4,0)$.

3.11.5 Practice Problems

1. Suppose you wanted to graph the equation $y = -4x - 1$.

    a. Describe the steps you would take to draw the graph.

b. How would you check that the graph you drew is correct?

2. Draw the following lines and then write an equation for each.

    a. Slope is 0, y-intercept is 5

    b. Slope is 2, y-intercept is -1

    c. Slope is -2, y-intercept is 1

    d. Slope is $\frac{-1}{2}$, y-intercept is -1

Unit 3: Linear Relationships

3. Write an equation for each line.

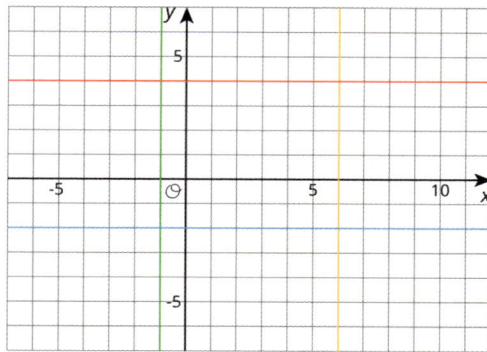

4. A publisher wants to figure out how thick their new book will be. The book has a front cover and a back cover, each of which have a thickness of $\frac{1}{4}$ of an inch. They have a choice of which type of paper to print the book on.

   a. Bond paper has a thickness of $\frac{1}{4}$ inch per one hundred pages. Write an equation for the width of the book, y, if it has x hundred pages, printed on bond paper.

   b. Ledger paper has a thickness of $\frac{2}{5}$ inch per one hundred pages. Write an equation for the width of the book, y, if it has x hundred pages, printed on ledger paper.

   c. If they instead chose front and back covers of thickness $\frac{1}{3}$ of an inch, how would this change the equations in the previous two parts?

Let's think about what it means to be a solution to a linear equation with two variables in it.

3.12.1 Warm-Up: Estimate Area

Which figure has the largest shaded region?

A   B   C

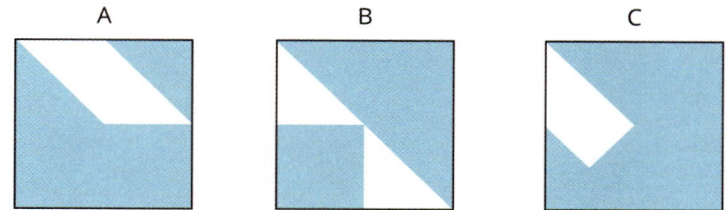

3.12.2a Exploration Activity: Apples and Oranges

At the corner produce market, apples cost $1 each and oranges cost $2 each.

1. Find the cost of:
   a. 6 apples and 3 oranges

   b. 4 apples and 4 oranges

   c. 5 apples and 4 oranges

   d. 8 apples and 2 oranges

2. Noah has $10 to spend at the produce market. Can he buy 7 apples and 2 oranges? Explain or show your reasoning.

3. What combinations of apples and oranges can Noah buy if he spends all of his $10?

4. Use two variables to write an equation that represents $10-combinations of apples and oranges. Be sure to say what each variable means.

5. What are 3 combinations of apples and oranges that make your equation true? What are three combinations of apples and oranges that make it false?

3.12.2b Exploration Extension: Are you ready for more?

1. Graph the equation you wrote relating the number of apples and the number of oranges.

2. What is the slope of the graph? What is the meaning of the slope in terms of the context?

3. Suppose Noah has $20 to spend. Graph the equation describing this situation. What do you notice about the relationship between this graph and the earlier one?

Unit 3: Linear Relationships

3.12.3 Exploration Activity: Solutions and Everything Else

You have two numbers. If you double the first number and add it to the second number, the sum is 10.

1. Let x represent the first number and let y represent the second number. Write an equation showing the relationship between x, y, and 10.

2. Draw and label a set of x- and y-axes. Plot at least five points on this coordinate plane that make the statement and your equation true. What do you notice about the points you have plotted?

3. List ten points that do *not* make the statement true. Using a different color, plot each point in the same coordinate plane. What do you notice about these points compared to your first set of points?

Lesson 12 Summary

Think of all the rectangles whose perimeters are 8 units. If x represents the width and y represents the length, then $2x + 2y = 8$ expresses the relationship between the width and length for all such rectangles.

For example, the width and length could be 1 and 3, since. $2 \cdot 1 + 2 \cdot 3 = 8$ or the width and length could be 2.75 and 1.25, since $2 \cdot (2.75) + 2 \cdot (1.25) = 8$.

We could find many other possible pairs of width and length, (x, y), that make the equation true—that is, pairs (x, y) that when substituted into the equation make the left side and the right side equal.

A **solution to an equation with two variables** is any pair of values (x, y) that make the equation true.

We can think of the pairs of numbers that are solutions of an equation as points on the coordinate plane. Here is a line created by all the points (x, y) that are solutions to $2x + 2y = 8$. Every point on the line represents a rectangle whose perimeter is 8 units. All points not on the line are not solutions to $2x + 2y = 8$.

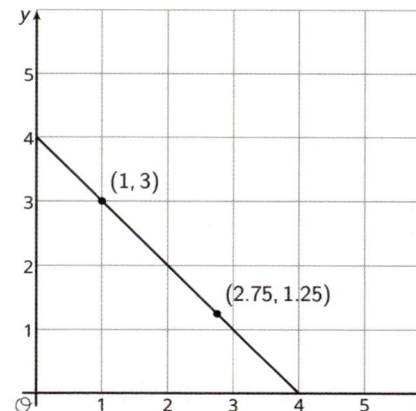

1. Select **all** of the ordered pairs (x, y) that are solutions to the linear equation $2x + 3y = 6$.

   ☐ $(0,2)$
   ☐ $(0,6)$
   ☐ $(2,3)$
   ☐ $(3,-2)$
   ☐ $(3,0)$
   ☐ $(6,-2)$

2. The graph shows a linear relationship between x and y.

   x represents the number of comic books Priya buys at the store, all at the same price, and y represents the amount of money (in dollars) Priya has after buying the comic books.

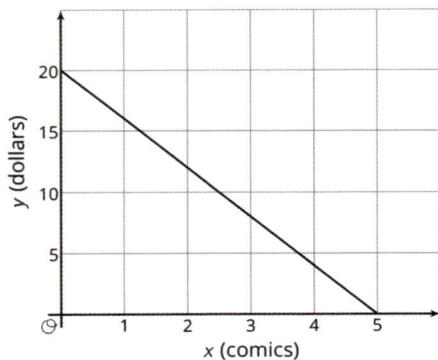

a. Find and interpret the x- and y-intercepts of this line.

b. Find and interpret the slope of this line.

c. Find an equation for this line.

d. If Priya buys 3 comics, how much money will she have remaining?

3. Match each equation with its three solutions.

   A. $y = 1.5x$
   B. $2x + 3y = 7$
   C. $x - y = 4$
   D. $3x = \frac{y}{2}$
   E. $y = -x + 1$

   I. $(14,21)$, $(2,3)$, $(8,12)$
   II. $(-3,-7)$, $(0,-4)$, $(-1,-5)$
   III. $\left(\frac{1}{2},\frac{1}{2}\right)$, $\left(\frac{1}{4},\frac{3}{4}\right)$, $\left(\frac{1}{8},\frac{7}{8}\right)$
   IV. $\left(1,1\frac{2}{3}\right)$, $(-1,3)$, $\left(0,2\frac{1}{3}\right)$
   V. $(0.5,3)$, $(1,6)$, $(1.2,7.2)$

4. A container of fuel dispenses fuel at the rate of 5 gallons per second. If y represents the amount of fuel remaining in the container, and x represents the number of seconds that have passed since the fuel started dispensing, then x and y satisfy a linear relationship.

   In the coordinate plane, will the slope of the line representing that relationship have a positive, negative, or zero slope? Explain how you know.

5. A sandwich store charges a delivery fee to bring lunch to an office building. One office pays $33 for 4 turkey sandwiches. Another office pays $61 for 8 turkey sandwiches. How much does each turkey sandwich add to the cost of the delivery? Explain how you know.

Let's find solutions to more linear equations.

3.13.1 Warm-Up: Coordinate Pairs

For each equation choose a value for x and then solve to find the corresponding y value that makes that equation true.

1. $6x = 7y$

2. $5x + 3y = 9$

3. $y + 5 - \frac{1}{3}x = 7$

3.13.2 Exploration Activity: True or False: Solutions in the Coordinate Plane

Here are graphs representing three linear relationships. These relationships could also be represented with equations.

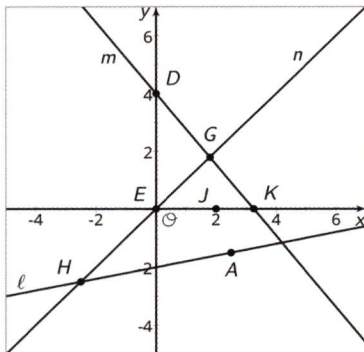

For each statement below, decide if it is true or false. Explain your reasoning.

1. $(4,0)$ is a solution of the equation for line m.

2. The coordinates of the point G make both the equation for line m and the equation for line n true.

3. $x = 0$ is a solution of the equation for line n.

4. $(2,0)$ makes both the equation for line m and the equation for line n true.

5. There is no solution for the equation for line ℓ that has $y = 0$.

6. The coordinates of point H are solutions to the equation for line ℓ.

7. There are exactly two solutions of the equation for line ℓ.

8. There is a point whose coordinates make the equations of all three lines true.

After you finish discussing the eight statements, find another group and check your answers against theirs. Discuss any disagreements.

Unit 3: Linear Relationships

3.13.3a Exploration Activity: I'll Take an X, Please

One partner has 6 cards labeled A through F and one partner has 6 cards labeled a through f. In each pair of cards (for example, Cards A and a), there is an equation on one card and a coordinate pair, (x, y), that makes the equation true on the other card.

1. The partner with the equation asks the partner with a solution for either the x-value or the y-value and explains why they chose the one they did.

2. The partner with the equation uses this value to find the other value, explaining each step as they go.

3. The partner with the coordinate pair then tells the partner with the equation if they are right or wrong. If they are wrong, both partners should look through the steps to find and correct any errors. If they are right, both partners move onto the next set of cards.

4. Keep playing until you have finished Cards A through F.

3.13.3b Exploration Extension: Are you ready for more?

Consider the equation $ax + by = c$, where a, b, and c are positive numbers.

1. Find the coordinates of the x- and y-intercepts of the graph of the equation.

2. Find the slope of the graph.

Lesson 13 Summary

Let's think about the linear equation $2x - 4y = 12$. If we know $(0, -3)$ is a solution to the equation, then we also know $(0, -3)$ is a point on the graph of the equation. Since this point is on the y-axis, we also know that it is the vertical intercept of the graph. But what about the coordinate of the horizontal intercept, when $y = 0$? Well, we can use the equation to figure it out.

$$\begin{aligned} 2x - 4y &= 12 \\ 2x - 4(0) &= 12 \\ 2x &= 12 \\ x &= 6 \end{aligned}$$

Since $x = 6$ when $y = 0$, we know the point $(6, 0)$ is on the graph of the line. No matter the form a linear equation comes in, we can always find solutions to the equation by starting with one value and then solving for the other value.

3.13.5 Practice Problems

1. For each equation, find y when $x = -3$. Then find x when $y = 2$

   a. $y = 6x + 8$

   b. $y = \frac{2}{3}x$

   c. $y = -x + 5$

Continued on next page

d. $y = \frac{3}{4}x - 2\frac{1}{2}$

e. $y = 1.5x + 11$

2. Match each graph of a linear relationship to a situation that most reasonably reflects its context.

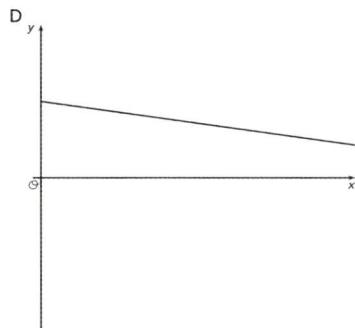

I. y is the weight of a kitten x days after birth.
II. y is the distance left to go in a car ride after x hours of driving at a constant rate toward its destination.
III. y is the temperature, in degrees C, of a gas being warmed in a laboratory experiment.
IV. y is the amount of calories consumed eating x crackers.

3. True or false: The points (6,13), (21,33), and (99,137) all lie on the same line. The equation of the line is $y = \frac{4}{3}x + 5$. Explain or show your reasoning.

4. Here is a linear equation: $y = \frac{1}{4}x + \frac{5}{4}$

a. Are (1,1.5) and (12,4) solutions to the equation? Explain or show your reasoning.

b. Find the x-intercept of the graph of the equation. Explain or show your reasoning.

Unit 3: Linear Relationships

5. Find the coordinates of B, C, and D given that $AB = 5$ and $BC = 10$.

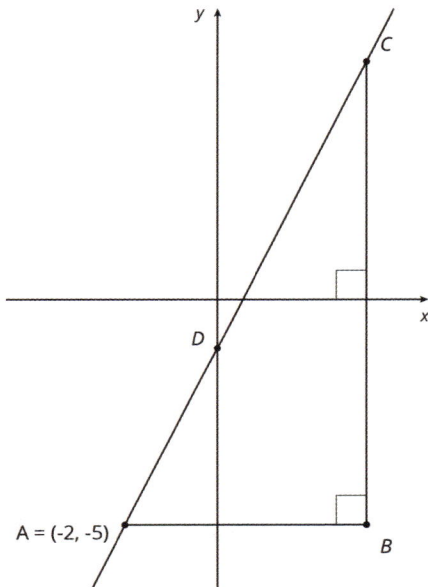

Let's write equations for real-world situations and think about their solutions.

🔔 3.14.1 Warm-Up: Buying Fruit

For each relationship described, write an equation to represent the relationship.

1. Grapes cost $2.39 per pound. Bananas cost $0.59 per pound. You have $15 to spend on g pounds of grapes and b pounds of bananas.

2. A savings account has $50 in it at the start of the year and $20 is deposited each week. After x weeks, there are y dollars in the account.

3.14.2 Exploration Activity: Five Savings Accounts

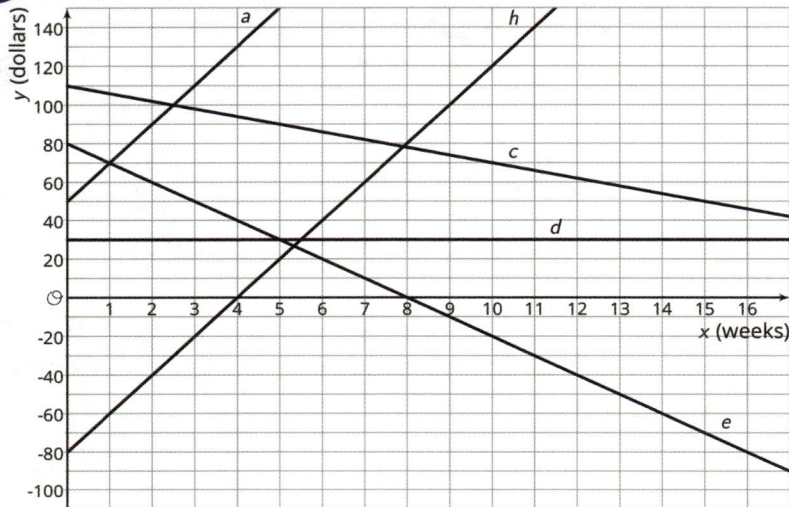

Each line represents one person's weekly savings account balance from the start of the year.

1. Choose one line and write a description of what happens to that person's account over the first 17 weeks of the year. Do not tell your group which line you chose.

2. Share your story with your group and see if anyone can guess your line.

3. Write an equation for each line on the graph. What do the slope, m, and vertical intercept, b, in each equation mean in the situation?

4. For which equation is (1,70) a solution? Interpret this solution in terms of your story.

5. Predict the balance in each account after 20 weeks.

3.14.3 Exploration Activity: Fabulous Fish

The Fabulous Fish Market orders tilapia, which costs $3 per pound, and salmon, which costs $5 per pound. The market budgets $210 to spend on this order each day.

1. What are five different combinations of salmon and tilapia that the market can order?

2. Define variables and write an equation representing the relationship between the amount of each fish bought and how much the market spends.

3. Sketch a graph of the relationship. Label your axes.

4. On your graph, plot and label the combinations A—F.

	A	B	C	D	E	F
pounds of tilapia	5	19	27	25	65	55
pounds of salmon	36	30.6	25	27	6	4

Which of these combinations can the market order? Explain or show your reasoning.

5. List two ways you can tell if a pair of numbers is a solution to an equation.

1. The owner of a new restaurant is ordering tables and chairs. He wants to have only tables for 2 and tables for 4. The total number of people that can be seated in the restaurant is 120.

   a. Describe some possible combinations of 2-seat tables and 4-seat tables that will seat 120 customers. Explain how you found them.

   b. Write an equation to represent the situation. What do the variables represent?

   c. Create a graph to represent the situation.

Continued on next page

d. What does the slope tell us about the situation?

e. Interpret the x and y intercepts in the situation.

2. Triangle A is an isosceles triangle with two angles of measure x degrees and one angle of measure y degrees.

   a. Find three combinations of x and y that make this sentence true.

   b. Write an equation relating x and y.

   c. If you were to sketch the graph of this linear equation, what would its slope be? How can you interpret the slope in the context of the triangle?

3. Select **all** the equations for which $(-6, -1)$ is a solution.

   ☐ $y = 4x + 23$

   ☐ $3x = \frac{1}{2}y$

   ☐ $2x - 13y = 1$

   ☐ $3y = \frac{1}{2}x$

   ☐ $2x + 6y = -6$

4. Consider the following graphs of linear equations. Decide which line has a positive slope, and which has a negative slope. Then calculate each line's exact slope.

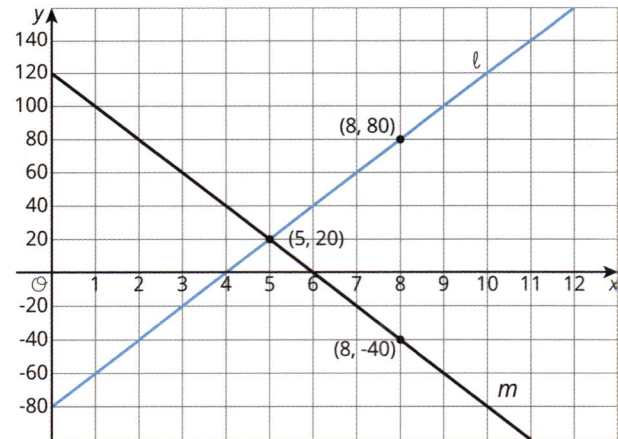

MATH NATION

Unit 4: Linear Equations and Linear Systems

Adapted from Open Up Resources 6-8 Math (authored by Illustrative Mathematics).
See inside front cover for details.

Section 3: Systems of Linear Equations

☐ *I can interpret ordered pairs that are solutions to an equation.*

☐ *I can identify ordered pairs that are solutions to an equation.*

☐ *I can use graphs to find an ordered pair that two real-world situations have in common.*

☐ *I can explain the solution to a system of equations in a real-world context. I can use patterns to write a linear equation to represent a situation.*

☐ *I can explain what a system of equations is.*

☐ *I can make graphs to find an ordered pair that two real-world situations have in common.*

☐ *I can graph a system of equations.*

☐ *I can solve systems of equations using algebra.*

☐ *I can use the structure of equations to help me figure out how many solutions a system of equations has.*

☐ *I can write a system of equations from a real-world situation.*

Section 4: Let's Put It to Work

☐ *I can use a system of equations to represent a real-world situation and answer questions about the situation.*

Adapted from Open Up Resources 6-8 Math (authored by Illustrative Mathematics).
See inside front cover for details.

Unit 4, Lesson 1: Number Puzzles

Let's solve some puzzles!

🔔 4.1.1 Warm-Up: Notice and Wonder: A Number Line

What do you notice? What do you wonder?

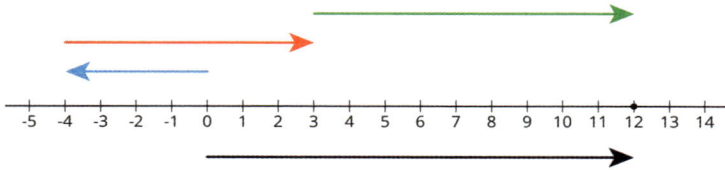

🔭 4.1.2 Exploration Activity: Telling Temperatures

Solve each puzzle. Show your thinking. Organize it so it can be followed by others.

1. The temperature was very cold. Then the temperature doubled.
   Then the temperature dropped by 10 degrees. Then the temperature increased by 40 degrees. The temperature is now 16 degrees. What was the starting temperature?

2. Lin ran twice as far as Diego. Diego ran 300 m farther than Jada. Jada ran $\frac{1}{3}$ the distance that Noah ran. Noah ran 1200 m. How far did Lin run?

🔭 4.1.3a Exploration Activity: Making a Puzzle

Write another number puzzle with at least three steps. On a different piece of paper, write a solution to your puzzle.

Trade puzzles with your partner and solve theirs. Make sure to show your thinking.

With your partner, compare your solutions to each puzzle. Did they solve them the same way you did? Be prepared to share with the class which solution strategy you like best.

Here is a number puzzle that uses math. Some might call it a magic trick!

1. Think of a number.
2. Double the number.
3. Add 9.
4. Subtract 3.
5. Divide by 2.
6. Subtract the number you started with.
7. The answer should be 3.

Why does this always work? Can you think of a different number puzzle that uses math (like this one) that will always result in 5?

- We can reason through it.

  Twice a number plus 4 is 18.
  Then twice the number is $18 - 4 = 14$.
  That means the number is 7.

- We can draw a diagram.

x	x	4
	18	

x	x
	14

x
7

- We can write and solve an equation.

$$2x + 4 = 18$$
$$2x = 14$$
$$x = 7$$

Reasoning and diagrams help us see what is going on and why the answer is what it is. But as number puzzles and story problems get more complex, those methods get harder, and equations get more and more helpful. We will use different kinds of diagrams to help us understand problems and strategies in future lessons, but we will also see the power of writing and solving equations to answer increasingly more complex mathematical problems.

📝 **4.1.5 Practice Problems**

1. Tyler reads $\frac{2}{15}$ of a book on Monday, $\frac{1}{3}$ of it on Tuesday, $\frac{2}{9}$ of it on Wednesday, and $\frac{3}{4}$ of the remainder on Thursday. If he still has 14 pages left to read on Friday, how many pages are there in the book?

📓 **Lesson 1 Summary**

Here is an example of a puzzle problem:

Twice a number plus 4 is 18. What is the number?

There are many different ways to represent and solve puzzle problems.

2. Clare asks Andre to play the following number puzzle:

- Pick a number
- Add 2
- Multiply by 3
- Subtract 7
- Add your original number

Andre's final result is 27. Which number did he start with?

3. In a basketball game, Elena scores twice as many points as Tyler. Tyler scores four points fewer than Noah, and Noah scores three times as many points as Mai. If Mai scores 5 points, how many points did Elena score? Explain your reasoning.

4. Select **all** of the given points in the coordinate plane that lie on the graph of the linear equation $4x - y = 3$.

- ☐ $(-1, -7)$
- ☐ $(0, 3)$
- ☐ $(\frac{3}{4}, 0)$
- ☐ $(1, 1)$
- ☐ $(2, 5)$
- ☐ $(4, -1)$

5. A store is designing the space for rows of nested shopping carts. Each row has a starting cart that is 4 feet long, followed by the nested carts (so 0 nested carts means there's just the starting cart). The store measured a row of 13 nested carts to be 23.5 feet long, and a row of 18 nested carts to be 31 feet long.

a. Create a graph of the situation.

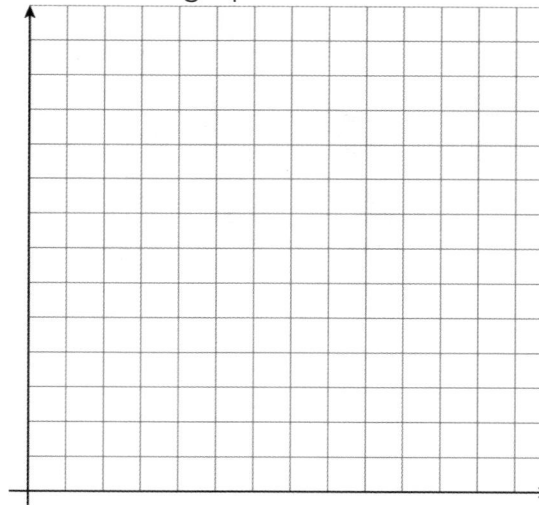

b. How much does each nested cart add to the length of the row? Explain your reasoning.

c. If the store design allows for 43 feet for each row, how many total carts fit in a row?

Unit 4, Lesson 2: Keeping the Equation Balanced

Let's figure out unknown weights on balanced hangers.

🔔 4.2.1 Warm-Up: Notice and Wonder: Hanging Socks

What do you notice?
What do you wonder?

🔭 4.2.2 Exploration Activity: Hanging Blocks

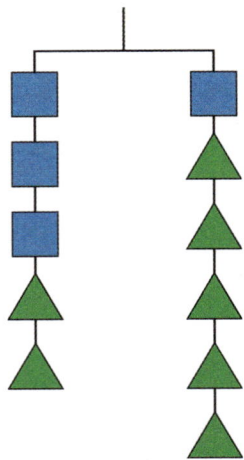

This picture represents a hanger that is balanced because the weight on each side is the same.

1. Elena takes two triangles off of the left side and three triangles off of the right side. Will the hanger still be in balance, or will it tip to one side? Which side? Explain how you know.

2. If a triangle weighs 1 gram, how much does a square weigh?

🔭 4.2.3a Exploration Activity: More Hanging Blocks

A triangle weighs 3 grams and a circle weighs 6 grams.

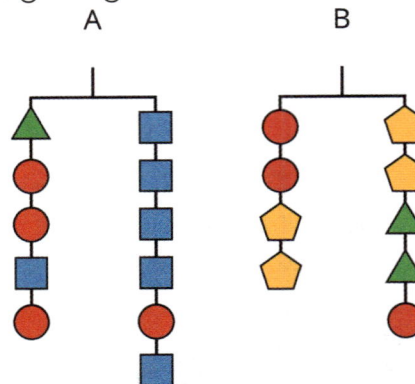

1. Find the weight of a square in Hanger A and the weight of a pentagon in Hanger B.

2. Write an equation to represent each hanger.

⚙ **4.2.3b Exploration Extension: Are you ready for more?**

What is the weight of a square on this hanger if a triangle weighs 3 grams?

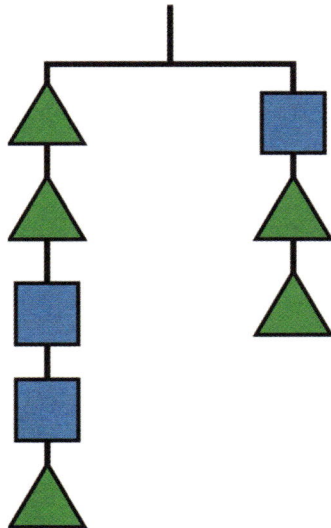

📖 **Lesson 2 Summary**

If we have equal weights on the ends of a hanger, then the hanger will be in balance. If there is more weight on one side than the other, the hanger will tilt to the heavier side.

We can think of a balanced hanger as a metaphor for an equation. An equation says that the expressions on each side have equal value, just like a balanced hanger has equal weights on each side.

If we have a balanced hanger and add or remove the same amount of weight from each side, the result will still be in balance.

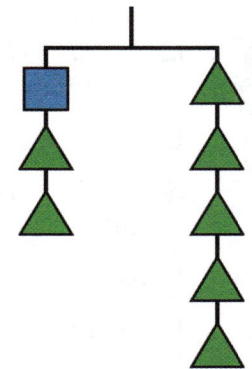

$a + 2b = 5b$

We can do these moves with equations as well: adding or subtracting the same amount from each side of an equation maintains the equality.

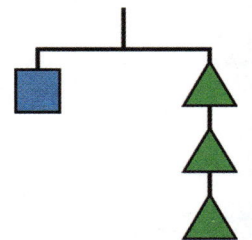

$a = 3b$

1. Which of the changes would keep the hanger in balance? Select all that apply.

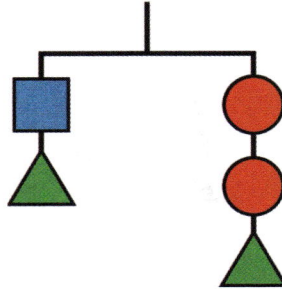

☐ Adding two circles on the left and a square on the right

☐ Adding 2 triangles to each side

☐ Adding two circles on the right and a square on the left

☐ Adding a circle on the left and a square on the right

☐ Adding a triangle on the left and a square on the right

2. Here is a balanced hanger diagram.

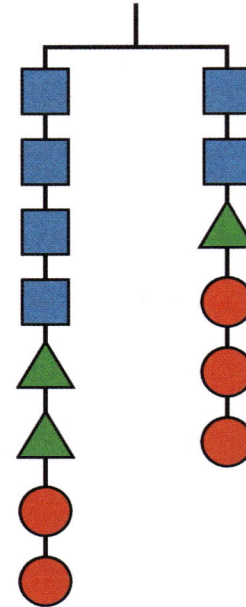

Each triangle weighs 2.5 pounds, each circle weighs 3 pounds, and x represents the weight of each square. Select *all* equations that represent the hanger.

☐ $x + x + x + x + 11 = x + 11.5$

☐ $2x = 0.5$

☐ $4x + 5 + 6 = 2x + 2.5 + 6$

☐ $2x + 2.5 = 3$

☐ $4x + 2.5 + 2.5 + 3 + 3 = 2x + 2.5 + 3 + 3 + 3$

3. What is the weight of a square if a triangle weighs 4 grams?

Explain your reasoning.

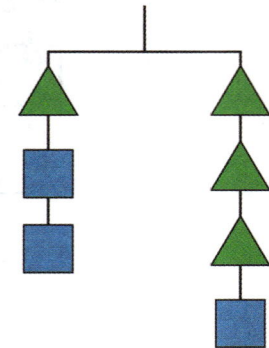

4. Andre came up with the following puzzle. "I am three years younger than my brother, and I am 2 years older than my sister. My mom's age is one less than three times my brother's age. When you add all our ages, you get 87. What are our ages?"

  a. Try to solve the puzzle.

  b. Jada writes this equation for the sum of the ages: $(x) + (x + 3) + (x - 2) + 3(x + 3) - 1 = 87$. Explain the meaning of the variable and each term of the equation.

  c. Write the equation with fewer terms.

  d. Solve the puzzle if you haven't already.

5. These two lines are parallel. Write an equation for each.

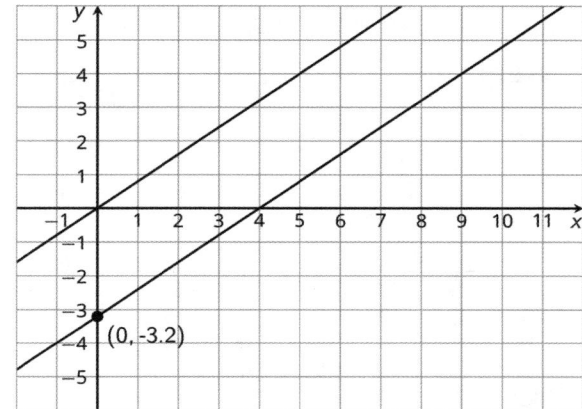

(0, -3.2)

Unit 4, Lesson 3: Balanced Moves

Let's rewrite equations while keeping the same solutions.

4.3.1 Warm-Up: Matching Hangers

Figures A, B, C, and D show the result of simplifying the hanger in Figure A by removing equal weights from each side.

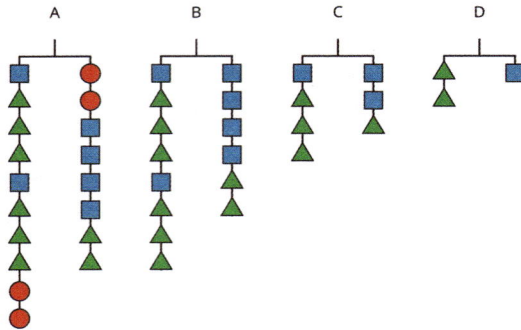

Here are some equations. Each equation represents one of the hanger diagrams.

$$2(x + 3y) = 4x + 2y$$

$$2y = x$$

$$2(x + 3y) + 2z = 2z + 4x + 2y$$

$$x + 3y = 2x + y$$

1. Write the equation that goes with each figure:

   A:

   B:

   C:

   D:

2. Each variable (x, y, and z) represents the weight of one shape. Which goes with which?

3. Explain what was done to each equation to create the next equation. If you get stuck, think about how the hangers changed.

4.3.2 Exploration Activity: Matching Equation Moves

Your teacher will give you some cards. Each of the cards 1 through 6 show two equations. Each of the cards A through E describe a move that turns one equation into another.

1. Match each number card with a letter card.

2. One of the letter cards will not have a match. For this card, write two equations showing the described move.

4.3.3a Exploration Activity: Keeping Equality

1. Noah and Lin both solved the equation $14a = 2(a - 3)$. Do you agree with either of them? Why?

Noah's solution:

$$14a = 2(a - 3)$$
$$14a = 2a - 6$$
$$12a = -6$$
$$a = -\frac{1}{2}$$

Lin's solution:

$$14a = 2(a - 3)$$
$$7a = a - 3$$
$$6a = -3$$
$$a = -\frac{1}{2}$$

2. Elena is asked to solve $15 - 10x = 5(x + 9)$. What do you recommend she does to each side first?

3. Diego is asked to solve $3x - 8 = 4(x + 5)$. What do you recommend he does to each side first?

4.3.3b Exploration Extension: Are you ready for more?

In a cryptarithmetic puzzle, the digits 0–9 are represented with letters of the alphabet. Use your understanding of addition to find which digits go with the letters A, B, E, G, H, L, N, and R.

HANGER + HANGER + HANGER = ALGEBRA

Lesson 3 Summary

An equation tells us that two expressions have equal value. For example, if $4x + 9$ and $-2x - 3$ have equal value, we can write the equation

$$4x + 9 = -2x - 3$$

Earlier, we used hangers to understand that if we add the same positive number to each side of the equation, the sides will still have equal value. It also works if we add *negative numbers*! For example, we can add -9 to each side of the equation.

$$4x + 9 + -9 = -2x - 3 + -9 \qquad \text{add} -9 \text{ to each side}$$
$$4x = -2x - 12 \qquad \text{combine like terms}$$

Since expressions represent numbers, we can also add *expressions* to each side of an equation. For example, we can add $2x$ to each side and still maintain equality.

$$4x + 2x = -2x - 12 + 2x \qquad \text{add } 2x \text{ to each side}$$
$$6x = -12 \qquad \text{combine like terms}$$

If we multiply or divide the expressions on each side of an equation by the same number, we will also maintain the equality (so long as we do not divide by zero).

$$6x \cdot \frac{1}{6} = -12 \cdot \frac{1}{6} \qquad \text{multiply each side by } \frac{1}{6}$$

or

$$6x \div 6 = -12 \div 6 \qquad \text{divide each side by } 6$$

Now we can see that $x = -2$ is the solution to our equation.

We will use these moves in systematic ways to solve equations in future lessons.

4.3.5 Practice Problems

1. In this hanger, the weight of the triangle is x and the weight of the square is y.

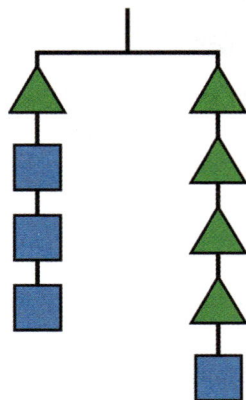

   a. Write an equation using x and y to represent the hanger.

   b. If x is 6, what is y?

2. Match each set of equations with the move that turned the first equation into the second.

   A. $6x + 9 = 4x - 3$
      $2x + 9 = -3$

   B. $-4(5x - 7) = -18$
      $5x - 7 = 4.5$

   C. $8 - 10x = 7 + 5x$
      $4 - 10x = 3 + 5x$

   D. $\frac{-5x}{4} = 4$
      $5x = -16$

   E. $12x + 4 = 20x + 24$
      $3x + 1 = 5x + 6$

   I. Multiply both sides by $\frac{-1}{4}$

   II. Multiply both sides by -4

   III. Multiply both sides by $\frac{1}{4}$

   IV. Add $-4x$ to both sides

   V. Add -4 to both sides

3. Andre and Diego were each trying to solve $2x + 6 = 3x - 8$. Describe the first step they each make to the equation.

   a. The result of Andre's first step was $-x + 6 = -8$.

   b. The result of Diego's first step was $6 = x - 8$.

Unit 4: Linear Equations and Linear Systems

4.

a. Complete the table with values for x or y that make this equation true: $3x + y = 15$.

x	2		6	0	3		
y		3				0	8

b. Create a graph, plot these points, and find the slope of the line that goes through them.

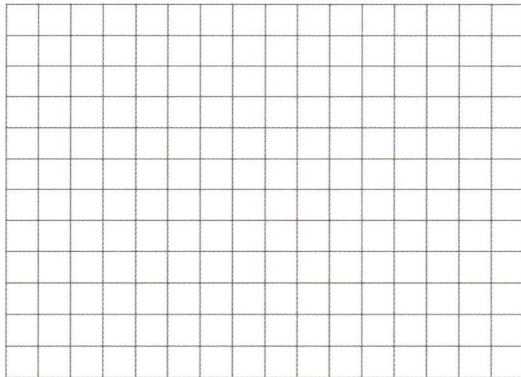

5. Select **all** the situations for which only zero or positive solutions make sense.

☐ Measuring temperature in degrees Celsius at an Arctic outpost each day in January.

☐ The height of a candle as it burns over an hour.

☐ The elevation above sea level of a hiker descending into a canyon.

☐ The number of students remaining in school after 6:00 p.m.

☐ A bank account balance over a year.

☐ The temperature in degrees Fahrenheit of an oven used on a hot summer day.

Unit 4, Lesson 4: More Balanced Moves

Let's rewrite some more equations while keeping the same solutions.

4.4.1 Warm-Up: Different Equations?

Equation 1

$$x - 3 = 2 - 4x$$

Which of these have the same solution as Equation 1? Be prepared to explain your reasoning.

Equation A

$$2x - 6 = 4 - 8x$$

Equation B

$$x - 5 = -4x$$

Equation C

$$2(1 - 2x) = x - 3$$

Equation D

$$-3 = 2 - 5x$$

4.4.2 Exploration Activity: Step by Step by Step by Step

Here is an equation, and then all the steps Clare wrote to solve it:

$$\begin{aligned}
14x - 2x + 3 &= 3(5x + 9) \\
12x + 3 &= 3(5x + 9) \\
3(4x + 1) &= 3(5x + 9) \\
4x + 1 &= 5x + 9 \\
1 &= x + 9 \\
-8 &= x
\end{aligned}$$

Here is the same equation, and the steps Lin wrote to solve it:

$$\begin{aligned}
14x - 2x + 3 &= 3(5x + 9) \\
12x + 3 &= 3(5x + 9) \\
12x + 3 &= 15x + 27 \\
12x &= 15x + 24 \\
-3x &= 24 \\
x &= -8
\end{aligned}$$

1. Are both of their *solutions* correct? Explain your reasoning.

2. Describe some ways the steps they took are alike and different.

3. Mai and Noah also solved the equation, but some of their steps have errors. Find the incorrect step in each solution and explain why it is incorrect.

Mai:

$$\begin{aligned}
14x - 2x + 3 &= 3(5x + 9) \\
12x + 3 &= 3(5x + 9) \\
7x + 3 &= 3(9) \\
7x + 3 &= 27 \\
7x &= 24 \\
x &= \frac{24}{7}
\end{aligned}$$

Noah:

$$\begin{aligned}
14x - 2x + 3 &= 3(5x + 9) \\
12x + 3 &= 15x + 27 \\
27x + 3 &= 27 \\
27x &= 24 \\
x &= \frac{24}{27}
\end{aligned}$$

4.4.3a Exploration Activity: Make Your Own Steps

Solve these equations for x.

1. $\frac{12+6x}{3} = \frac{5-9}{2}$

2. $x - 4 = \frac{1}{3}(6x - 54)$

3. $-(3x - 12) = 9x - 4$

4.4.3b Exploration Extension: Are you ready for more?

I have 24 pencils and 3 cups. The second cup holds one more pencil than the first. The third holds one more than the second. How many pencils does each cup contain?

Lesson 4 Summary

How do we make sure the solution we find for an equation is correct? Accidentally adding when we meant to subtract, missing a negative when we distribute, forgetting to write an x from one line to the next—there are many possible mistakes to watch out for!

Fortunately, each step we take solving an equation results in a new equation with the same solution as the original. This means we can check our work by substituting the value of the solution into the original equation. For example, say we solve the following equation:

$$\begin{aligned} 2x &= -3(x + 5) \\ 2x &= -3x + 15 \\ 5x &= 15 \\ x &= 3 \end{aligned}$$

Substituting 3 in place of x into the original equation,

$$\begin{aligned} 2(3) &= -3(3 + 5) \\ 6 &= -3(8) \\ 6 &= -24 \end{aligned}$$

we get a statement that isn't true! This tells us we must have made a mistake somewhere. Checking our original steps carefully, we made a mistake when distributing -3. Fixing it, we now have

$$\begin{aligned} 2x &= -3(x + 5) \\ 2x &= -3x - 15 \\ 5x &= -15 \\ x &= -3 \end{aligned}$$

Substituting -3 in place of x into the original equation to make sure we didn't make another mistake:

$$\begin{aligned} 2(-3) &= -3(-3 + 5) \\ -6 &= -3(2) \\ -6 &= -6 \end{aligned}$$

This equation is true, so $x = -3$ is the solution.

1. Mai and Tyler work on the equation $\frac{2}{5}b + 1 = -11$ together. Mai's solution is $b = -25$ and Tyler's is $b = -28$. Here is their work:

Mai:
$$\frac{2}{5}b + 1 = -11$$
$$\frac{2}{5}b = -10$$
$$b = -10 \cdot \frac{5}{2}$$
$$b = -25$$

Tyler:
$$\frac{2}{5}b + 1 = -11$$
$$2b + 1 = -55$$
$$2b = -56$$
$$b = -28$$

Do you agree with their solutions? Explain or show your reasoning.

2. Solve $3(x - 4) = 12x$

3. Describe what is being done in each step while solving the equation.

   a. $2(-3x + 4) = 5x + 2$

   b. $-6x + 8 = 5x + 2$

   c. $8 = 11x + 2$

   d. $6 = 11x$

   e. $x = \frac{6}{11}$

4. Andre solved an equation, but when he checked his answer he saw his solution was incorrect. He knows he made a mistake, but he can't find it. Where is Andre's mistake and what is the solution to the equation?

$$
\begin{aligned}
-2(3x - 5) &= 4(x + 3) + 8 \\
-6x + 10 &= 4x + 12 + 8 \\
-6x + 10 &= 4x + 20 \\
10 &= -2x + 20 \\
-10 &= -2x \\
5 &= x
\end{aligned}
$$

Unit 4: Linear Equations and Linear Systems

5. Choose the equation that has solutions (5,7) and (8,13).

    A. $3x - y = 8$

    B. $y = x + 2$

    C. $y - x = 5$

    D. $y = 2x - 3$

6. A length of ribbon is cut into two pieces to use in a craft project. The graph shows the length of the second piece, x, for each length of the first piece, y.

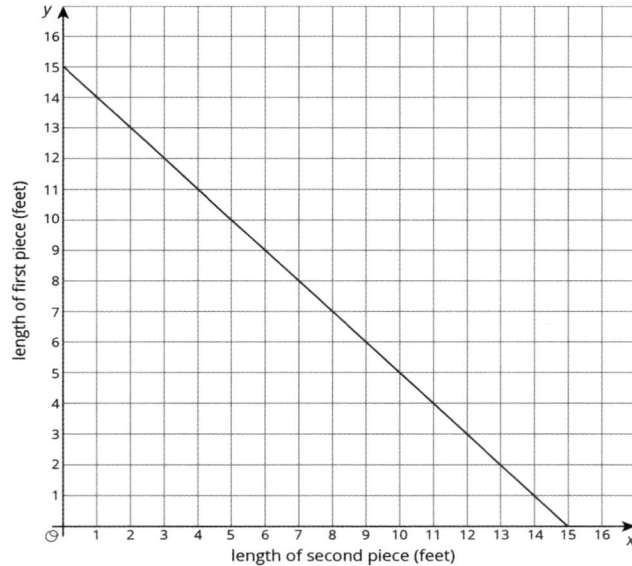

length of first piece (feet)

length of second piece (feet)

    a. How long is the ribbon? Explain how you know.

b. What is the slope of the line?

c. Explain what the slope of the line represents and why it fits the story.

Unit 4, Lesson 5: Solving Any Linear Equation

Let's solve linear equations.

4.5.1 Warm-Up: Equation Talk

1. $5 - x = 8$

2. $-1 = x - 2$

3. $-3x = 9$

4. $-10 = -5x$

4.5.2 Exploration Activity: Trading Moves

Your teacher will give you 4 cards, each with an equation.

1. With your partner, select a card and choose who will take the first turn.
2. During your turn, decide what the next move to solve the equation should be, explain your choice to your partner, and then write it down once you both agree. Switch roles for the next move. This continues until the equation is solved.
3. Choose a second equation to solve in the same way, trading the card back and forth after each move.
4. For the last two equations, choose one each to solve and then trade with your partner when you finish to check one another's work.

4.5.3 Exploration Activity: A Puzzling Puzzle

Tyler says he invented a number puzzle. He asks Clare to pick a number, and then asks her to do the following:

- Triple the number
- Subtract 7
- Double the result
- Subtract 22
- Divide by 6

Clare says she now has a -3. Tyler says her original number must have been a 3. How did Tyler know that? Explain or show your reasoning. Be prepared to share your reasoning with the class.

Unit 4: Linear Equations and Linear Systems

When we have an equation in one variable, there are many different ways to solve it. We generally want to make moves that get us closer to an equation like

$$variable = some\ number$$

For example, $x = 5$ or $t = \frac{7}{3}$. Since there are many ways to do this, it helps to choose moves that leave fewer terms or factors. If we have an equation like

$$3t + 5 = 7,$$

adding -5 to each side will leave us with fewer terms. The equation then becomes

$$3t = 2.$$

Dividing each side of this equation by 3 will leave us with t by itself on the left and that $t = \frac{2}{3}$.

Or, if we have an equation like

$$4(5 - a) = 12,$$

dividing each side by 4 will leave us with fewer factors on the left, $5 - a = 3$.

Some people use the following steps to solve a linear equation in one variable:

1. Use the distributive property so that all the expressions no longer have parentheses.

2. Collect like terms on each side of the equation.

3. Add or subtract an expression so that there is a variable on just one side.

4. Add or subtract an expression so that there is just a number on the other side.

5. Multiply or divide by a number so that you have an equation that looks like *variable = some number*.

For example, suppose we want to solve $9 - 2b + 6 = -3(b + 5) + 4b$.

$9 - 2b + 6$	$= -3b - 15 + 4b$	Use the distributive property
$15 - 2b$	$= b - 15$	Gather like terms
15	$= 3b - 15$	Add $2b$ to each side
30	$= 3b$	Add 15 to each side
10	$= b$	Divide each side by 3

Following these steps will always work, although it may not be the most efficient method. From lots of experience, we learn when to use different approaches.

🔴 **4.5.5 Practice Problems**

1. Solve each of these equations. Explain or show your reasoning.

   $$2(x + 5) = 3x + 1$$

   $$3y - 4 = 6 - 2y$$

   $$3(n + 2) = 9(6 - n)$$

2. Clare was solving an equation, but when she checked her answer she saw her solution was incorrect. She knows she made a mistake, but she can't find it. Where is Clare's mistake and what is the solution to the equation?

$$
\begin{aligned}
12(5 + 2y) &= 4y - (5 - 9y) \\
72 + 24y &= 4y - 5 - 9y \\
72 + 24y &= -5y - 5 \\
24y &= -5y - 77 \\
29y &= -77 \\
y &= \frac{-77}{29}
\end{aligned}
$$

3. Solve each equation, and check your solution.

$$\frac{1}{9}(2m - 16) = \frac{1}{3}(2m + 4)$$

$$-4(r + 2) = 4(2 - 2r)$$

$$12(5 + 2y) = 4y - (6 - 9y)$$

4. Here is the graph of a linear equation.

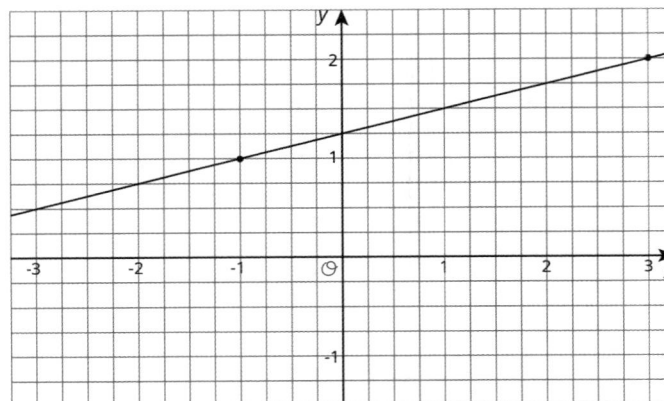

Select **all** true statements about the line and its equation.

☐ One solution of the equation is (3,2).
☐ One solution of the equation is (−1,1).
☐ One solution of the equation is $\left(1, \frac{3}{2}\right)$.
☐ There are 2 solutions.
☐ There are infinitely many solutions.
☐ The equation of the line is $y = \frac{1}{4}x + \frac{5}{4}$.
☐ The equation of the line is $y = \frac{5}{4}x + \frac{1}{4}$.

5. A participant in a 21-mile walkathon walks at a steady rate of 3 miles per hour. He thinks, "The relationship between the number of miles left to walk and the number of hours I already walked can be represented by a line with slope −3." Do you agree with his claim? Explain your reasoning.

Unit 4: Linear Equations and Linear Systems

MATH NATION

Let's solve linear equations like a boss.

4.6.1 Warm-Up: Equal Perimeters

The triangle and the square have equal perimeters.

1. Find the value of x.

2. What is the perimeter of each of the figures?

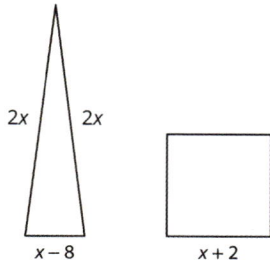

4.6.2 Exploration Activity: Predicting Solutions

Without solving, identify whether these equations have a solution that is positive, negative, or zero.

1. $\frac{x}{6} = \frac{3x}{4}$

2. $7x = 3.25$

3. $7x = 32.5$

4. $3x + 11 = 11$

5. $9 - 4x = 4$

6. $-8 + 5x = -20$

7. $-\frac{1}{2}(-8 + 5x) = -20$

4.6.3a Exploration Activity: Which Would You Rather Solve?

Here are a lot of equations:

A. $-\frac{5}{6}(8 + 5b) = 75 + \frac{5}{3}b$

B. $-\frac{1}{2}(t + 3) - 10 = -6.5$

C. $\frac{10-v}{4} = 2(v + 17)$

D. $2(4k + 3) - 13 = 2(18 - k) - 13$

E. $\frac{n}{7} - 12 = 5n + 5$

F. $3(c - 1) + 2(3c + 1) = -(3c + 1)$

G. $\frac{4m-3}{4} = -\frac{9+4m}{8}$

H. $p - 5(p + 4) = p - (8 - p)$

I. $2(2q + 1.5) = 18 - q$

J. $2r + 49 = -8(-r - 5)$

1. Without solving, identify 3 equations that you think would be least difficult to solve and 3 equations you think would be most difficult to solve. Be prepared to explain your reasoning.

2. Choose 3 equations to solve. At least one should be from your "least difficult" list and one should be from your "most difficult" list.

4.6.3b Exploration Extension: Are you ready for more?

Mai gave half of her brownies, and then half a brownie more, to Kiran. Then she gave half of what was left, and half a brownie more, to Tyler. That left her with one remaining brownie. How many brownies did she have to start with?

Unit 4: Linear Equations and Linear Systems

Lesson 6 Summary

Sometimes we are asked to solve equations with a lot of things going on on each side. For example,

$$x - 2(x + 5) = \frac{3(2x - 20)}{6}$$

This equation has variables on each side, parentheses, and even a fraction to think about. Before we start distributing, let's take a closer look at the fraction on the right side. The expression $2x - 20$ is being multiplied by 3 and divided by 6, which is the same as just dividing by 2, so we can re-write the equation as

$$x - 2(x + 5) = \frac{2x - 20}{2}$$

But now it's easier to see that all the terms on the numerator of right side are divisible by 2, which means we can re-write the right side again as

$$x - 2(x + 5) = x - 10$$

At this point, we could do some distribution and then collect like terms on each side of the equation. Another choice would be to use the structure of the equation. Both the left and the right side have something being subtracted from x. But, if the two sides are equal, that means the "something" being subtracted on each side must also be equal. Thinking this way, the equation can now be re-written with less terms as

$$2(x + 5) = 10$$

Only a few steps left! But what can we tell about the solution to this problem right now? Is it positive? Negative? Zero? Well, the 2 and the 5 multiplied together are 10, so that means the 2 and the x multiplied together cannot have a positive or a negative value. Finishing the steps we have:

$$\begin{aligned} 2(x + 5) &= 10 \\ x + 5 &= 5 \qquad \text{Divide each side by 2} \\ x &= 0 \qquad \text{Subtract 5 from each side} \end{aligned}$$

Neither positive nor negative. Just as predicted.

4.6.5 Practice Problems

1. Solve each of these equations. Explain or show your reasoning.

   a. $2b + 8 - 5b + 3 = -13 + 8b - 5$

   b. $2x + 7 - 5x + 8 = 3(5 + 6x) - 12x$

   c. $2c - 3 = 2(6 - c) + 7c$

2. Solve each equation and check your solution.

   a. $-3w - 4 = w + 3$

   b. $3(3 - 3x) = 2(x + 3) - 30$

Continued on next page

c. $\frac{1}{3}(z+4) - 6 = \frac{2}{3}(5-z)$

3. Elena said the equation $9x + 15 = 3x + 15$ has no solutions because $9x$ is greater than $3x$. Do you agree with Elena? Explain your reasoning.

4. The table gives some sample data for two quantities, x and y, that are in a proportional relationship.

x	y
14	21
64	
	39
1	

   a. Complete the table.

   b. Write an equation that represents the relationship between x and y shown in the table.

c. Graph the relationship. Use a scale for the axes that shows all the points in the table.

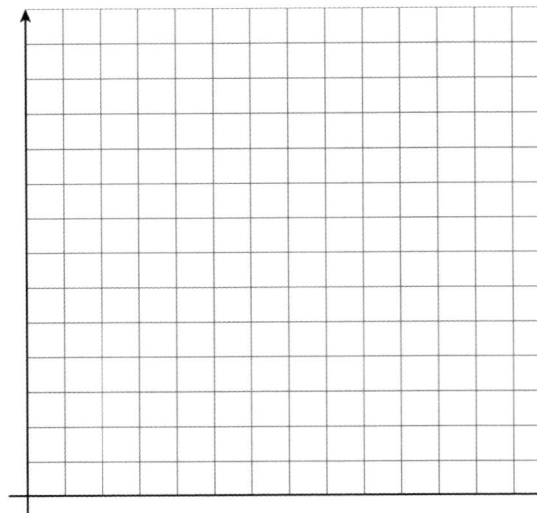

Unit 4: Linear Equations and Linear Systems

MATH NATION

Unit 4, Lesson 7: All, Some, or No Solutions

Let's think about how many solutions an equation can have.

🔔 4.7.1 Warm-Up: Which One Doesn't Belong: Equations

Which one doesn't belong?

A. $5 + 7 = 7 + 5$

B. $5 \cdot 7 = 7 \cdot 5$

C. $2 = 7 - 5$

D. $5 - 7 = 7 - 5$

🔭 4.7.2a Exploration Activity: Thinking About Solutions

$$n = n$$

$$2t + 6 = 2(t + 3)$$

$$3(n + 1) = 3n + 1$$

$$\frac{1}{4}(20d + 4) = 5d$$

$$5 - 9 + 3x = -10 + 6 + 3x$$

$$\frac{1}{2} + x = \frac{1}{3} + x$$

$$y \cdot -6 \cdot -3 = 2 \cdot y \cdot 9$$

$$v + 2 = v - 2$$

1. Sort these equations into the two types: true for all values and true for no values.

2. Write the other side of this equation so that this equation is true for all values of u. $6(u - 2) + 2 =$

3. Write the other side of this equation so that this equation is true for no values of u. $6(u - 2) + 2 =$

⚙ 4.7.2b Exploration Extension: Are you ready for more?

Consecutive numbers follow one right after the other. An example of three consecutive numbers is 17, 18, and 19. Another example is -100, -99, -98.

How many sets of two or more consecutive positive integers can be added to obtain a sum of 100?

4.7.3 Exploration Activity: What's the Equation?

1. Complete each equation so that it is true for all values of x.

   a. $3x + 6 = 3(x + \underline{})$

   b. $x - 2 = -(\underline{} - x)$

   c. $\frac{15x-10}{5} = \underline{} - 2$

2. Complete each equation so that it is true for no values of x.

   a. $3x + 6 = 3(x + \underline{})$

   b. $x - 2 = -(\underline{} - x)$

   c. $\frac{15x-10}{5} = \underline{} - 2$

3. Describe how you know whether an equation will be true for all values of x or true for no values of x.

Lesson 7 Summary

An equation is a statement that two expressions have an equal value. The equation

$$2x = 6$$

is a true statement if x is 3:

$$2 \cdot 3 = 6$$

It is a false statement if x is 4:

$$2 \cdot 4 = 6$$

The equation $2x = 6$ has *one and only one solution*, because there is only one number (3) that you can double to get 6.

Some equations are true no matter what the value of the variable is. For example:

$$2x = x + x$$

is always true, because if you double a number, that will always be the same as adding the number to itself. Equations like $2x = x + x$ have an *infinite number of solutions*. We say it is true for all values of x.

Some equations have *no solutions*. For example:

$$x = x + 1$$

has no solutions, because no matter what the value of x is, it can't equal one more than itself.

When we solve an equation, we are looking for the values of the variable that make the equation true. When we try to solve the equation, we make allowable moves assuming it *has* a solution. Sometimes we make allowable moves and get an equation like this:

$$8 = 7$$

This statement is false, so it must be that the original equation had no solution at all.

MATH NATION

1. For each equation, decide if it is always true or never true.

   a. $x - 13 = x + 1$

   b. $x + \frac{1}{2} = x - \frac{1}{2}$

   c. $2(x + 3) = 5x + 6 - 3x$

   d. $x - 3 = 2x - 3 - x$

   e. $3(x - 5) = 2(x - 5) + x$

2. Mai says that the equation $2x + 2 = x + 1$ has no solution because the left hand side is double the right hand side. Do you agree with Mai? Explain your reasoning.

3.

   a. Write the other side of this equation so it's true for all values of x: $\frac{1}{2}(6x - 10) - x =$

   b. Write the other side of this equation so it's true for no values of x: $\frac{1}{2}(6x - 10) - x =$

4. Here is an equation that is true for all values of x: $5(x + 2) = 5x + 10$. Elena saw this equation and says she can tell $20(x + 2) + 31 = 4(5x + 10) + 31$ is also true for any value of x. How can she tell? Explain your reasoning.

5. Elena and Lin are trying to solve $\frac{1}{2}x + 3 = \frac{7}{2}x + 5$. Describe the change they each make to each side of the equation.

   a. Elena's first step is to write $3 = \frac{7}{2}x - \frac{1}{2}x + 5$.

   b. Lin's first step is to write $x + 6 = 7x + 10$.

6. Solve each equation and check your solution.

$$3x - 6 = 4(2 - 3x) - 8x$$

$$\frac{1}{2}z + 6 = \frac{3}{2}(z + 6)$$

$$9 - 7w = 8w + 8$$

7. The point $(-3,6)$ is on a line with a slope of 4.

   a. Find two more points on the line.

   b. Write an equation for the line.

Let's solve equations with different numbers of solutions.

4.8.1 Warm-Up: Matching Solutions

Consider the unfinished equation $12(x - 3) + 18 =$ ____

Match the following expressions with the number of solutions the equation would have with that expression on the right hand side.

A. $6(2x - 3)$	I. One solution?
B. $4(3x - 3)$	II. No solutions?
C. $4(2x - 3)$	III. All solutions?

4.8.2 Exploration Activity: Thinking About Solutions Some More

Your teacher will give you some cards.

1. With your partner, solve each equation.
2. Then, sort them into categories.
3. Describe the defining characteristics of those categories and be prepared to share your reasoning with the class.

4.8.3a Exploration Activity: Make Use of Structure

For each equation, determine whether it has no solutions, exactly one solution, or is true for all values of x (and has infinitely many solutions). If an equation has one solution, solve to find the value of x that makes the statement true.

1.

   a. $6x + 8 = 7x + 13$

   b. $6x + 8 = 2(3x + 4)$

   c. $6x + 8 = 6x + 13$

2.

   a. $\frac{1}{4}(12 - 4x) = 3 - x$

   b. $x - 3 = 3 - x$

   c. $x - 3 = 3 + x$

3.

   a. $-5x - 3x + 2 = -8x + 2$

   b. $-5x - 3x - 4 = -8x + 2$

   c. $-5x - 4x - 2 = -8x + 2$

4.

   a. $4(2x - 2) + 2 = 4(x - 2)$

   b. $4x + 2(2x - 3) = 8(x - 1)$

Continued on next page

c. $4x + 2(2x - 3) = 4(2x - 2) + 2$

5.

a. $x - 3(2 - 3x) = 2(5x + 3)$

b. $x - 3(2 + 3x) = 2(5x - 3)$

c. $x - 3(2 - 3x) = 2(5x - 3)$

6. What do you notice about equations with one solution? How is this different from equations with no solutions and equations that are true for every x?

Consecutive numbers follow one right after the other. An example of three consecutive numbers is 17, 18, and 19. Another example is -100, -99, -98.

1. Choose any set of three consecutive numbers. Find their average. What do you notice?

2. Find the average of another set of three consecutive numbers. What do you notice?

3. Explain why the thing you noticed must always work, or find a counterexample.

Unit 4: Linear Equations and Linear Systems

Sometimes it's possible to look at the structure of an equation and tell if it has infinitely many solutions or no solutions. For example, look at

$$2(12x + 18) + 6 = 18x + 6(x + 7).$$

Using the distributive property on the left and right sides, we get

$$24x + 36 + 6 = 18x + 6x + 42.$$

From here, collecting like terms gives us

$$24x + 42 = 24x + 42.$$

Since the left and right sides of the equation are the same, we know that this equation is true for any value of x without doing any more moves!

Similarly, we can sometimes use structure to tell if an equation has no solutions. For example, look at

$$6(6x + 5) = 12(3x + 2) + 12.$$

If we think about each move as we go, we can stop when we realize there is no solution:

$\frac{1}{6} \cdot 6(6x + 5)$	$= \frac{1}{6} \cdot (12(3x + 2) + 12)$	Multiply each side by $\frac{1}{6}$.
$6x + 5$	$= 2(3x + 2) + 2$	Distribute $\frac{1}{6}$ on the right
$6x + 5$	$= 6x + 4 + 2$	Distribute 2 on the right s

The last move makes it clear that the **constant terms** on each side, 5 and $4 + 2$, are not the same. Since adding 5 to an amount is always less than adding $4 + 2$ to that same amount, we know there are no solutions.

Doing moves to keep an equation balanced is a powerful part of solving equations, but thinking about what the structure of an equation tells us about the solutions is just as important.

4.8.5 Practice Problem

1. Lin was looking at the equation $2x - 32 + 4(3x - 2462) = 14x$. She said, "I can tell right away there are no solutions, because on the left side, you will have $2x + 12x$ and a bunch of constants, but you have just $14x$ on the right side." Do you agree with Lin? Explain your reasoning.

2. Han was looking at the equation $6x - 4 + 2(5x + 2) = 16x$. He said, "I can tell right away there are no solutions, because on the left side, you will have $6x + 10x$ and a bunch of constants, but you have just $16x$ on the right side." Do you agree with Han? Explain your reasoning.

3. Decide whether each equation is true for all, one, or no values of x.

   a. $6x - 4 = -4 + 6x$

   b. $4x - 6 = 4x + 3$

   c. $-2x + 4 = -3x + 4$

4. Solve each of these equations. Explain or show your reasoning.

   a. $3(x - 5) = 6$

   b. $2\left(x - \frac{2}{3}\right) = 0$

   c. $4x - 5 = 2 - x$

5. The points $(-2,0)$ and $(0,-6)$ are each on the graph of a linear equation. Is $(2,6)$ also on the graph of this linear equation? Explain your reasoning.

6. In the picture triangle $A'B'C'$ is an image of triangle ABC after a rotation. The center of rotation is E.

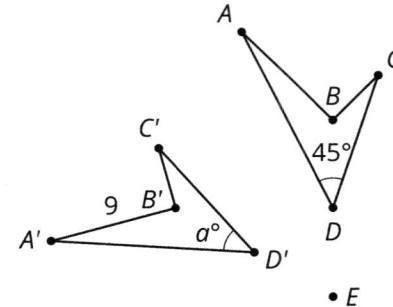

   a. What is the length of side AB? Explain how you know.

Unit 4: Linear Equations and Linear Systems

b. What is the measure of angle D'? Explain how you know.

Unit 4, Lesson 9: When Are They the Same?

Let's use equations to think about situations.

4.9.1 Warm-Up: Which Would You Choose?

If you were babysitting, would you rather

- Charge $5 for the first hour and $8 for each additional hour?

Or

- Charge $15 for the first hour and $6 for each additional hour?

Explain your reasoning.

4.9.2 Exploration Activity: Water Tanks

The amount of water in two tanks every 5 minutes is shown in the table.

time (minutes)	tank 1 (liters)	tank 2 (liters)
0	25	1000
5	175	900
10	325	800
15	475	700
20	625	600
25	775	500
30	925	400
35	1075	300
40	1225	200
45	1375	100
50	1525	0

1. Describe what is happening in each tank. Either draw a picture, say it verbally, or write a few sentences.

2. Use the table to estimate when the tanks will have the same amount of water.

3. The amount of water (in liters) in tank 1 after t minutes is $30t + 25$. The amount of water (in liters) in tank 2 after t minutes is $-20t + 1000$. Find the time when the amount of water will be equal.

4.9.3a Exploration Activity: Elevators

A building has two elevators that both go above and below ground.

At a certain time of day, the travel time it takes elevator A to reach height h in meters is $0.8h + 16$ seconds.

The travel time it takes elevator B to reach height h in meters is $-0.8h + 12$ seconds.

ground level

1. What is the height of each elevator at this time?

2. How long would it take each elevator to reach ground level at this time?

MATH NATION

3. If the two elevators travel toward one another, at what height do they pass each other? How long would it take?

4. If you are on an underground parking level 14 meters below ground, which elevator would reach you first?

4.9.3b Exploration Extension: Are you ready for more?

1. In a two-digit number, the ones digit is twice the tens digit. If the digits are reversed, the new number is 36 more than the original number. Find the number.

2. The sum of the digits of a two-digit number is 11. If the digits are reversed, the new number is 45 less than the original number. Find the number.

3. The sum of the digits in a two-digit number is 8. The value of the number is 4 less than 5 times the ones digit. Find the number.

Lesson 9 Summary

Imagine a full 1,500 liter water tank that springs a leak, losing 2 liters per minute. We could represent the number of liters left in the tank with the expression $-2x + 1,500$, where x represents the number of minutes the tank has been leaking.

Now imagine at the same time, a second tank has 300 liters and is being filled at a rate of 6 liters per minute. We could represent the amount of water in liters in this second tank with the expression $6x + 300$, where x represents the number of minutes that have passed.

Since one tank is losing water and the other is gaining water, at some point they will have the same amount of water—but when? Asking when the two tanks have the same number of liters is the same as asking when $-2x + 1,500$ (the number of liters in the first tank after x minutes) is equal to $6x + 300$ (the number of liters in the second tank after x minutes),

$$-2x + 1,500 = 6x + 300.$$

Solving for x gives us $x = 150$ minutes. So after 150 minutes, the number of liters of the first tank is equal to the number of liters of the second tank. But how much water is actually in each tank at that time? Since both tanks have the same number of liters after 150 minutes, we could substitute $x = 150$ minutes into either expression.

Using the expression for the first tank, we get $-2(150) + 1,500$ which is equal to $-300 + 1,500$, or 1,200 liters.

If we use the expression for the second tank, we get $6(150) + 300$, or just $900 + 300$, which is also 1,200 liters. That means that after 150 minutes, each tank has 1,200 liters.

4.9.5 Practice Problems

1. Cell phone Plan A costs $70 per month and comes with a free $500 phone. Cell phone Plan B costs $50 per month but does not come with a phone. If you buy the $500 phone and choose Plan B, how many months is it until your cost is the same as Plan A's?

2. Priya and Han are biking in the same direction on the same path.

   a. Han is riding at a constant speed of 16 miles per hour. Write an expression that shows how many miles Han has gone after t hours.

   b. Priya started riding a half hour before Han. If Han has been riding for t hours, how long has Priya been riding?

   c. Priya is riding at a constant speed of 12 miles per hour. Write an expression that shows how many miles Priya has gone after Han has been riding for t hours.

   d. Use your expressions to find when Han and Priya meet.

3. Which story matches the equation $-6 + 3x = 2 + 4x$?

   A. At 5 p.m., the temperatures recorded at two weather stations in Antarctica are -6 degrees and 2 degrees. The temperature changes at the same constant rate, x degrees per hour, throughout the night at both locations. The temperature at the first station 3 hours after this recording is the same as the temperature at the second station 4 hours after this recording.

   B. Elena and Kiran play a card game. Every time they collect a pair of matching cards, they earn x points. At one point in the game, Kiran has -6 points and Elena has 2 points. After Elena collects 3 pairs and Kiran collects 4 pairs, they have the same number of points.

4. For what value of x do the expressions $\frac{2}{3}x + 2$ and $\frac{4}{3}x - 6$ have the same value?

5. Decide whether each equation is true for all, one, or no values of x.

   a. $2x + 8 = -3.5x + 19$

   b. $9(x - 2) = 7x + 5$

   c. $3(3x + 2) - 2x = 7x + 6$

6. Solve each equation. Explain your reasoning.

   a. $3d + 16 = -2(5 - 3d)$

   b. $2k - 3(4 - k) = 3k + 4$

c. $\dfrac{3y-6}{9} = \dfrac{4-2y}{-3}$

7. Describe a rigid transformation that takes Polygon A to Polygon B.

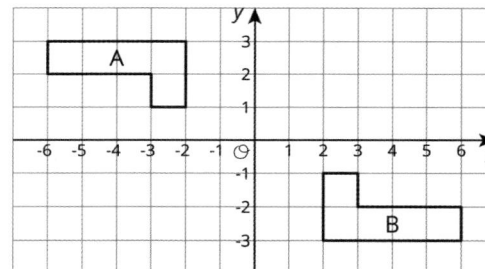

Let's interpret the meaning of points in a coordinate plane.

4.10.1 Warm-Up: Which One Doesn't Belong: Lines in the Plane

Which one doesn't belong? Explain your reasoning.

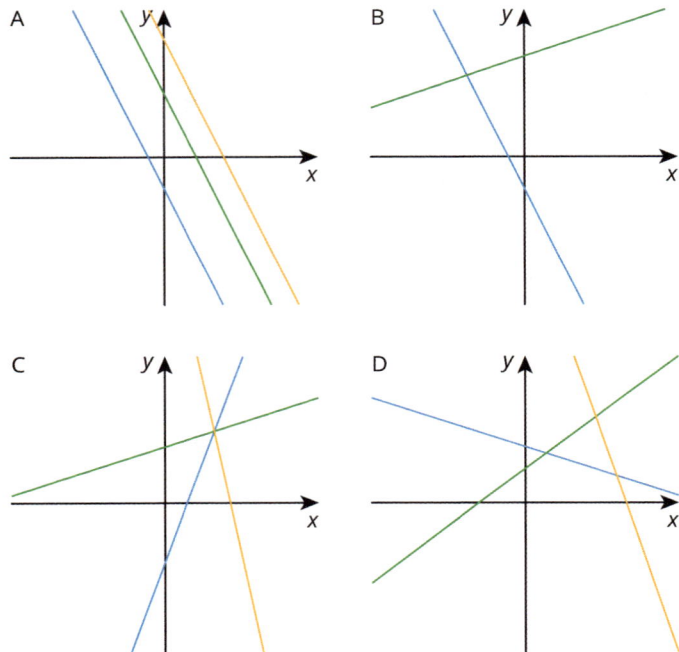

4.10.2 Exploration Activity: Pocket Full of Change

Jada told Noah that she has $2 worth of quarters and dimes in her pocket and 17 coins all together. She asked him to guess how many of each type of coin she has.

1. Here is a table that shows some combinations of quarters and dimes that are worth $2. Complete the table.

number of quarters	number of dimes
0	20
4	
	0
	5

2. Here is a graph of the relationship between the number of quarters and the number of dimes when there are a total of 17 coins.

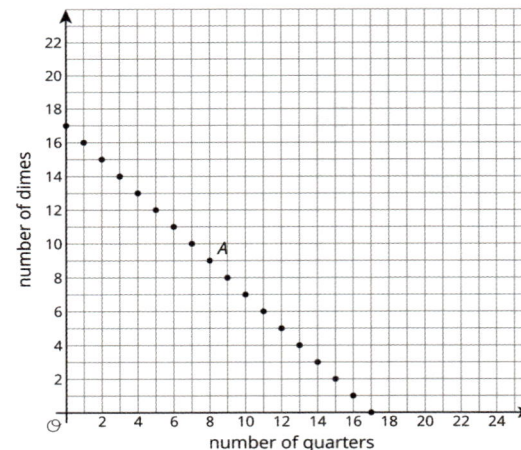

a. What does Point A represent?

b. How much money, in dollars, is the combination represented by Point A worth?

3. Is it possible for Jada to have 4 quarters and 13 dimes in her pocket? Explain how you know.

4. How many quarters and dimes must Jada have? Explain your reasoning.

4.10.3a Exploration Activity: Making Signs

Clare and Andre are making signs for all the lockers as part of the decorations for the upcoming spirit week. Yesterday, Andre made 15 signs and Clare made 5 signs. Today, they need to make more signs. Each person's progress today is shown in the coordinate plane.

Based on the lines, mark the statements as true or false for each person.

point	what it says	Clare	Andre
A	At 40 minutes, I have 25 signs completed.		
B	At 75 minutes, I have 42 and a half signs completed.		
C	At 0 minutes, I have 15 signs completed.		
D	At 100 minutes, I have 60 signs completed.		

4.10.3b Exploration Extension: Are you ready for more?

- 4 toothpicks make 1 square
- 7 toothpicks make 2 squares
- 10 toothpicks make 3 squares

Do you see a pattern? If so, how many toothpicks would you need to make 10 squares according to your pattern? Can you represent your pattern with an expression?

We studied linear relationships in an earlier unit. We learned that values of x and y that make an equation true correspond to points (x, y) on the graph. For example, if we have x pounds of flour that costs $0.80 per pound and y pounds of sugar that costs $0.50 per pound, and the total cost is $9.00, then we can write an equation like this to represent the relationship between x and y:

$$0.8x + 0.5y = 9$$

Since 5 pounds of flour costs $4.00 and 10 pounds of sugar costs $5.00, we know that $x = 5$, $y = 10$ is a solution to the equation, and the point $(5,10)$ is a point on the graph. The line shown is the graph of the equation:

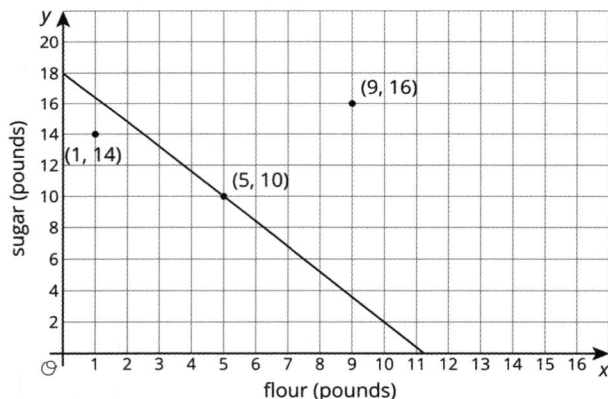

Notice that there are two points shown that are not on the line. What do they mean in the context? The point $(1,14)$ means that there is 1 pound of flour and 14 pounds of sugar. The total cost for this is $0.8 \cdot 1 + 0.5 \cdot 14$ or $7.80. Since the cost is not $9.00, this point is not on the graph. Likewise, 9 pounds of flour and 16 pounds of sugar costs $0.8 \cdot 9 + 0.5 \cdot 16$ or $15.20, so the other point is not on the graph either.

Suppose we also know that the flour and sugar together weigh 15 pounds. That means that

$$x + y = 15$$

If we draw the graph of this equation on the same coordinate plane, we see it passes through two of the three labeled points:

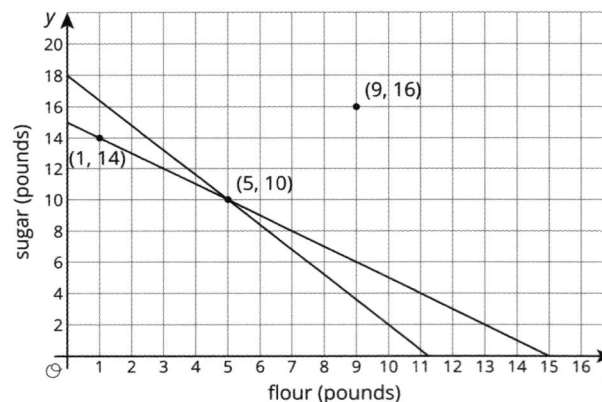

The point $(1,14)$ is on the graph of $x + y = 15$ because $1 + 14 = 15$. Similarly, $5 + 10 = 15$. But $9 + 16 \neq 15$, so $(9,16)$ is *not* on the graph of $x + y = 15$. In general, if we have two lines in the coordinate plane,

- The coordinates of a point that is on both lines makes both equations true.

- The coordinates of a point on only one line makes only one equation true.

- The coordinates of a point on neither line make both equations false.

Unit 4: Linear Equations and Linear Systems

1.

a. Match the lines m and n to the statements they represent:

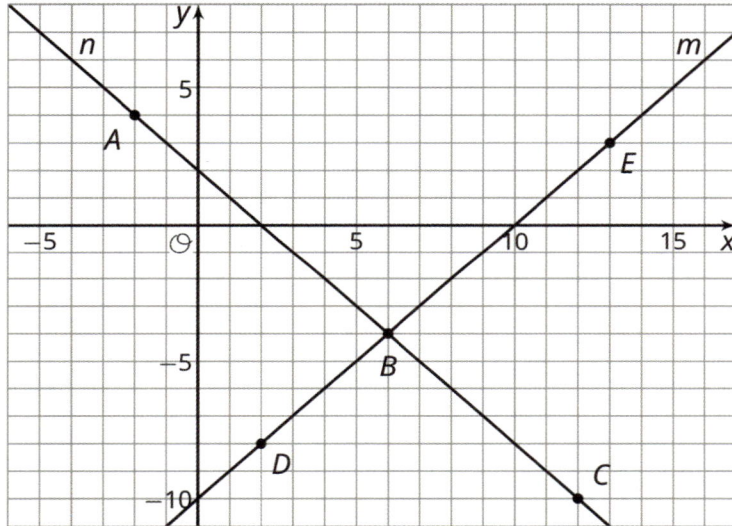

i. A set of points where the coordinates of each point have a sum of 2

ii. A set of points where the y-coordinate of each point is 10 less than its x-coordinate

b. Match the labeled points on the graph to statements about their coordinates:

i. Two numbers with a sum of 2

ii. Two numbers where the y-coordinate is 10 less than the x-coordinate

iii. Two numbers with a sum of 2 and where the y-coordinate is 10 less than the x-coordinate

2. Here is an equation: $4x - 4 = 4x +$ ___. What could you write in the blank so the equation would be true for:

a. No values of x

b. All values of x

c. One value of x

3. Mai earns $7 per hour mowing her neighbors' lawns. She also earned $14 for hauling away bags of recyclables for some neighbors.

Priya babysits her neighbor's children. The table shows the amount of money, m, she earns in h hours. Priya and Mai have agreed to go to the movies the weekend after they have earned the same amount of money for the same number of work hours.

h	m
1	$8.40
2	$16.80
4	$33.60

Continued on next page

a. How many hours do they have to work before they go to the movies?

b. How much will they have earned?

c. Explain where the solution can be seen in tables of values, graphs, and equations that represent Priya's and Mai's hourly earnings.

b. $\frac{3(2-r)}{4} = \frac{3+r}{6}$

c. $\frac{4p+3}{8} = \frac{p+2}{4}$

d. $\frac{2(a-7)}{15} = \frac{a+4}{6}$

4. For each equation, explain what you could do first to each side of the equation so that there would be no fractions. You do not have to solve the equations (unless you want more practice).

a. $\frac{3x-4}{8} = \frac{x+2}{3}$

Unit 4, Lesson 11: On Both of the Lines

Let's use lines to think about situations.

4.11.1 Warm-Up: Notice and Wonder: Bugs Passing in the Night

What do you notice? What do you wonder?

4.11.2 Exploration Activity: Bugs Passing in the Night, Continued

A different ant and ladybug are a certain distance apart, and they start walking toward each other. The graph shows the ladybug's distance from its starting point over time and the labeled point (2.5,10) indicates when the ant and the ladybug pass each other.

The ant is walking 2 centimeters per second.

1. Write an equation representing the relationship between the ant's distance from the ladybug's starting point and the amount of time that has passed.

2. If you haven't already, draw the graph of your equation on the same coordinate plane.

4.11.3 Exploration Activity: A Close Race

Elena and Jada were racing 100 meters on their bikes. Both racers started at the same time and rode at constant speed. Here is a table that gives information about Jada's bike race:

time from start (seconds)	distance from start (meters)
6	36
9	54

1. Graph the relationship between distance and time for Jada's bike race. Make sure to label and scale the axes appropriately.

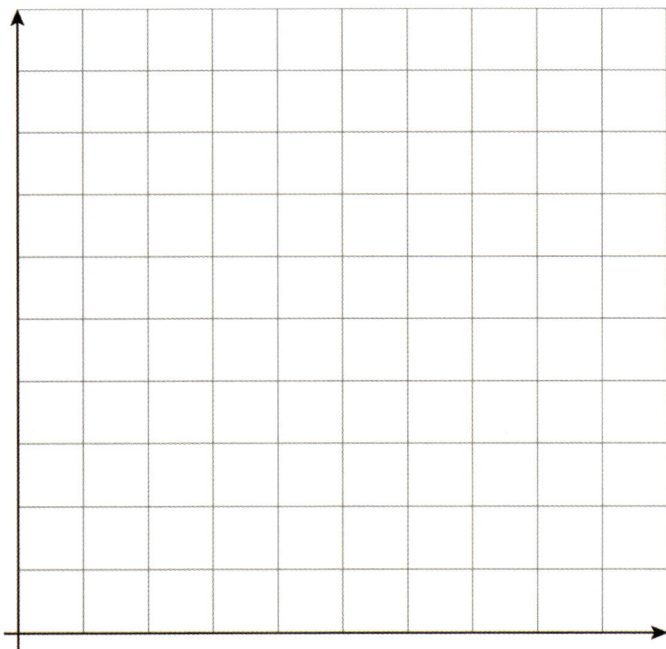

2. Elena traveled the entire race at a steady 6 meters per second. On the same set of axes, graph the relationship between distance and time for Elena's bike race.

3. Who won the race?

Lesson 11 Summary

The solutions to an equation correspond to points on its graph. For example, if Car A is traveling 75 miles per hour and passes a rest area when $t = 0$, then the distance in miles it has traveled from the rest area after t hours is

$$d = 75t$$

The point (2,150) is on the graph of this equation because $150 = 75 \cdot 2$: two hours after passing the rest area, the car has traveled 150 miles.

If you have *two* equations, you can ask whether there is an ordered pair that is a solution to *both* equations simultaneously. For example, if Car B is traveling towards the rest area and its distance from the rest area is

$$d = 14 - 65t$$

we can ask if there is ever a time when the distance of Car A from the rest area is the same as the distance of Car B from the rest area. If the answer is "yes", then the solution will correspond to a point that is on both lines.

(0.1, 7.5)

Looking at the coordinates of the intersection point, we see that Car A and Car B will both be 7.5 miles from the rest area after 0.1 hours (which is 6 minutes).

Unit 4: Linear Equations and Linear Systems

Now suppose another car, Car C, had also passed the rest stop at time $t = 0$ and traveled in the same direction as Car A, also going 75 miles per hour. It's equation would also be $d = 75t$. Any solution to the equation for Car A would also be a solution for Car C, and any solution to the equation for Car C would also be a solution for Car A. The line for Car C would land right on top of the line for Car A. In this case, every point on the graphed line is a solution to both equations, so that there are infinitely many solutions to the question "when are Car A and Car C the same distance from the rest stop?" This would mean that Car A and Car C were side by side for their whole journey.

When we have two linear equations that are equivalent to each other, like $y = 3x + 2$ and $2y = 6x + 4$, we will get two lines that are "right on top" of each other. Any solution to one equation is also solution to the other, so these two lines intersect at infinitely many points.

4.11.5 Practice Problems

1. Diego has $11 and begins saving $5 each week toward buying a new phone. At the same time that Diego begins saving, Lin has $60 and begins spending $2 per week on supplies for her art class. Is there a week when they have the same amount of money? How much do they have at that time?

2. Use a graph to find x and y values that make both $y = \frac{-2}{3}x + 3$ and $y = 2x - 5$ true.

3. The point where the graphs of two equations intersect has y-coordinate 2. One equation is $y = -3x + 5$. Find the other equation if its graph has a slope of 1.

4. A farm has chickens and cows. All the cows have 4 legs and all the chickens have 2 legs. All together, there are 82 cow and chicken legs on the farm. Complete the table to show some possible combinations of chickens and cows to get 82 total legs.

number of chickens (x)	number of cows (y)
35	
7	
	10
19	
	5

Here is a graph that shows possible combinations of chickens and cows that add up to 30 animals:

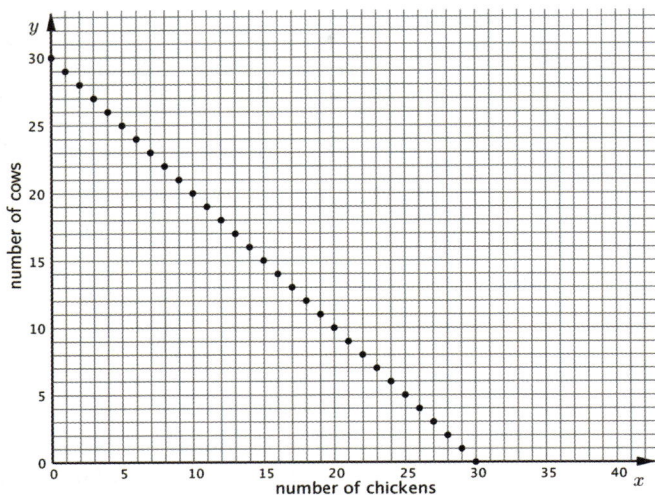

If the farm has 30 chickens and cows, and there are 82 chicken and cow legs all together, then how many chickens and how many cows could the farm have?

Let's learn what a system of equations is.

4.12.1 Warm-Up: Milkshakes

Diego and Lin are drinking milkshakes. Lin starts with 12 ounces and drinks $\frac{1}{4}$ an ounce per second. Diego starts with 20 ounces and drinks $\frac{2}{3}$ an ounce per second.

1. How long will it take Lin and Diego to finish their milkshakes?

2. Without graphing, explain what the graphs in this situation would look like. Think about slope, intercepts, axis labels, units, and intersection points to guide your thinking.

3. Discuss your description with your partner. If you disagree, work to reach an agreement.

4.12.2 Exploration Activity: Passing on the Trail

There is a hiking trail near the town where Han and Jada live that starts at a parking lot and ends at a lake. Han and Jada both decide to hike from the parking lot to the lake and back, but they start their hikes at different times.

At the time that Han reaches the lake and starts to turn back, Jada is 0.6 miles away from the parking lot and hiking at a constant speed of 3.2 miles per hour towards the lake. Han's distance, d, from the parking lot can be expressed as $d = -2.4t + 4.8$, where t represents the time in hours since he left the lake.

1. What is an equation for Jada's distance from the parking lot as she heads toward the lake?

2. Draw both graphs: one representing Han's equation and one representing Jada's equation. It is important to be very precise! Be careful, work in pencil, and use a ruler.

3. Find the point where the two graphs intersect each other. What are the coordinates of this point?

4. What do the coordinates mean in this situation?

5. What has to be true about the relationship between these coordinates and Jada's equation?

6. What has to be true about the relationship between these coordinates and Han's equation?

4.12.3 Exploration Activity: Stacks of Cups

A stack of n small cups has a height, h, in centimeters of $h = 1.5n + 6$. A stack of n large cups has a height, h, in centimeters of $h = 1.5n + 9$.

1. Graph the equations for each cup on the same set of axes. Make sure to label the axes and decide on an appropriate scale.

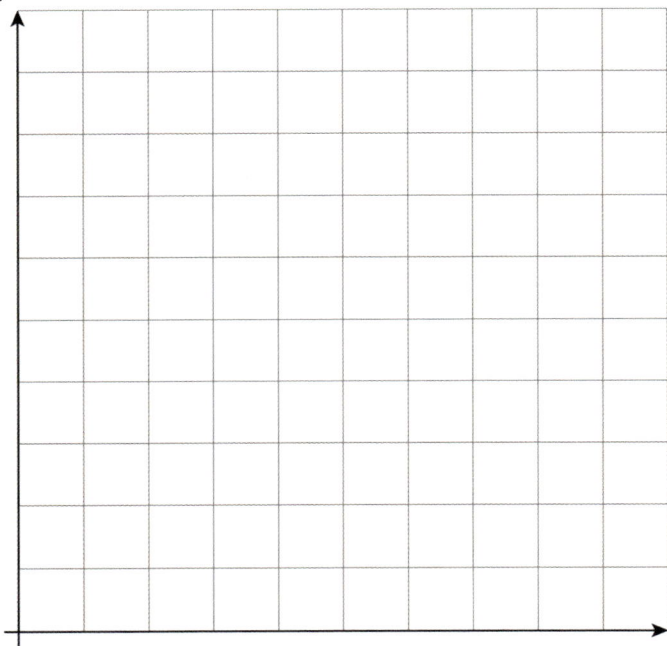

2. For what number of cups will the two stacks have the same height?

Lesson 12 Summary

A **system of equations** is a set of 2 (or more) equations where the variables represent the same unknown values. For example, suppose that two different kinds of bamboo are planted at the same time. Plant A starts at 6 ft tall and grows at a constant rate of $\frac{1}{4}$ foot each day. Plant B starts at 3 ft tall and grows at a constant rate of $\frac{1}{2}$ foot each day. We can write equations $y = \frac{1}{4}x + 6$ for Plant A and $y = \frac{1}{2}x + 3$ for Plant B, where x represents the number of days after being planted, and y represents height. We can write this system of equations.

$$\begin{cases} y = \dfrac{1}{4}x + 6 \\ y = \dfrac{1}{2}x + 3 \end{cases}$$

Solving a system of equations means to find the values of x and y that make both equations true at the same time. One way we have seen to find the solution to a system of equations is to graph both lines and find the intersection point. The intersection point represents the pair of x and y values that make both equations true. Here is a graph for the bamboo example:

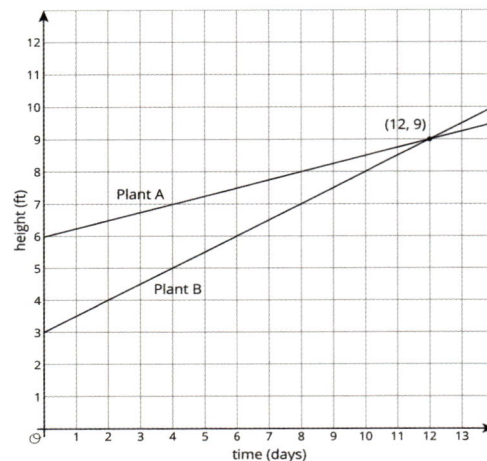

Unit 4: Linear Equations and Linear Systems

The solution to this system of equations is (12,9), which means that both bamboo plants will be 9 feet tall after 12 days.

We have seen systems of equations that have no solutions, one solution, and infinitely many solutions.

- When the lines do not intersect, there is no solution. (Lines that do not intersect are *parallel*.)
- When the lines intersect once, there is one solution.
- When the lines are right on top of each other, there are infinitely many solutions.

In future lessons, we will see that some systems cannot be easily solved by graphing, but can be easily solved using algebra.

4.12.5 Practice Problems

1. Here is the graph for one equation in a system of equations:

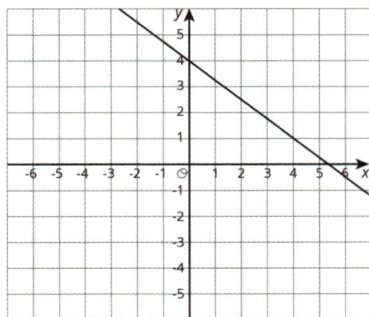

a. Write a second equation for the system so it has infinitely many solutions.

b. Write a second equation whose graph goes through (0,1) so the system has no solutions.

c. Write a second equation whose graph goes through (0,2) so the system has one solution at (4,1).

2. Create a second equation so the system has no solutions.

$$\begin{cases} y = \dfrac{3}{4}x - 4 \end{cases}$$

3. Andre is in charge of cooking broccoli and zucchini for a large group. He has to spend all $17 he has and can carry 10 pounds of veggies. Zucchini costs $1.50 per pound and broccoli costs $2 per pound. One graph shows combinations of zucchini and broccoli that weigh 10 pounds and the other shows combinations of zucchini and broccoli that cost $17.

a. Name one combination of veggies that weighs 10 pounds but does not cost $17.

Continued on next page

b. Name one combination of veggies that costs $17 but does not weigh 10 pounds.

c. How many pounds each of zucchini and broccoli can Andre get so that he spends all $17 and gets 10 pounds of veggies?

4. The temperature in degrees Fahrenheit, F, is related to the temperature in degrees Celsius, C, by the equation

$$F = \frac{9}{5}C + 32.$$

a. In the Sahara desert, temperatures often reach 50 degrees Celsius. How many degrees Fahrenheit is this?

b. In parts of Alaska, the temperatures can reach -60 degrees Fahrenheit. How many degrees Celsius is this?

c. There is one temperature where the degrees Fahrenheit and degrees Celsius are the same, so that $C = F$. Use the expression from the equation, where F is expressed in terms of C, to solve for this temperature.

Unit 4, Lesson 13: Solving Systems of Equations

Let's solve systems of equations.

🔔 **4.13.1 Warm-Up: True or False: Two Lines**

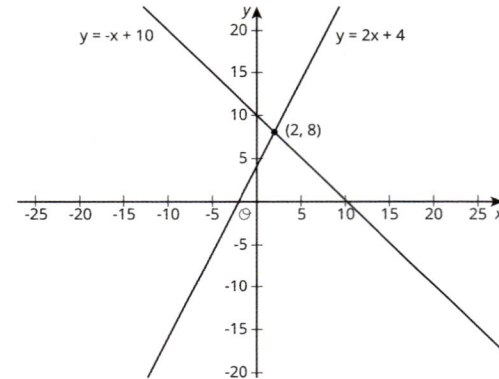

Use the lines to decide whether each statement is true or false. Be prepared to explain your reasoning using the lines.

1. A solution to $8 = -x + 10$ is 2.

2. A solution to $2 = 2x + 4$ is 8.

3. A solution to $-x + 10 = 2x + 4$ is 8.

4. A solution to $-x + 10 = 2x + 4$ is 2.

5. There are no values of x and y that make $y = -x + 10$ and $y = 2x + 4$ true at the same time.

MATH NATION

4.13.2 Exploration Activity: Matching Graphs to Systems

Here are three **systems of equations** graphed on a coordinate plane:

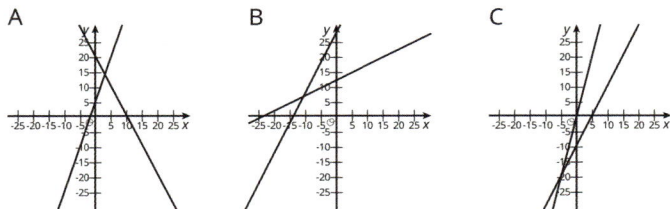

1. Match each figure to one of the systems of equations shown here.

   a. $\begin{cases} y = 3x + 5 \\ y = -2x + 20 \end{cases}$

   b. $\begin{cases} y = 2x - 10 \\ y = 4x - 1 \end{cases}$

   c. $\begin{cases} y = 0.5x + 12 \\ y = 2x + 27 \end{cases}$

2. Find the solution to each system and check that your solution is reasonable based on the graph.

4.13.3a Exploration Activity: Different Types of Systems

Your teacher will give you a page with some systems of equations.

1. Graph each system of equations carefully on the provided coordinate plane.

2. Describe what the graph of a system of equations looks like when it has . . .

   a. 1 solution

   b. 0 solutions

   c. infinitely many solutions

4.13.3b Exploration Extension: Are you ready for more?

The graphs of the equations $Ax + By = 15$ and $Ax - By = 9$ intersect at $(2,1)$. Find A and B. Show or explain your reasoning.

📖 Lesson 13 Summary

Sometimes it is easier to solve a system of equations without having to graph the equations and look for an intersection point. In general, whenever we are solving a system of equations written as

$$\begin{cases} y = [\text{some stuff}] \\ y = [\text{some other stuff}] \end{cases}$$

we know that we are looking for a pair of values (x, y) that makes both equations true. In particular, we know that the value for y will be the same in both equations. That means that

$$[\text{some stuff}] = [\text{some other stuff}]$$

For example, look at this system of equations:

$$\begin{cases} y = 2x + 6 \\ y = -3x - 4 \end{cases}$$

Since the y value of the solution is the same in both equations, then we know $2x + 6 = -3x - 4$

We can solve this equation for x:

$2x + 6$	$= -3x - 4$	
$5x + 6$	$= -4$	add $3x$ to each side
$5x$	$= -10$	subtract 6 from each side
x	$= -2$	divide each side by 5

But this is only half of what we are looking for: we know the value for x, but we need the corresponding value for y. Since both equations have the same y value, we can use either equation to find the y-value:

$$y = 2(-2) + 6$$

$$\text{Or} \quad y = -3(-2) - 4$$

In both cases, we find that $y = 2$. So the solution to the system is $(-2, 2)$. We can verify this by graphing both equations in the coordinate plane.

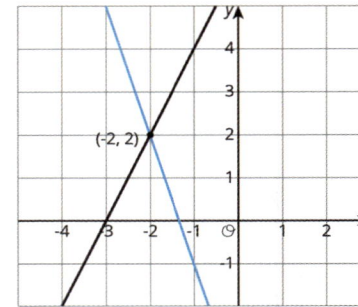

In general, a system of linear equations can have:

- No solutions. In this case, the lines that correspond to each equation never intersect.
- Exactly one solution. The lines that correspond to each equation intersect in exactly one point.
- An infinite number of solutions. The graphs of the two equations are the same line!

🔴 4.13.5 Practice Problems

1.

a. Write equations for the lines shown.

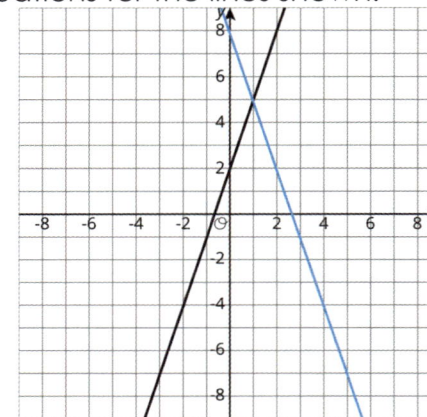

b. Describe how to find the solution to the corresponding system by looking at the graph.

c. Describe how to find the solution to the corresponding system by using the equations.

2. The solution to a system of equations is $(5, -19)$. Choose two equations that might make up the system.

- ☐ $y = -3x - 6$
- ☐ $y = 2x - 23$
- ☐ $y = -7x + 16$
- ☐ $y = x - 17$
- ☐ $y = -2x - 9$

3. Solve the system of equations: $\begin{cases} y = 4x - 3 \\ y = -2x + 9 \end{cases}$

4. Solve the system of equations: $\begin{cases} y = \frac{5}{4}x - 2 \\ y = \frac{-1}{4}x + 19 \end{cases}$

5. Here is an equation: $\frac{15(x-3)}{5} = 3(2x - 3)$

a. Solve the equation by using the distributive property first.

b. Solve the equation without using the distributive property.

c. Check your solution.

Unit 4, Lesson 14: Solving More Systems

Let's solve systems of equations.

4.14.1 Warm-Up: Algebra Talk: Solving Systems Mentally

Solve these without writing anything down:

$$\begin{cases} x = 5 \\ y = x - 7 \end{cases}$$

$$\begin{cases} y = 4 \\ y = x + 3 \end{cases}$$

$$\begin{cases} x = 8 \\ y = -11 \end{cases}$$

4.14.2 Exploration Activity: Challenge Yourself

Here are a lot of systems of equations:

A $\begin{cases} y = 4 \\ x = -5y + 6 \end{cases}$

B $\begin{cases} y = 7 \\ x = 3y - 4 \end{cases}$

C $\begin{cases} y = \frac{3}{2}x + 7 \\ x = -4 \end{cases}$

D $\begin{cases} y = -3x + 10 \\ y = -2x + 6 \end{cases}$

E $\begin{cases} y = -3x - 5 \\ y = 4x + 30 \end{cases}$

F $\begin{cases} y = 3x - 2 \\ y = -2x + 8 \end{cases}$

G $\begin{cases} y = 3x \\ x = -2y + 56 \end{cases}$

H $\begin{cases} x = 2y - 15 \\ y = -2x \end{cases}$

I $\begin{cases} 3x + 4y = 10 \\ x = 2y \end{cases}$

J $\begin{cases} y = 3x + 2 \\ 2x + y = 47 \end{cases}$

K $\begin{cases} y = -2x + 5 \\ 2x + 3y = 31 \end{cases}$

L $\begin{cases} x + y = 10 \\ x = 2y + 1 \end{cases}$

1. Without solving, identify 3 systems that you think would be the least difficult to solve and 3 systems that you think would be the most difficult to solve. Be prepared to explain your reasoning.

2. Choose 4 systems to solve. At least one should be from your "least difficult" list and one should be from your "most difficult" list.

Unit 4: Linear Equations and Linear Systems

Tyler was looking at this system of equations:

$$\begin{cases} x + y = 5 \\ x + y = 7 \end{cases}$$

He said, "Just looking at the system, I can see it has no solution. If you add two numbers, that sum can't be equal to two different numbers."

Do you agree with Tyler?

In rectangle $ABCD$, side AB is 8 centimeters and side BC is 6 centimeters. F is a point on BC and E is a point on AB. The area of triangle DFC is 20 square centimeters, and the area of triangle DEF is 16 square centimeters. What is the area of triangle AED?

When we have a system of linear equations where one of the equations is of the form $y = $ [stuff] or $x = $ [stuff], we can solve it algebraically by using a technique called *substitution*. The basic idea is to replace a variable with an expression it is equal to (so the expression is like a substitute for the variable). For example, let's start with the system:

$$\begin{cases} y = 5x \\ 2x - y = 9 \end{cases}$$

Since we know that $y = 5x$, we can substitute $5x$ for y in the equation $2x - y = 9$,

$$2x - (5x) = 9,$$

and then solve the equation for x,

$$x = -3.$$

We can find y using either equation. Using the first one: $y = 5 \cdot -3$. So

$$(-3, -15)$$

is the solution to this system. We can verify this by looking at the graphs of the equations in the system:

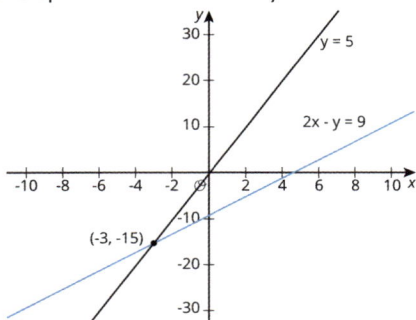

Sure enough! They intersect at $(-3, -15)$.

We didn't know it at the time, but we were actually using substitution in the last lesson as well. In that lesson, we looked at the system

$$\begin{cases} y = 2x + 6 \\ y = -3x - 4 \end{cases}$$

and we substituted $2x + 6$ for y into the second equation to get $2x + 6 = -3x - 4$. Go back and check for yourself!

1. Solve: $\begin{cases} y = 6x \\ 4x + y = 7 \end{cases}$

2. Solve: $\begin{cases} y = 3x \\ x = -2y + 70 \end{cases}$

3. Which equation, together with $y = -1.5x + 3$, makes a system with one solution?

   A. $y = -1.5x + 6$

   B. $y = -1.5x$

   C. $2y = -3x + 6$

   D. $2y + 3x = 6$

   E. $y = -2x + 3$

4. The system $x - 6y = 4$, $3x - 18y = 4$ has no solution.

   a. Change one constant or coefficient to make a new system with one solution.

b. Change one constant or coefficient to make a new system with an infinite number of solutions.

5. Match each graph to its equation.

A

B

C

D
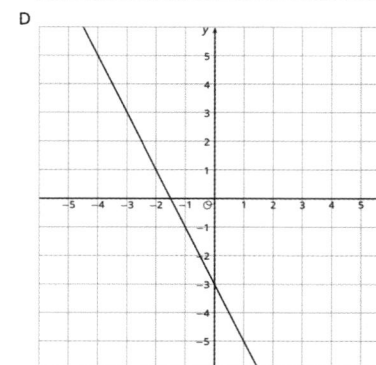

   I. $y = 2x + 3$

   II. $y = -2x + 3$

   III. $y = 2x - 3$

   IV. $y = -2x - 3$

6. Here are two points: $(-3,4)$, $(1,7)$. What is the slope of the line between them?

A. $\frac{4}{3}$

B. $\frac{3}{4}$

C. $\frac{1}{6}$

D. $\frac{2}{3}$

Let's write systems of equations from real-world situations.

4.15.1 Warm-Up: How Many Solutions? Matching

Match each system of equations with the number of solutions the system has.

A. $\begin{cases} y = -\frac{4}{3}x + 4 \\ y = -\frac{4}{3}x - 1 \end{cases}$

B. $\begin{cases} y = 4x - 5 \\ y = -2x + 7 \end{cases}$

C. $\begin{cases} 2x + 3y = 8 \\ 4x + 6y = 17 \end{cases}$

D. $\begin{cases} y = 5x - 15 \\ y = 5(x - 3) \end{cases}$

I. No Solutions

II. One Solution

III. Infinitely many solutions

4.15.2 Exploration Activity: Situations and Systems

For each situation:

- Create a system of equations.
- Then, without solving, interpret what the solution to the system would tell you about the situation.

A. Lin's family is out for a bike ride when her dad stops to take a picture of the scenery. He tells the rest of the family to keep going and that he'll catch up. Lin's dad spends 5 minutes taking the photo and then rides at 0.24 miles per minute until he meets up with the rest of the family further along the bike path. Lin and the rest were riding at 0.18 miles per minute.

B. Noah is planning a kayaking trip. Kayak Rental A charges a base fee of $15 plus $4.50 per hour. Kayak Rental B charges a base fee of $12.50 plus $5 per hour.

C. Diego is making a large batch of pastries. The recipe calls for 3 strawberries for every apple. Diego used 52 fruits all together.

D. Flour costs $0.80 per pound and sugar costs $0.50 per pound. An order of flour and sugar weighs 15 pounds and costs $9.00.

4.15.3 Exploration Activity: Solving Systems Practice

Here is a lot of systems of equations:

A. $\begin{cases} y = -2x + 6 \\ y = x - 3 \end{cases}$

B. $\begin{cases} y = 5x - 4 \\ y = 4x + 12 \end{cases}$

C. $\begin{cases} y = \frac{2}{3}x - 4 \\ y = -\frac{4}{3}x + 9 \end{cases}$

D. $\begin{cases} 4y + 7x = 6 \\ 4y + 7x = -5 \end{cases}$

E. $\begin{cases} y = 0.24x \\ y = 0.18x + 0.9 \end{cases}$

F. $\begin{cases} y = 4.5x + 15 \\ y = 5x + 12.5 \end{cases}$

G. $\begin{cases} y = 3x \\ x + y = 52 \end{cases}$

a. Without solving, identify 3 systems that you think would be the least difficult for you to solve and 3 systems you think would be the most difficult. Be prepared to explain your reasoning.

b. Choose 4 systems to solve. At least one should be from your "least difficult" list and one should be from your "most difficult" list.

Lesson 15 Summary

We have learned how to solve many kinds of systems of equations using algebra that would be difficult to solve by graphing. For example, look at

$$\begin{cases} y = 2x - 3 \\ x + 2y = 7 \end{cases}$$

The first equation says that $y = 2x - 3$, so wherever we see y, we can substitute the expression $2x - 3$ instead. So the second equation becomes $x + 2(2x - 3) = 7$.

We can then solve for x:

$$
\begin{array}{lll}
x + 4x - 6 & = 7 & \text{distributive property} \\
5x - 6 & = 7 & \text{combine like terms} \\
5x & = 13 & \text{add 6 to each side} \\
x & = \dfrac{13}{5} & \text{multiply each side by } \dfrac{1}{5}
\end{array}
$$

We know that the y value for the solution is the same for either equation, so we can use either equation to solve for it. Using the first equation, we get:

$$
\begin{array}{lll}
y & = 2\left(\dfrac{13}{5}\right) - 3 & \text{substitute } x = \dfrac{13}{5} \text{ into the equation} \\
y & = \dfrac{26}{5} - 3 & \text{multiply } 2\left(\dfrac{13}{5}\right) \text{ to make } \dfrac{26}{5} \\
y & = \dfrac{26}{5} - \dfrac{15}{5} & \text{rewrite 3 as } \dfrac{15}{5} \\
y & = \dfrac{11}{5}
\end{array}
$$

If we substitute $x = \frac{13}{5}$ into the other equation, $x + 2y = 7$, we get the same y value. So the solution to the system is $\left(\frac{13}{5}, \frac{11}{5}\right)$.

There are many kinds of systems of equations that we will learn how to solve in future grades, like $\begin{cases} 2x + 3y = 6 \\ -x + 2y = 3 \end{cases}$

Or even $\begin{cases} y = x^2 + 1 \\ y = 2x + 3 \end{cases}$

Unit 4: Linear Equations and Linear Systems

1. Kiran and his cousin work during the summer for a landscaping company. Kiran's cousin has been working for the company longer, so his pay is 30% more than Kiran's. Last week his cousin worked 27 hours, and Kiran worked 23 hours. Together, they earned $493.85. What is Kiran's hourly pay? Explain or show your reasoning.

2. Decide which story can be represented by the system of equations $y = x + 6$ and $x + y = 100$. Explain your reasoning.

   A. Diego's teacher writes a test worth 100 points. There are 6 more multiple choice questions than short answer questions.

   B. Lin and her younger cousin measure their heights. They notice that Lin is 6 inches taller, and their heights add up to exactly 100 inches.

3. Clare and Noah play a game in which they earn the same number of points for each goal and lose the same number of points for each penalty. Clare makes 6 goals and 3 penalties, ending the game with 6 points. Noah earns 8 goals and 9 penalties and ends the game with −22 points.

   a. Write a system of equations that describes Clare and Noah's outcomes. Use x to represent the number of points for a goal and y to represent the number of points for a penalty.

Continued on next page

b. Solve the system. What does your solution mean?

4. Solve: $\begin{cases} y = 6x - 8 \\ y = -3x + 10 \end{cases}$

5.

a. Estimate the coordinates of the point where the two lines meet.

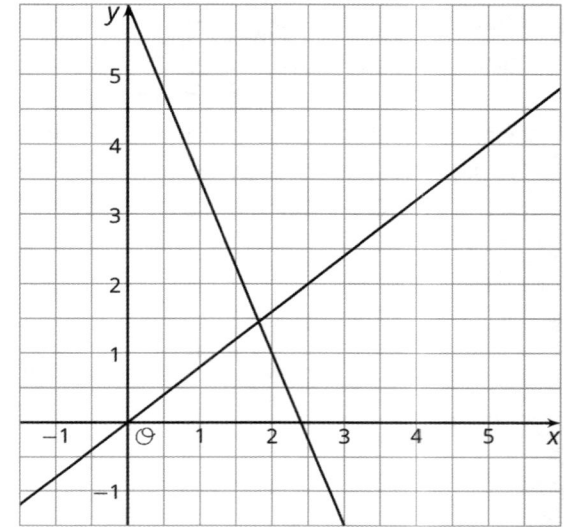

b. Choose two equations that make up the system represented by the graph.

☐ $y = \dfrac{5}{4}x$

☐ $y = 6 - 2.5x$

☐ $y = 2.5x + 6$

☐ $y = 6 - 3x$

☐ $y = 0.8x$

c. Solve the system of equations and confirm the accuracy of your estimate.

Unit 4: Linear Equations and Linear Systems

Unit 4, Lesson 16: Solving Problems with Systems of Equations

Let's solve some gnarly problems.

4.16.1 Warm-Up: Are We There Yet?

A car is driving towards home at 0.5 miles per minute. If the car is 4 miles from home at $t = 0$, which of the following can represent the distance that the car has left to drive?

A. $0.5t$

B. $4 + 0.5t$

C. $4 - 0.5t$

D. $4 \cdot (0.5t)$

4.16.2a Exploration Activity: Cycling, Fundraising, Working, and ___?

Solve each problem. Explain or show your reasoning.

1. Two friends live 7 miles apart. One Saturday, the two friends set out on their bikes at 8 am and started riding towards each other. One rides at 0.2 miles per minute, and the other rides at 0.15 miles per minute. At what time will the two friends meet?

2. Students are selling grapefruits and nuts for a fundraiser. The grapefruits cost $1 each and a bag of nuts cost $10 each. They sold 100 items and made $307. How many grapefruits did they sell?

3. Jada earns $7 per hour mowing her neighbors' lawns. Andre gets paid $5 per hour for the first hour of babysitting and $8 per hour for any additional hours he babysits. What is the number of hours they both can work so that they get paid the same amount?

4. Pause here so your teacher can review your work. Then, invent another problem that is like one of these, but with different numbers. Solve your problem.

5. Create a visual display that includes:
   o The new problem you wrote, without the solution.

   o Enough work space for someone to show a solution.

6. Trade your display with another group, and solve each other's new problem. Make sure that you explain your solution carefully. Be prepared to share this solution with the class.

7. When the group that got the problem you invented shares their solution, check that their answer is correct.

⚙ **4.16.2b Exploration Extension: Are you ready for more?**

MATH NATION

On a different Saturday, two friends set out on bikes at 8:00 am and met up at 8:30 am. (The same two friends who live 7 miles apart.) If one was riding at 10 miles per hour, how fast was the other riding?

Unit 4: Linear Equations and Linear Systems